Brihadaranyaka Upanishad

With Devanagari Script, Translation and Notes

Translated from the original Sanskrit text by

Jayaram V

First Edition 2013. Revised 2024

Published by
Pure Life Vision LLC
New Albany, Ohio

Brihadaranyaka Upanishad

Copyright © 2013, 2024 by Jayaram V
Published and Distributed Worldwide by Pure Life Vision LLC., USA.
First edition 2013. Revised 2024.

This book is copyrighted under International and Pan-American conventions and printed in the USA. All rights reserved. No part of this publication may be reproduced, stored in a retrieval system, or transmitted in any form or by any means, electronic, mechanical, photocopying, recording, scanning, or otherwise, without the prior written permission of the publisher or the author. Requests to the publisher for permission or bulk purchase of the book should be made online at http://www.PureLifeVision.com.

Without in any way limiting the author's [and publisher's] exclusive rights under copyright, any use of this publication to "train" generative artificial intelligence (AI) technologies to generate text is expressly prohibited. The author reserves all rights to license uses of this work for generative AI training and development of machine learning language models.

Limit of Liability/Disclaimer of Warranty: While the publisher and the author have used their best efforts in preparing this book, they make no representation or warranties with respect to the accuracy or completeness of the contents of this book and specifically disclaim any implied warranties of merchantability or fitness for a particular purpose. No warranty may be created or extended by sales representatives or written sales materials. The advice and strategies contained herein may not be suitable for your situation. You should consult with a professional where appropriate. Neither the publisher nor the author shall be liable for any loss of profit or any other commercial damages, including but not limited to special, incidental, consequential, or other damages.

Pure Life Vision books and products are available through bookstores and online websites. For Enquiries, please visit https://www.PureLifeVision.com.

Cover illustration Vedic imagery © Jayaram V

Publisher Cataloging-in-Publication Data

V, Jayaram, (Vemulapalli)
Brihadaranyaka Upanishad
       p. cm
       Includes bibliographical references
       ISBN- 13: 978-1-935760-07-8
       ISBN- 10: 1-935760-076
       1. Upanishads. 2. Upanishads. English. 3. Upanishads. Commentaries. I. Title.

       BL1124.7. B752. V15 2013
294.5/9218—dc22   2013905114

Printed in the United States of America
10 9 8 7 6 5 4 3 2 1
First Edition 2013. Revised Edition 2024

About the Author

Jayaram V, a renowned author with a unique perspective, has penned 15 books, including Brahman, The Awakened Life, An Introduction to Hinduism, Bhagavadgita: Unveiling the Gita's Secrets, Essays on the Bhagavadgita, Selected Upanishads, Brihadaranyaka and Chandogya Upanishads, and Shiva Sutras: Mystic Knowledge Explained. Jayaram's insightful writings, appreciated worldwide, delve into Hinduism, Buddhism, Jainism, Sikhism, Zoroastrianism, Spirituality and Self-improvement. He is the Founder and President of Hinduwebsite.com, a comprehensive website on Hinduism, Buddhism, and related religions, where most of his writings can be found. To learn more about Jayaram V, please visit https://www.jayaramv.com.

Books By Jayaram V

1. The Bhagavadgita: Unveiling the Gita's Secrets
2. Shiva Sutras: Mystic Knowledge Explained
3. The Awakened Life: Spiritual Knowledge from India's Sacred Traditions
4. Brahman
5. Essays on the Bhagavadgita
6. The Bhagavadgita: A Complete Translation
7. The Bhagavadgita: A Simple Translation
8. Introduction to Hinduism
9. Selected Upanishads
10. Brihadaranyaka Upanishad
11. Chandogya Upanishad
12. Think Success: Essays on Self-help
13. Being the Best: Practical Advice for Peace and Happiness
14. Thoughts and Quotations
15. Sadhana Panchakam - The Fivefold Spiritual Practice

Contents

Preface to the Revised Edition 9
Author's Note 11
Introduction 13
Chapter 1 23
    The Symbolism of Horse Sacrifice 23
    Creation and Separation of Worlds and Beings 25
    Gods and Demons and the Superiority of Breath 30
    Creation of Duality and Diversity 40
    Seven Types of Food Created by Prajapati 50
    Name, Form, and Action, The Threefold Diversity 60

Chapter 2 62
    The Right and Wrong Knowledge of Brahman 62
    Breath and Other Deities in the Body 68
    The Two Forms of Brahman 70
    A Conversation Between Yajnavalkya and Maitreyi 72
    The Sweetness of God Inherent in Creation 78
    The Line of Teachers and Students 83

Chapter 3 85
    Yajnavalkya on Sacrificial Rites 85
    Yajnavalkya on Senses and Sense Objects 89
    Yajnavalkya on Where Horse Sacrificers Go 92
    Yajnavalkya on the Unknowability of Self 93
    Yajnavalkya on Renunciation and Liberation 95
    Yajnavalkya on the Worlds and Their Support 96
    Yajnavalkya on the Inner Controller 97
    Yajnavalkya on Imperishable, Unseen Brahman 102
    Yajnavalkya on Many Gods and One God 106

Chapter 4 117
    Yajnavalkya on Partial Definitions of Brahman 117
    Yajnavalkya on the Person in the Body 123
    Yajnavalkya on the Light Within 125
    The Fate of the Departing Souls 137
    Yajnavalkya and Maitreyi 145
    The Line of Teachers and Students 150

Chapter 5 152

Invocation to Brahman, the Full 152
Prajapati's Advice to Gods, Humans and Demons 152
Brahman as Hrdayam - The Heart 154
Brahman as That and Sat 154
Brahman as Satyam - the Truth 155
Brahman as the Person in the Mind 157
Brahman as the Lightning 157
Speech Symbolized as the Cow 157
The Digestive Fire Within the Body 158
The Journey of Souls After Death 158
Death and Illness as Austerities 159
The Interconnection Between Food and Breath 159
Breath as Ukta, the Hymn of Praise 160
The Four Feet of Gayatri 162
Prayer to Pusan and Agni by a Dying Person 166

Chapter 6 168

Breath is Superior to the Organs of the Body 168
The Path of Gods and the Path of Ancestors 172
A Sacrifice for Greatness and Prosperity 178
Methods to Obtain a Good Son 184
The Line of Teachers and Students 191

Bibliography 193
Cover Page Symbolism 201

Preface to the Revised Edition

This is a revised edition of the first edition published in 2013, a result of our continuous dialogue with you, our readers. In this revision, we corrected a few spelling mistakes, improved punctuation, revised the translation of a few verses, improved a few existing annotations, changed their font size, and added new annotations to some verses we felt needed further explanation. We also removed information about previous publications since some of them have also undergone revisions. Overall, this is the same edition published in 2013 with a few changes, which will improve the quality and content of the book and make it more readable and useful, thanks to your valuable feedback.

Publishers
August 8, 2024

To

My Teachers and My Parents

Author's Note

The Brihadaranyaka Upanishad, a monumental text of the Vedic times, stands as one of the largest, oldest, and most comprehensive Upanishads associated with the Vedas. More specifically, it belongs to the Shukla Yajurveda. Its sheer size surpasses that of the Bhagavadgita and falls short only to the Chandogya Upanishad. The translations of these two Upanishads are integral to any comprehensive understanding of the Upanishads, encapsulating much of their essence. They are useful to know how ritual Vedism shifted its gears and veered steadily toward the spiritual thought process of the Upanishads. As part of my endeavor to translate the 16 Upanishads, I chose to include the Brihadaranyaka Upanishad. This decision was driven by my quest to unravel its enigmatic symbolism and delve into its profound ritual and spiritual knowledge.

If you are interested in Hinduism and want to know its early development, I believe a critical study of this scripture is necessary and helpful. The Upanishad contains references to early Vedic practices, such as the horse sacrifice and procreation ceremonies, knowledge of Brahman and Self, nature of creation, constitution of the human personality, importance of food and breath, father-to-son transmission ceremony, nature of sleep, and afterlife. Whoever reads it is presented with the vision of the human body as a universe in itself and the hidden presence of Brahman in the sweetness (honey) of life.

The Upanishad also illuminates the greatness of sages Yajnavalkya, Ajatasatru, Janaka, and Pavahana Jaivali, who were undoubtedly the greatest seers and teachers Hinduism has ever produced. The unique conversation between Yajnavalkya and his wife, Maitreyi, presented twice with minor variations, challenges our modern values and attitudes. This translation, like all my previous ones, has been a journey of self-study and contemplation of Hinduism. The process has enriched me, and I am eager to share this transformative knowledge with others.

Wherever necessary, I included explanatory notes to explain the meaning of critical words and phrases and their hidden symbolism. A translation is an attempt to render an existing text truly in another language. It does not require originality but authenticity, except when you add critical notes and commentary and interpret the original text according to your knowledge and understanding. Overall, the effort requires humility, tenacity, the austerity of discipline, and fealty to the original text. Even then, translators will face limitations when they translate ancient scriptures written thousands of years ago in archaic languages into other languages that are culturally and historically different from where the texts originated.

In translating an ancient text, you enter into a silent communication with the masters of ancient worlds. You become a medium between an ancient thought process and a modern mindset. In this process, a translator excels to the extent he remains true to the original thought and reflects its light and wisdom like a mirror without the impurity of his own ego. Also, in translating an ancient scripture, at times, you may find yourself standing on your own ground because of your unique insight or intuitive knowledge and interpret it differently. That is where I believe a translation gains merit or demerit and comes under scrutiny. I hope scholars and serious practitioners of Hinduism alike will find this translation useful.

Jayaram V

Introduction

The Brihadaranyaka Upanishad, one of the most comprehensive Upanishads in the Vedas, is a treasure trove of information on the ritual, mystical, and philosophical aspects of the Vedic religion. These aspects are the foundation of present-day Hinduism. This Upanishad is ideal for contemplation upon the mysteries of Brahman and ourselves. By studying this Upanishad, we gain a comprehensive understanding of the history of ancient India, the lives of the Vedic people, and their beliefs about creation, the universe, man's place in the cosmos, the constitution of the human body, and the relationship between the individual Self and the Universal Self. We also gain a deep insight into concepts such as karma, dharma, austerity, afterlife, liberation, rebirth, the inner Self, duality, truth, Brahman, Nature, renunciation, creation, family, sacrifice, procreation, and progeny.

Brihadaranyaka means a great forest. As the name implies, it is both an Aranyaka (forest book) and an Upanishad (secret teaching), and by arrangement, forms part of a Brahmana, namely the Satapatha Brahmana of the White Yajurveda. As a Brahmana, it dwells upon the knowledge of Vedic sacrifices, such as the horse sacrifice and rituals associated with procreation. As an Aranyaka, it deals with the knowledge of advanced rituals and their hidden symbolism. In the true tradition of an Upanishad, it contains the knowledge of the Self, Brahman, and liberation. The famous saying (Mahavakya), "Aham Brahmasmi," meaning I am Brahman, is found in this one only.

An overview

The Upanishad is divided into three parts (khandas), each containing two chapters, namely the Madhu Khanda, Muni Khanda, and Khila Khanda. Khanda means division or part. Madhu means honey. Muni means an ascetic or a hermit who practices the austerity of silence. Khila means supplemental. Madhu Khanda deals with ritual symbolism, the essential nature of Brahman (honey) hidden in creation, and the body as an abode of gods and aspects of Brahman. The Second chapter in this section compares the entire creation to honey or the sweetness of

Brahman. Hence, the name. The second division, Muni Khanda, also known as Yajnavalkya Khanda, deals with the teachings of Yajnavalkya, a great debater and exponent of early Vedic philosophy. The name 'muni' is most likely a reference to Yajnavalkya himself, who dominates the entire section with his knowledge and erudition. The third one, namely Khila Khanda, deals with the nature, aspects, and infinity of Brahman and procedural knowledge of certain ceremonies meant to gain wealth, fame, and progeny. The six chapters under the three divisions are divided into 47 sections and contain 427 verses. Although the number of verses is less, the Upanishad is larger in volume than the Bhagavadgita since it contains long verses of multiple lines. An overview of the Upanishad, along with the number of verses and sections in each chapter, is provided below.

Chapter	Khanda	No. of Brahmanas	No. of Verses
Chapter 1	Madhu Khanda	6	80
Chapter 2	Madhu Khanda	6	66
Chapter 3	Muni Khanda	9	85
Chapter 4	Muni Khanda	6	91
Chapter 5	Khila Khanda	15	30
Chapter 6	Khila Khanda	5	75
Total		47	**427**

Important concepts

The Brihadaranyaka Upanishad contains many ideas of the Vedanta philosophy. However, unlike the Bhagavadgita, it does not emphasize devotional theism but the pursuit of knowledge and duty. The scripture deals with both ritual knowledge (karma kanda) and spiritual knowledge (jnana kanda). It is believed that the three sections of the Upanishad once existed as independent texts belonging to three lineages of teachers and were grouped subsequently into one. Most of the ideas and concepts found in the Upanishad are found in other Upanishads also. Yet, it stands out in comparison to them because of its sheer size and antiquity. Some important themes from the Upanishad are discussed below.

The symbolism of the sacrificial horse

The Upanishad begins with a description of the sacrificial horse after it has been killed and spread out on the ritual ground in the prescribed manner. The beginning verses draw a comparison between the sacrificial horse and the Cosmic Person (Purusha) or the Macrocosm (Prajapati or Viraj). Its parts are compared to various aspects of creation. The horse sacrifice, known as Ashvamedha Yajna, which is now defunct, was popular in the days when kings and emperors of the original Kshatriya clans ruled ancient India. The sacrifice was the means by which kings declared their power and displayed their valor. The ritual itself is described in the Ashvamedha chapter of the Vajasaneyi Samhita (22-25) of the White Yajurveda and the Atharvaveda (9-7). Procedurally, it was a long ritual performed in the aftermath of a king's conquest, involving the king, his sons, queens, court officials, and hosts of priests aimed to consolidate the king's power and glory and bring peace and prosperity to the kingdom. In the concluding part of the sacrifice, the horse was sacrificed ritually, and its meat was cooked in the sacrificial fire and shared by the king, his family, and the performing priests. The sacrifice was meant to remind the king that his power emanated from the heavens and that while he was entitled to rule the lands he occupied, the true inhabitant, owner, and enjoyer of all the universe was Brahman. As a ruler, he was expected to consider the world as a manifestation of Brahman and perform his duties with detachment and renunciation, subduing his ego and upholding the eternal law of God.

The superiority and invincibility of breath

The Upanishad, like many other Upanishads, projects the body as a replica of the Cosmic Being, Purusha. Like the cosmos, the body has three spheres. The head represents the heavenly region. The middle part represents the mid-region, and the lower body is comparable to the earth. The body housed several deities in the form of sense-organs, with breath as their superior, the mind and intelligence as their inner controller, and the Self as the enjoyer. The superiority of breath is described in the first chapter (1.3.1-18) as well as in the last chapter (6.1). It is superior to all the organs inside the body because it is subtle, impervious to evil, vital for their existence, and distributes the energy (prana) in the body among them according to their due share. It is the essence of the limbs (Ayasa Angirasa) because they are filled with its presence. The verses suggest that breath is not only impervious to evil but also acts as a purifier by carrying away the evil associated with them out of the body to the end of the quarters. The organs in the body are comparable to deities. However, all the deities located in them are vulnerable to evil and death., except breath, which is invincible and incorruptible. Hence, one can take refuge in breath to protect oneself from evil during one's life and when departing from the body.

Knowing Brahman

The fourth Brahmana of the first chapter says that one should realize Brahman as oneself. This awareness should spring not intellectually but from self-realization when all desires, duality, and attachments are overcome. He who knows Brahman as oneself (Aham Brahmasmi) becomes all. Duality arises when one wakes up from the state of "I am Brahman" to "I am so and so." Duality and diversity arise because we desire company; we seek sense objects for our enjoyment and engage in desire-ridden actions. When names and forms disappear from knowing awareness, the Self alone remains.

The triple aspects of creation

According to the Upanishad, name, form, and obligatory duty (or actions) are the triple aspects of creation. Brahman manifests worlds and beings with their help. He does it because He wants to flourish in His creation and enjoy the worlds He creates. He desires the company of a female companion (duality) for the same reason. By creating different forms of food, names, forms, and duties, He becomes many and manifests as many. As part of the diversity and for the sake of dharma (duty), He creates four classes of gods and four castes, namely, the Brahmanas, the Kshatriyas, the Vaisyas, and the Sudras. The Upanishad also describes the deities associated with each of the castes.

Significance of dreams and deep sleep

Duality and diversity of names, forms, and actions exist in the wakeful state. Our experience of these may lead to mistaken notions of Brahman, such as the ones explained by the proud scholar Balaki to Ajatasatru in the second chapter as the sun, the moon, the mind, etc. These analogies are not without a basis because they do symbolically represent Brahman. However, the absolute reality of Brahman is realized only when we transcend all objectivity and enter transcendental states comparable in our consciousness to deep sleep.

The gross and subtle aspects of creation

In creation, Brahman manifests as both with form (murtam) and without form (amurtam). They are also known as the gross and subtle aspects of creation. They are present in us also. Our gross bodies are made up of fire, air, and water, and our subtle bodies of air and space. Both are perishable. Only the Self in the body is imperishable. The gross manifestations of Brahman are mortal and fixed. The subtle ones of the higher realms, represented by gods and Brahman's highest manifestations, are immortal and not fixed.

The Self alone is dearer

In a conversation between himself and his wife, Maitreyi, Yajnavalkya explains that if there is a reason to love creation and its numerous manifestations, it is not because things are lovable in themselves but because they are the numerous manifestations of the indivisible truth. A person becomes lovable not because he is a husband, son, or father but because of the Self that is present in him. Duality arises, and we regard others as separate or different when we do not perceive the Self in them. A thing is known by its source, and the source of all is the same Self. He is the essence of all, just as the salt in the water or the air in space, and He alone is dearer.

The one and many gods

The monotheistic elements of Hinduism are presented in the third chapter, in which Yajnavalkya explains that although the gods are numerous, they all are, indeed, aspects of one universal truth and depend upon one eternal truth only. The gods are the numerous manifestations of Brahman. Based on their immediate support, nature, or functions, we may classify them into different classes. But they can be reduced by their worlds into just three, namely the earth, the mid-region, and the heaven. They can be further reduced into two on the basis of their dependence upon food and breath. However, in the ultimate analysis, the entire creation rests upon one supreme truth only, and that is Brahman. He is the support of all existence.

Duality and non-duality

In the fourth chapter of the third Brahmana, Yajnavalkya explains to King Janaka that duality arises when we focus on the material aspects of Brahman and regard Him as speech, breath, etc. He suggests that we should regard Brahman as the light within, which is not dependent upon any external source, such as the light coming from the sun, the moon, or a torch. The Self is beyond all duality. He is without desires, free from impurities, and has no fear. In that absolute state, there is no second and no perception arising from the senses but an uninterrupted seeing of the seer without any intermediary agency such as the mind or the senses. Whoever enters into that state becomes one, like the water in a river or stream joining an ocean. It is the highest goal, the highest wealth, and the highest world. There, one enjoys the bliss of Brahman, which is a million times more intense than the ordinary pleasures we enjoy on earth.

Karma, desires, and life after death

In the next Brahmana (4.4), Yajnavalkya explains the different paths by which souls departing from here travel to the next worlds. In the same section, he also explains the importance of renunciation, austerities, and performing righteous actions. The concept of karma is briefly touched on here with the statement that the doer of good deeds becomes good, and the doer of evil becomes evil. Desires are the root cause of evil actions, and one should, therefore, practice renunciation. Those who perform desire-ridden actions and obligatory duties go to the world of ancestors but return from there to continue their bondage to samsara in another birth. However, those who transcend desires and achieve liberation become immortal and go to the world of Brahman.

The importance of three virtues

The fifth chapter of the second Brahmana contains an interesting story about how Prajapati taught the three most important virtues to the three classes of his progeny, namely, the gods, humans, and demons. To the gods, who are by nature pleasure-loving, he advised them to practice self-restraint (data). To the humans who are by nature greedy and selfish, he instructed them to practice charity (data), and to the demons who are by nature cruel, he counseled them to practice compassion (daydream). These three virtues are indeed relevant and important for humans since they possess both divine and demonic nature. Further, the gods and demons reside in their bodies and influence their thoughts and actions.

The significance of Gayatri

According to the Upanishad, Brahman is four-footed a symbolic reference to his all-pervading nature and the fact that he is spread in all directions. He is compared to the horse as well as to the Gayatri chant (5.14. Both are four-footed; the horse has four legs, and the Gayatri has four meters. The three worlds, namely the earth, the mid-region, and the heaven, make up his one foot. The hymns of the three Vedas make up one foot. The five breaths, namely Prana, Apana, Vyana, Samana, and Udana, make up one foot. The fourth foot is the sun itself, which shines high above the dark skies upon truth. It is the same as Turiya, the deep sleep state. By knowing the significance of Gayatri, its fourth and visible foot, and by chanting it, one can overcome adversity, subdue enemies, and fulfill one's desires.

Brihadaranyaka Upanishad

Procreation as an act of sacrifice

The sixth chapter of the Upanishad (6.4) describes sexual intercourse as a sacrifice in itself. Right knowledge of sexual intercourse is important. Without it, one may incur bad karma (6.4.3). According to the verses, Prajapati created a woman for procreation and made her compatible with male sexual organs, which is compared to the sacrificial pit and the intercourse itself to Vajapeya sacrifice. The next few verses explain how a man may engage himself in a sexual union with her, if necessary, by using force or a spell to produce the offspring. The section also contains formulas to produce different types of male children and methods to harm an adulterer who seduces another man's wife.

Conclusion

The Brihadaranyaka Upanishad contains the germs of many thoughts that now form an integral part of Hinduism. It also contains verses that are very ancient in origin and give credence to the argument that, at least in parts, it is earlier than the rest of the principal Upanishads. The Upanishad itself might have come to us from different sources and later compiled together into one text, as indicated by their arrangement into three sections (Khandas) ascribed to three different lineages of teachers, who are mentioned at the end of each respective section. The Upanishad also portrays the importance of Kshatriya teachers and the contribution they made to the development of Vedic wisdom.

Jayaram V

Translation

Brihadaranyaka Upanishad

Jayaram V

Chapter 1

First Brahmana

The Symbolism of Horse Sacrifice

1. aum! usa va asvasya medhyasya sirah, suryas caksuh, vatahpranah, vyattam agnir vaisvanarah; samvatsara atmasvasyamedhyasya, dyauh prstham, antariksam udaram, prthivipajasyam, disah parsve, avantaradisah parsavah,rtavongani, masas cardhamasas ca parvani, ahoratranipratisthah, naksatrany asthini, nabho mamsani; uvadhyamsikatah, sindhavo gudah, yakrc ca klomanas ca parvatah, osadhayas ca vanaspatayas ca lomani, udyan purvardhahnimlocan jaghanardhah, yad vijrmbhate tad vidyotate, yadvidhunute tat stanayati, yan mehati tad varsati; vag evasyavak.

1. Aum! The dawn is the head of the sacrificial horse. The sun is its eyes, the wind is its vital breath, and the Vaisvanarah fire is its open mouth. The year is the very body of the sacrificial horse; the sky is its back; the mid-region is its belly; the earth is its hoof; the quarters are its sides; the intermediate quarters its ribs; the seasons its limbs; the months and half-months its joints, days and nights its feet. The stars are its bones; the clouds are its flesh; the sand is its food in the stomach; the rivers are its blood vessels; the mountains are its liver and lungs; and the herbs and trees are its hair. The rising sun is its anterior; the setting sun is its posterior. When it yawns, then lightning; when it stirs, then thunder; when it relieves itself, it rains; and when it makes noise, it is speech itself.

Notes: The sacrificial horse is compared to the entire material manifestation. It is compared part by part to Purusha, the Cosmic Self. This is the description of a horse that was part of an ancient Vedic ceremony called the Horse Sacrifice (*Ashvamedha Yajna*), in which it would eventually be killed and deified to signify the divine authority the king commanded as the earthly representative of Prajapati himself. Horse sacrifices were common in ancient India when the kings of the original Kshatriya clans ruled the land. By all means, it was an ancient Vedic tradition that is now defunct. It was customary for the kings to perform this sacrifice to extend their empires and conquer new lands. The horse was set free to herald their intention to launch the conquest, using it as the symbol of their royalty, authority, sway, and lordship. The ritual usually lasted until the king concluded his conquest and returned to his capital, having established his divine authority and sovereignty.

At the beginning of the sacrifice, the king who intended to host the sacrifice would choose an able horse and set it free in a public ceremony, declaring his intent to conquer new lands. Once the horse was decorated and set free with royal fanfare, he and his army would follow it as it galloped into the open country and pasture lands according to its will. Whatever places it passed through, the king would claim them as a part of his conquered territory. If anyone caught the horse and held it captive, it signaled that his sovereignty was challenged and he must prove his prowess by fighting the opposing party. At the end of the expedition, if the king remained unopposed or survived all the challenges and remained victorious, he would return from the conquest with the sacrificial horse and formally complete the concluding part of the sacrifice by performing a ceremony along with his queens in which he would formally and ritually sacrifice the horse under the guidance of the royal priests. The meat from the sacrificial horse would be consumed by the king, his queens, and his relations. By that sacrifice, the king would consolidate his position as the lord of the four directions, just as the all-pervading Brahman, the Lord of the universe, symbolically represented by the horse. Brahma Prajapati, who was the chief deity of the Kshatriyas during their heydays, figures prominently in this Upanishad as the Cosmic Being (Purusha). The Horse sacrifice was thus an ancient Vedic tradition practiced by kings, which vested them with the divine power and authority of Brahman, the lord of the sacrifices with unsurpassed strength and power. The practice fell into disuse subsequently, as the ancient lineages of kings and their dynasties perished.

The symbolism of the sacrifice has been well documented in this section of the Brihadaranyaka Upanishad. The horse is compared to Brahman. Like the horse, Brahman has four feet or four quarters. Like the horse, Brahman is swift and moving. Like the horse, Brahman is the support for the king and his lands. Like the horse, Brahman also underwent a self-sacrifice. Just as the horse carries the intention of the king across the earth, Brahman carries the intentions of the sacrificer across the space to heaven. With the sacrifice of the horse, the king attained sameness or oneness with Brahman as the Lord of the Four Directions with unsurpassable power and glory.

Spiritually speaking, a Vedic sacrifice is a creative and transformative process. Through the sacrifices, you seek divine help to increase your powers or manifest your desires and wishes. Through the sacrifices, you also transform yourself and your life and destiny with the help of the gods. Through sacrificial actions, you enter into the realm of Brahman and end your association with Nature and the mortal world and the possibility of another birth. The horse sacrifice deified the horse as well as the king who performed it. Through the sacrifice, a worshipper also elevates all the offerings to the level of the Cosmic Being since the Cosmic Being Himself is the sacrificed and the sacrificer in every sacrifice. The same happened in the case of the horse also. Through sacrifice, the horse, the offering, became the Cosmic Being (Brahman or Purusha) and the worshipper, too, as the sacrificer. The horse represented the materiality or the corporeality of the creation. It was the body of the Cosmic Being, the mighty Purusha, who spread across the endless empyrean. It was the Prajapati Himself who used parts of Himself to manifest creation.

The comparison is usually called *Nasya*. The sacrificial horse is laid down in an easterly direction, with its head towards the east and tail to the west. Vaisvanara fire is the fire in the body, which is responsible for the body's warmth and its various functions. Its visible aspect is speech. Its hidden aspect is digestion. Its subtle aspect is breath or the flow of prana. The year is viewed as the body of Kala (Time) since it has months as its organs, parts, or divisions. Dhyau is heaven, beyond the sky. The sky is actually the mid-region. Since it is hollow, it is compared to the belly. The horse's bones are compared to the stars because they are white like them. The clouds are compared to the flesh because clouds have water, while flesh has blood and water.

2. ahar va asvam purastan mahima nvajayata. tasya purvesamudre yonih, ratrir enam pascan mahima nvajayata, tasyapare samudre yonih, etau va asvam mahimanavabhitah sambabhuvatuh hayo bhutva devan avahat, vajigandharvan, arvasuran, asvo manusyan; samudra evasyabandhuh, samudro yonih.

2. The sacrificial golden vessel called Mahiman placed in front of the horse is clearly the day. Its source is (in) the eastern sea. The night is the sacrificial silver vessel called Mahiman placed behind the horse. Its source is (in) the western sea. These two, called Mahiman, appeared on both sides of the horse. Having become Haya, it carried the gods, as Vaji the celestial beings, as Arva the demons and as Asva the humans. The sea is its relation, and the sea is its womb.

Notes: In the previous verse, the emphasis was on the bodily parts of the sacrificial horse. Here, it is on the ritual elements or the utensils used in the sacrifice. In the horse sacrifice, as per tradition, they used to place two sacrificial cups, one gold and one silver, on the front and back sides of the sacrificial horse. Water in these cups was used for different purposes. The golden cup is compared to the day because it has the color of the sun and the silver cup to the night because it has the color of the moon. The horse represents the body of the Cosmic Self as well as the body of all beings in all the worlds. Hence, it is given different names in different worlds, namely Haya, Vaji, Arva, and Asva. Shankara interpreted samudra as the Supreme Self and translated the last line as," The Supreme Self is its stable, and the Supreme Self (or the sea) is its source."

Second Brahmana

Creation and Separation of Worlds and Beings

1. naiveha kimcanagra asit, mrtyunaivedam avrtam asit, asanayaya, asanaya hi mrtyuh; tan mano'kuruta atmanvisyam iti. so'rcann acarat, tasyarcata. apojayanta, arcate vaime kam abh-

ud iti; tad evarkasya arkatvam; kam ha va asmaibhavati, ya evam etad arkasya arkatvam veda.

1. In the beginning, there was nothing here whatsoever. Indeed, by Death only all this was enveloped, or by hunger, because hunger is death only. He created the mind, thinking, "Let me have a mind." Then, He performed worship. From that worship, water was produced. He thought, "Truly, while I was worshipping, water was produced. That is why water is called Arca. Surely, water comes to him who thus knows why water came to be known as Arca."

Notes: Death is Time (*Kala*). In our scriptures, death and time are used synonymously. Everything that is born has to die. Everything emerges out of time and then is lost in time. Therefore, Death is depicted here as the source of all or Prajapati, the Lord of all beings. In the *Bhagavadgita* also, Arjuna envisions the universal form of God as Time only. Death is also used here synonymously with hunger. Shankara says Death is hunger because when we are hungry, we kill animals and eat them. Symbolically, in the context of this verse, hunger means desire, which sets in motion the cycle of creation. It is also the source of all modifications and actions within the Field of Nature. Desires cause the jivas' embodiment, bondage, and mortality. Desire or hunger, therefore, is also death because it causes death and rebirth.

This verse also speaks about how diversity came into existence. The first phenomenon to manifest was the Cosmic Mind or intelligence. From that emerged duality and individuality (ego). This individuation was the "self" that Death decided to have before it performed the ritual worship to produce water. The water that was produced in the ritual was rain in general and sperm, the source of life, in particular. Life on earth is sustained by both. Both arise from heat, the heat from the sun in the case of rain, and the heat from the body (Vaisvanara fire) in the case of sperm. Therefore, water is always available to those who know its source and how it is produced.

2. apo va arkah. tad yad apam sara asit, tat samahanyata, saprithivy abhavat, tasyam asramyat. tasya srantasya taptasyatejo raso niravartatagnih.

2. Water, truly, is arca. What was there as froth on the water solidified and became the earth. He (Death) became tired and rested upon it. While He was thus tired and resting, heat arose in Him and turned His vigor into fire.

Notes: The separation of the earth from water (primordial sea) is described here. The earth stands not only for the planet on which we live but also for the primordial egg consisting of all material aspects of Nature and creation. Its subtle aspect is the smell. Due to internal heat, fire separated from the earth. According to Shankara, Viraj was the first embodied being to arise from the Cosmic egg.

3. sa tredhatmanam vyakuruta, adityam trtiyam, vayumtrtiyam, sa esa pranas tredha vihitah. tasya praci dik sirah,asau casau cairmau; atha asya pratici dik puccham, asaucasau ca sakthyau; daksina codici ca parsve, dyauh prstham,antariksam udaram, iyam urah, sa eso 'psu pratisthitah,yatra kva caiti tad eva pratitisthaty evam vidvan.

3. He divided Himself into three, the sun (fire) as one-third, and the air as one-third. He also divided His vital breath (prana) into three. His head is the eastern direction; his arms are that and this (northeast and southeast). Now, His tail is the western direction and his two legs are this and that (southwest and northwest). His sides are the southern and northern directions. The sky is His back. The mid-region is His belly. The earth is His chest. Whoever knows that (truth) stands firm wherever he goes.

Notes: Creation is a process of diversification or separation. How the Comic Self, the One indivisible reality, divided itself into many aspects, directions, components of life, and materiality is being discussed here. We may not fully understand the symbolism hidden in these verses since the original meanings of many of the words used in them have changed over time. Therefore, we can only speculate what they imply. Symbolically, we may assume that three worlds became separated in the initial stages of creation, namely the heaven, the mid-religion, and the earth. In the case of the human body, the three are represented by the head, the trunk, and the legs. The sun represents the heaven. The air represents the mid-region of celestial planes, and the vital breath (*prana*) represents the mortal world.

4. so 'kamayata dvitiyo ma atma jayeteti, sa manasa vacam mithunam samabhavad asanaya mrtyuh, tad yad reta asit, sa samvatsaro 'bhavat; na ha pura tatah samvatsara asa. tam etavantam kalam abhibhah. yavan samvatsarah, tam etavatah, kalasya parastad asrjata; tam jatam abhivyadadat, sa bhan akarot saiva vag abhavat.

4. He desired, "Let me have a second self to arise from Me." He, hunger or death, joined the speech with the mind. Whatever was the seed of it, He let it become the year. Prior to that, there was no year. He bore him for a year and, after that period, delivered him. When he was born, (Death) opened his mouth (to devour him). He cried," Bhan," and it became (his) speech.

Notes: With these verses, we are still in a world of abstract ideas and cryptic symbolism. Hence, we cannot be certain what these associations and descriptions imply. We are still in the middle of the cosmic events that happened in the early stages of creation, which led to the formation of many cosmic deities of the highest order. This verse suggests that a Being with a name and form (Viraj) emerged out of Time as a result of a great meditation or austerity performed by Death using His mind as the seed of thought and some powerful chants (*mantras*) as the force to manifest them. The meditation lasted for one full Brahma year, spanning billions of Earth years. At the end of it, a great Being emerged. He was Viraj, the world itself. Death tried to swallow him because He was hungry, but the newborn one managed to avoid it with a forceful cry, which became his very speech and saving mantra. Even now, if someone cries in distress, people take pity on him and leave him alone. It was what Death did. Thus, through these happenings, Death or Prajapati divided Himself into three parts and, using His mind-born power and, with the help of the mantras, produced Viraj, the Being of universal proportions who had a name, form, and body. At the microcosmic level, we may compare this shining one, for that is what Viraj means, to a jiva, a being, or an embodied self. In the macrocosm, he is Purusha, the Cosmic Being. From the time beings are born, Death tries to swallow them constantly. They manage to survive so long as they keep it away with the help of the *Vedas* and sacrifices. Eventually, in the end times, He will swallow Viraj, the Cosmic Being, too.

5. sa aiksata: yadi va imam abhimamsye, kaniyo 'nnam karisya iti: sa taya vaca tenatmanedam sarvam asrjata yad idam kim ca, rco yajumsi samani chandamsi yajnan prajah pasun. sa yad yad evasrjata, tad tad attum adhriyata; sarvam va attiti tad aditer aditvam, sarvasyaitasyatta bhavati, sarvam asyannam bhavati, ya evam etad aditer aditvam veda.

5. He thought, "If I kill him, I shall have but little supply of food." Therefore, with that speech and that mind, He brought forth whatever that exists here, the hymns of the Rigveda, Yajurveda, and Samaveda, the meters, the sacrifices, humans and animals. Whatever He manifested, all that He decided to eat. Because He eats everything, indeed the nature of Aditi is called Aditi. He who knows how Aditi got this nature of Aditi becomes an eater of everything here, and everything becomes His food.

Notes: Death spared the firstborn because it would have ended the creation of life and existence there itself. Since He wanted to have more manifestations and further diversity, He continued with His act of creation and brought out the other aspects of Nature into existence. All the things that are mentioned in this verse are part of this world and subject to Nature (Prakriti). Death consumes them all in its own mysterious ways through numerous modifications. They are part of Nature (Aditi) and serve Death. Aditi is the Mother of all. She, as Death's consort, is also the consumer of all. As the producer, she is the creator, and as the consumer, she is Death itself. Eating also means enjoyment. All the sense objects that are enjoyed by the beings represent food only. That enjoyment arising from desires is also their source of suffering, mortality, birth, and rebirth.

Chapter 1

6. so 'kamayata, bhuyasa yajñena bhuyo yajeyeti; so 'sramyat, sa tapo 'tapyata: tasya srantasya taptasya yaso viryam udakramat. prana vai yaso viryam; tat pranesutkrantesu sariram svayitum adhriyata, tasya sarira eva mana asit.

6. He desired, "Let me sacrifice again with a bigger sacrifice." He toiled, performing austerities. While He was thus tired and engaged in austerities, His fame, and vigor departed from Him. Fame and vigor were indeed His vital breaths. When they departed, His body began to swell, yet His mind remained fixed on the body.

7. so 'kamayata, medhyam ma idam syat, atmanvy anena syam iti; tato 'svah samabhavat, yad asvat, tan medhyam abhud iti tad evasva-medhasyasva-medhatvam; esa ha va asva medham veda, ya enam evam veda. Tam anavarudhyaivamanyata; tam samvatsarasya parastad atmana alabhata: pasun devatabhyah pratyauhat. Tasmat sarva-devatyam proksitam prajapatyam alabhante; esa ha va asva-medho ya esa tapati: tasya samvatsara atma, ayam agnir arkah, tasyeme loka atmanah; tav etav arkasvamedhau. so punar ekaiva devata bhavati, mrtyur eva; apa punar-mrtyum jayati, nainam mrtyurm apnoti, mrtyur asyatma bhavati, etasam devatanam eko bhavati.

7. He (Prajapati) desired, "Let this body of mine be fit for a sacrifice and let me become embodied through it." Then He became a horse. Because it swelled (asvat) to become a horse and fit for sacrifice (medhya), the horse came to be known as Asva and the horse sacrifice Ashvamedha. Truly, he who knows it thus knows the Ashvamedha. Then, letting the horse go free, He (Prajapati) reflected upon it (imagining Himself as the horse). At the end of a year, He sacrificed it to Himself and offered other animals to the deities. Therefore, to this day, when the priests sacrifice to Prajapati the horse sanctified (by the mantras), they consider that it has been dedicated to all other gods. Truly, the sun, which produces heat, is the horse sacrifice. Of Him, the year is His body (because it is subject to divisions). This (earthly) fire is the sacrificial fire (Arca) (arising from the Sun, who is the horse sacrifice), and the worlds are His bodies. Thus, these are the two: the sacrificial fire and the horse sacrifice. They are one and the same: Death. He who knows this overcomes further death. Death cannot seize him. Death becomes His very Self, and he becomes one with the deities.

Chapter 1
Third Brahmana

Gods and Demons and the Superiority of Breath

1. dvaya ha prajapatyah, devas casuras ca. tatah kaniyasa eva devah, jyayasa asurah, ta esu lokesv aspardhanta, te ha deva ucuh, hantasuran yajña udgithenatyayameti.

1. There were two (classes) of Prajapati's sons, the gods and the demons. Of them the gods were younger and the demons older. They were struggling to control these worlds. The gods said, "Let us overcome the demons in the sacrifice through Udgita."

Notes: The gods and the demons are part of the cosmic body and our bodies also. They exist in us as bodily organs. When humans perform virtuous and selfless actions as ordained by the scriptures and purify their minds and bodies, the organs become divine instruments of righteousness and shine with the vigor and effulgence of gods, but when they perform actions with evil or selfish thoughts and intentions or desires, under the influence of the gunas, they become impure, dark and demonic with impurities and transform into instruments of evil. According to the Vedas, all selfish actions are evil. When organs are used for selfish purposes, they produce sinful karma. Hence, the Bhagavadgita recommends karma sannyasa yoga, in which actions are performed as a service or offering to God without desiring their fruit and offering that fruit to God only. Actions performed thus will not produce karma. In this section, we will realize that all the organs except the breath are susceptible to selfish desires and, thereby, vulnerable to evil influences. Udgita refers to the stotras, chants, or Samans of the Samaveda sung by Udgatris in the second part of the sacrifices, starting with Aum. They energize and lift the vibrations emanating from them and propel them higher into the atmosphere (mid-region) and toward the gods in heaven.

2. te ha vacam ucuh, tvam na udgaya iti, tatheti: tebhyo vag udagayat. yo vaci bhogas tam devebhya agayat. yat kalyanam vadati tad atmane; te vidur, anena vai na udgatratyesya ntiti tam abhidrutya papmanavidhyan, sa yah sa papma yad evedam apratirupam vadati, sa eva sa papma.

2. They said to the organ of speech, "Chant for us (the Udgita). "Surely," said speech and chanted for them. Whatever enjoyment was there in the speech, it made it available to the gods, but whatever good or auspiciousness was there in the speech, it kept to itself. The demons knew, "Truly, by this singer, they will overpower us." Therefore, they rushed upon it and polluted it with evil. That evil, which consists in saying what is sinful, it is that evil.

Notes: In chanting the Samans during the sacrifice, the Udgatir priests chant three Pavamanas for the gods and nine for themselves. The speech organ followed the same practice. It sang for the pleasure of gods but, at the same time, sang for its own good. The demons took advantage of this selfish behavior of the speech (organ) and overpowered it. It is not uncommon for humans to use speech for selfish or evil purposes to speak about themselves, speak untruths or falsehoods, hurt others with harsh and violent words, or reflect the evils of pride, anger, lust, envy, and greed in their speech. These are the vulnerabilities of speech to evil and selfish desires. The same speech may also be used to speak pleasant words, spread knowledge, peace, and happiness, chant mantras and prayers, worship God, or speak truth. Thus, human speech is vulnerable to both good and evil.

3. atha ha pranam ucuh, tvam na udgaya iti, tatheti: tebhyah prana udagayat. yah prane bhogas tam devebhya agayat, yat kalyanam jighrati tad atmane, te vidur anena vai naudgatr atyesyantiti. tam abhidrutya papmanavidhyan, sa yah sa papma yad evedam apratirupam jighrati sa eva sa papma.

3. *Then they said to the nose, "Chant for us (the Udgita)." "Surely," said the nose and chanted for them. Whatever enjoyment was there in the smell, it made it available to the gods, but whatever good or auspiciousness was there in the smell it kept to itself. The demons knew, "Truly, by this singer, they will overpower us." Therefore, they rushed upon it and polluted it with evil. That evil, which consists in smelling what is foul, it is that evil.*

Notes: The reference here is to the nose, not to the breath or prana. Reference to the breath will come later. The organ of smell is subject to attraction and aversion and can be used for both good and bad purposes and selfish enjoyment. Hence, it is not a reliable instrument or a safe haven for the gods.

4. atha ha caksur ucuh, tvam na udgaya iti tatheti: tebhyas caksur udagayat. yas caksusi bhogas tam devebhya agayat, yat kalyanam pasyati tad atmane; te vidur anena vai na udgatratyesyantiti. tam abhidrutya papmanavidhyan, sa yah sa papma yad evedam apratirupam pasyati, sa eva sa papma.

4. *Then, they said to the eye, "Chant for us (the Udgita)." "Surely," said the eye and chanted for them. Whatever enjoyment was there in seeing, it made it available to the gods, but whatever good or auspiciousness was there in seeing, it kept to itself. The demons knew, "Truly, by this singer, they will overpower us." Therefore, they rushed upon it and polluted it with evil. That evil, which lies in seeing what is unpleasant or improper, it is that evil.*

Notes: The eyes are also subject to attraction and aversion and good and evil influences of passions and emotions. The world is a mixture of good and evil or pure and impure. We cannot avoid seeing evil with our eyes, nor do we always succeed in looking away from temptations. The eyes are, therefore, unfit as the abode of gods.

5. atha ha srotram ucuh, tvam na udgaya iti, tatheti: tebhyah srotram udagayat. yah srotre bhogas tam devebhya agayat, yat kalyanam srnoti tad atmane; te vidur anena vai na udgatratyesyantiti. tam abhidrutya papmanavidhyan; sa yah sa papma yad evedam apratirupam srnoti, sa eva sa papma.

5. Then, they said to the ear, "Chant for us (the Udgita)." "Surely," said the ear and chanted for them. Whatever enjoyment was there in the hearing, it made it available to the gods, but whatever good or auspiciousness was there in hearing, it kept to itself. The demons knew, "Truly, by this singer, they will overpower us." Therefore, they rushed upon it and polluted it with evil. That evil, which lies in hearing what is unpleasant or improper, it is that evil.

6. atha ha mana ucuh, tvam na udgaya iti, tatheti: tebhyo mana udagayat. yo manasi bhogas tam devebhya agayat, yat kalyanam samkalpayati tad atmane; te vidur anena vai na udgatratyesyantiti. tam abhidrutya papmanavidhyan; sa yah sa papma yad evedam apratirupam samkalpayati, sa eva sa papma; evam u khalv eta devatah papmabhir upasrjan, evam enah papmanavidhyan.

6. Then, they said to the mind, "Chant for us (the Udgita)." "Surely," said the mind and chanted for them. Whatever enjoyment was there in the mind, it made it available to the gods, but whatever good or auspiciousness was there in the mind, it kept to itself. The demons knew, "Truly, by this singer, they will overpower us." Therefore, they rushed upon it and polluted it with evil. That evil, which lies in thinking what is unpleasant or improper, it is that evil. Thus, they overwhelmed these (other) deities and polluted them with evil.

Notes: The organs failed to uphold the gods and their righteous virtues because, in performing their duties, they were motivated by desires, attachments, and selfishness. They served not only the gods in nourishing them but also the demons under the influence of desires, selfish thoughts, and intentions. Selfishness is a demonic quality. The gods, in contrast, do not live for themselves. They live for others, stand for righteousness, and serve the Supreme Lord. Their selfless service is truly admirable, and hence, we look to them for help. If you are selfish, you will weigh the pros and cons of your actions and decisions before helping others. The gods do not have such consideration. They respond to everyone equally when they are invoked properly. For the same reason, they also do not make food for themselves, but rather depend upon us. When one makes things for oneself, including cooking food for one's own survival or enjoyment, it is deemed selfish and an evil action. The demons live and work for themselves. Humans who live selfishly or perform actions out of selfish desires are tainted with evil. Their actions lead to karma and bondage. The gods realized that none of the organs of the body was fit enough to serve them or protect them from evil without being influenced by evil desires.

7. atha hemam asanyam pranam ucuh, tvam na udgaya iti, tatheti: tebhya esa prana udagayat; te vidur anena vai na udgatratyesyantiti. tam abhidrutya papmanavidhyan; sa yatha asmanam rtva losto vidhvamseta, evam haiva vidhvamsamana visvanco vinesuh, tato deva abhavan, parasurah; bhavaty atmana parasya dvisan bhratrvyo bhavati ya evam veda.

7. Then, they said to the breath in the mouth, "Chant for us (the Udgita).) "Breath said, "Surely," and chanted for them. The demons knew, "Truly, by this singer, they will overpower us." Therefore, they rushed upon it and wanted to pollute it with evil. Now, as a lump of earth would be shattered and scattered in all directions when it is hit by a rock, so were they shattered and flung in all directions, whereby they perished. Thus, the gods prevailed, and the demons perished. He who knows this becomes his true Self, and his envious kinsman who hates him is crushed.

Notes: The demons succeeded in attacking the organs in the body and tainting them with evil because the organs, such as the speech, eyes, ears, nose, etc., were influenced by the gunas and the desires and attachment induced by them. They were unable to rise above their identification with the body and the ego and perform their obligatory duties for the sake of the creation. However, with the breath, it was different. Breath does not work for a motive or purpose. It is not subject to attraction and aversion or any passions and emotions. One does not breathe for enjoyment or fulfilling desires but for living. One can be selective in the actions of all other organs, but not so in the case of the breath. Breathing is an autonomous process. It is under its own control. Hence it is not susceptible to selfishness. Since it is free from attachment and selfish desires and works autonomously and selflessly, the demons cannot influence it or control it. Prana that enters our bodies through breathing is also not associated with any particular organ. It is not associated with the body even. Its source is also not the body but the sun and the air in the atmosphere (antariksham), and the energy that flows in the whole universe. It sustains the body but does not depend upon it. It does not utilize the energy produced by the body. It rather distributes it. It also upholds and unites the various parts of the body. Hence, breath, truly, is a divinity, pure and resplendent, and qualifies as the lord of all other organs. Because of this, breathing exercises, or Pranayama, are recommended in Yoga to control and discipline the mind and body.

8. te hocuh, kva nu so 'bhud yo na ittham asakteti, ayam asye 'ntar iti, so 'yasya angirasah, anganam hi rasah.

8. They said, "Where was he who has empowered us in this way? He is here within the mouth. He is called Ayasya Angirasa because he is the essence of the limbs.

Notes: Ayasa Angirasah means the sap (rasa) of the organs (angas) that removes their tiredness (ayasa). It is most likely a reference to Prana, the subtle energy that flows through the nerve and breath channels in the body due to breathing.

9. sa va esa devata dur nama, duram hy asya mrtyuh, duram ha va asman mrtyur bhavati ya evam veda.

9. That deity goes by the name Dur because Death stays away from him. Indeed, Death stays away from him, who knows him thus.

Notes: As long as the body has breath, Death cannot enter that body. Death comes only when the breath in the body departs. This is the meaning.

10. sa va esa devataitasam devatanam papmanam mrtyum apahatya, yatrasam disam antah, tad gamayamcakara, tad asam pamano vinyadadhat, tasman na janam iyat, nantam iyat, net papmanam mrtyum anvavayaniti.

10. That deity, verily, took away the evil of the gods (limbs), including death, to the end of the quarters. There, he dropped their evils. Therefore, one should neither go to a being (of that region) nor go to the end (of the quarters). Otherwise, he will meet there with the evil, with death.

Notes: The end of the quarters means the end of the world of gods, the mid-region, and the mortal world. Breath flows in these regions and keeps them clean. The gods live in the world of light. The celestial beings live in the mid-region pervaded by the light rays of the sun. Mortal beings live on the Earth, which is also energized by the sun every day. Beyond these three is the world of darkness, where the demons live. Their evil reigns because all the evil in all creation was taken and dumped there by the Shaktis, who personify breath. Because of this action of breath, evil is now confined to the evil world. When one performs evil actions, one enters those regions and picks up the evils from the demons who support them. Therefore, one should not resort to evil actions, however tempting they are, because by indulging in selfish actions and evil desires, beings succumb to karma, suffering, death, and rebirth.

11. sa va esa devataitasam devatanam papmanam mrtyum apahatya athaina mrtyum atyavahat.

11. That deity, having removed death, the evil of the gods, next carried them beyond death.

12. sa vai vacam eva prathamam atyavahat, sa yada mrtyum atyamucyata, so 'gnir abhavat, so 'yam agnih parena mrtyum atikranto dipyate.

12. It carried first the organ of speech (beyond death). When it was freed from death, it became fire. This fire, having transcended death, shines beyond its limits.

Notes: Pure speech is fire. It burns away all evils. It connects us with gods. It facilitates good actions. It promotes cooperation, sharing, and orderly living.

13. atha pranam atyavahat, sa yada mrtyum atyamucyata, sa vayur abhavat. so'yam vayuh parena mrtyum atikrantah pavate.

13. Then, it carried the organ of smell (beyond death). When it was freed from death, it became air. That air, having transcended death, blows beyond its limits.

14. atha caksur atyavahat, tad yada mrtyum atyamucyata, saadityo'bhavat, so'sav adityah parena mrtyum atikrantas tapati.

14. Then it carried the eye (beyond death). When it was freed from death, it became the sun. That sun, having transcended death, shines beyond its limits.

15. atha srotram atyavahat, tad yada mrtyum atyamucyata, ta diso'bhavan, ta ima disah parena mrtyum atikrantah.

15. Then it carried the ear (beyond death). When it was freed from death, it became quarters. The quarters, having transcended death, extend beyond its limits.

16. atha mano 'tyavahat, tad yada mrtyum atyamucyata, sa cand-ama abhavat, so'sau candrah parena mrtyum atikranto bhati, evam ha va enam esa devata mrtyum ativahati, ya evam veda.

16. Then it carried the mind (beyond death). When it was freed from death, it became the moon. That moon, having transcended death, shines beyond its limits. Thus, verily, this deity carries beyond death the one who knows thus.

17. athatmane 'nnadyam agayat, yadd hi kim cannam adyate, anenaiva tad adyate, iha pratitisthati.

17. Then, it secured food for itself by chanting, for it alone eats whatever food it eats and rests firmly upon that.

Notes: The subtle energy (prana), which is of the nature of the sun, coming out of the food we eat joins with the breath and is circulated throughout the body through the breath. Thus, whatever food we eat is eaten by breath only. Just as fire receives all the sacrificial offerings in a sacrifice on behalf of other gods, the breath (prana) in the body receives all the subtle energy coming out of the food. Then, unlike the other organs, which are prone to selfishness, it selflessly distributes the energy from the food it has eaten among the various parts of the body. The body, which is made up of the food eaten by the breath, is where the breath rests. That is what "rests firmly upon that" means. Although it rests in the body, it is not dependent on the body or the food, whereas the opposite is true in the case of the body and all the organs. Thus, the breath exemplifies karma sannyasa by performing its obligatory duty without desiring the fruit of its actions.

18. te deva abruvan, etavad va idam sarvam yad annam, tad atmana agasih, anu no 'sminn anna abhajasveti, te vai ma 'bhisamvisateti; tatheti: tam samantam parinyavisanta, tasmad yad ananenannam atti, tenaitas trpyanti; evam ha va enam sva abhisamvisanti, bharta svanam sresthah, pura eta bhavaty annado 'dhipatih, ya evam veda; ya u haivamvidam svesu pratipratir bubhusati, na haivalam bharyebhyo bhavati; atha ya evaitam anubhavati, yo vaitam anu bharyan bubhursati, sa haivalam bh aryebhyo bhavati.

18. The gods said, "Whatever is here, all of it you have secured for yourself as food by chanting. Now, share that food with us." "Now gather around facing me." "Surely." They gathered around him. Therefore, whatever food is eaten through the breath, the gods (limbs) are satisfied by it. In the same manner, relatives gather around a person who knows this. He becomes their supporter, the best, and a leader among them. He becomes an eater of food and ruler of them. However, none who desires to be equal to the one who knows this would be able to support his own dependents, but whoever follows him or desires to follow him to support his dependents also becomes capable of supporting them.

Notes: This verse suggests that the organs depend upon breath for their nourishment. Whatever vital energy the breath consumes from the food is automatically shared by the deities in the organs since they turn to the breath and look to him for their nourishment. Breath is selfless. Hence, when the gods asked him to share the food with them, he readily obliged. He who knows this follows the example of breath and shares whatever wealth or food he secures through his actions with the others who depend upon him or look to him for help. Hence, he becomes like the breath, the nourishers and supporters and others naturally follow him because of his benevolence.

19. so 'yasya angirasah, anganam hi rasah, prano va anganam rasah, prano hi va anganam rasah, tasmad yasmat kasmac cangat prana utkramati, tad eva tat susyati; esa hi va anganam rasah.

19. It is Ayasya Angirasa, for it is the sap. Truly, breath is the sap of the limbs. Yes, breath is the sap of the limbs. Therefore, from whichever limb breath departs, that dries up, for indeed, it is the sap of the limbs.

Notes: In the eighth verse it has already been stated that the vital energy (prana) produced by breath from the food is the essence of the limbs in the body. It is repeated here. Ayasa Angirasa means the essence, sap, or energy (rasa) of the striving (ayasa) organs (angas). Breath, indeed, is the essence of the working organs for it flows in the body as the essence of the food and nourishes and strengthens them by moving through them continuously until it departs from the body.

20. esa u eva brhaspatih, vag vai brhati tasya esa patih, tasmad u brhaspatih.

20. And it is also Brahaspati. Speech is Brihati, and this (breath) is its lord. Therefore, it is Brihaspati, the lord of Brihati.

Notes: Brihati means speech which includes all the letters, meters, intelligence, and sounds used in chanting the Riks, the hymns of the Rigveda. Breath is its support in the throat. Hence, it is Brihaspati, the Lord of Brihati.

21. esa u eva brahmanas-patih, vag vai brahma, tasya esa patih, tasmad u brahmanas-patih.

21. And it is also Brahmanaspati. Indeed, speech is Brahmana. This is its lord. Therefore, it is Brahmanaspati, the lord of Brahmanas.

Notes: According to Shankara, Brahmana represents the Yajus or the hymns of the Yajurveda.

22. esa u eva sama, vag vai sama, esa sa camasceti, tat samnah samatvam; yad veva samah plusina, samo masakena, samo nagena, sama ebhis tribhir lokaih, samo 'nena sarvena, tasmad veva sama, asnute samnah sayujyam salokatam, ya evam etat sama veda.

22. And it is the same as the Saman. Speech is indeed the chant. Speech is Sa, and breath is Ama. Hence the name Sama, for the chant. The chant is also Sama because it is the same (sama) with (the sounds made by) a white ant, a mosquito, an elephant, (all the beings in) the three worlds, and the entire universe. He who knows this about the chant (Saman) attains oneness with it or lives in the world of sameness.

Notes: The hymns or songs of Samaveda are called Samans. Sa represents speech, and Ama represents prana, the subtle energy. Both are needed to sing the Samans. Saman is also sama (equality) because its singing stabilizes the mind and establishes sameness or equanimity.

23. esa u va udgithah; prano va ut, pranena hidam sarvam uttabdham, vag eva githa, uc ca githa ceti, sa udgithah.

23. And indeed, it is the high chant (Udgita). Breath is indeed Ut (support), for by breath only all this is supported. Speech, indeed, is the chant (gita). Breath is the support (ut) of the chant (gita). Hence it is Udgita, the support of the chant.

Notes: When you take long and deep breaths, it becomes Udgita, the uplifting Saman.

24. taddhapi brahmadattas caikitaneyo rajanam bhaksayann uvaca, ayam tyasya raja murdhanam vipatayatat, yad ito 'yasya angiraso 'nyenodagayad iti, vaca ca hy eva sa pranena codagayad iti.

24. Also, regarding this, there is this reference. While drinking Soma, the king among the drinks, Brahmadatta Caikitaneya, once said this, "May this kingly drink strike off this head of mine if I say that Ayasa Angirasa chanted the high chant by any other means, for by the speech and by the breath alone he chanted the Udigita.

Notes: This is to reinforce the conviction that none but breath is the support of Udgita, the uplifting Saman.

25. tasya haitasya samno yah svam veda, bhavati hasya svam; tasya vai svara eva svam; tasmad artvijyam karisyan vaci svaram iccheta; taya vaca svara-sampannayartvijyam kuryat; tasmad yajñe svaravantam didrksanta eva; atho yasya svam bhavati; bhavati hasya svam, ya evam etat samnah, svam veda.

25. He who knows the wealth of the chant gains wealth. Indeed, voice is its wealth. Hence, he who wants to assume the duties of a Rtviz priest should desire to have a good voice for his chants. Possessing such a voice, he should perform his duties as a Rtvij priest. For this reason only, at a sacrifice, people desire to see a priest who is endowed with a good voice and regard him as the one who has the wealth. He who knows the wealth of a chant as such attains wealth.

26. tasya haitasya samno yah suvarnam veda, bhavati hasya suvarnam, tasya vai svara eva suvarnam, bhavati hasya suvarnam, ya evam etat samnah suvarnam veda.

26. He who knows the gold hidden in the chant attains gold. Truly, the gold of a Saman is svara, the voice (that sings it). He who knows about this gold of a chant attains gold.

Notes: These verses refer to the importance of voice, tone, pronunciation, and intonation in chanting the hymns during sacrificial ceremonies. The deities do not respond if the chanting or singing is incorrect or inaccurate.

27. tasya haitasya samno yah pratistham veda, prati ha tisthati, tasya vai vageva pratistha, vaci hi khalv esa etat pranah pratisthito giyate. anna ity u haika ahuh.

27. He who knows the support for the chant obtains the support (of breath, gods, and patrons). Speech is indeed the support; for resting on speech, breath emits the chant. Some say resting on food (the body).

Notes: The support of the Saman is prana or subtle energy. Obtaining the support of the breath means a long lifespan and the benefits of a successful career as a priest or singer of Samans.

28. athatah pavamananam evabhyarohah, sa vai khalu prastota sama prastauti, sa yatra prastuyat, tad etani japet: 'asato ma sad gamaya, tamaso ma jyotir gamaya, mrtyor mamrtam gamaya' iti, sa yad aha, asato ma sad gamaya iti, mrtyur va asat, sad amrtam, mrtyor mamrtam gamaya, amrtam ma kurv ity evaitad aha; tamaso ma jyotir gamaya iti, mrtyur vai tamah, jyotir amrtam, mrtyor ma amrtam gamaya, amrtam kurv ity evaitad aha; mrtyor mamrtam gamaya iti, natra tirohitam ivasti. atha yanitarani stotrani, tesv atmane'nnadyam agayet; tasmad u tesu varam vrnita, yam kamam, kamayeta, tam, sa esa evam-vid udgatatmane va yajamanaya va yam kamam kamayate tam agayati; taddhaital loka-jid eva, na haiva lokyataya asasti, ya evam etat sama veda.

28. Now, as to the repetition (Abhyaroha) of only the purifying hymns called Pavamanas. The Prastotr priest chants the Saman. While he does it, the sacrificer should repeat with him these (three Yaju mantras): from untruth lead me towards truth, from darkness lead me towards light, and from death lead me towards immortality. When he says, "From untruth lead me towards truth," the untruth (asat), verily, is death itself, and the truth (sat) is immortality. Thus, he is actually saying, "From death lead me towards immortality," or saying, "Make me immortal." When he says, "From darkness lead me towards light," darkness means death, and light means immorality. Thus, he is saying, "From death lead me towards light," or saying, "Make me immortal." In the third chant- "From death lead me towards immortality," there is no hidden meaning that requires explanation. He should then recite the remaining Pavamanas to procure food for himself. While they are being chanted, the sacrificer should ask for whatever boon he may desire. Whichever Udgatir priest knows this, whatever boon he desires for himself or for the sacrificer, he secures them by chanting. This chanting certainly leads to the conquest of the world. He who knows the (sup-

port) for the chant (Saman), for him there is no fear of being left without (the objects of) the world.

Notes: The Pavamanas are special mantras. This verse says that the Prastotr priest should chant the first three mantras, known as Yaju mantras, regarding death and immortality for the sake of the sacrificer and the remaining ones for himself. The chanting is meant to establish a connection with the divinity (the Self) seated in the body and gain control over the body and the mortal world so that one is freed from the want of wealth and from the cycle of births and deaths. This verse is the last of this section. In the first part of this section, we read that breath carried away all the evil present in the organs and placed them beyond the three worlds. So, when we pray, saying, "Lead me from death or lead from darkness or lead me from mortality," we are actually seeking the help of the divine breath, the Lord, who is called Ayasa Angiras, Brihaspati and Brahmanaspati, to keep us safe from these three evils: death, darkness, and mortality.

Fourth Brahmana

Creation of Duality and Diversity

1. atmaivedam agra asit purusavidhah, so'nuviksya nanyad atmano'pasyat, so'ham asmity agre vyaharat; tato'ham namabhavat, tasmad apy etarhy amantritah; aham ayam ity evagra uktva, athanyan nama prabrute yad asya bhavati. sa yat purvo'smat sarvasmat sarvan papmana ausat, tasmat purusah; osati ha vai sa tam, yo'smat purvo bubhusati, ya evam veda.

1. In the beginning, this was but one Self in the form of a person (purusha). Looking around, he saw nothing but himself. His first utterance was, "I am He." Thus, the name "I" came into existence. Therefore, to this day, when a person is greeted, he first says, "It is I," and then says whatever other name he may have. Because he was the first before all (puru) to burn all evils, he is accordingly called Purusha. He who knows thus indeed burns up one who wants to be before him.

Notes: All this was but oneself means all this existence was but one reality without diversity or differentiation. It then manifested into various individualities, each with a form and name. The individuality or the personality, described here as the 'I' or aham, was the first. Therefore, it is called Purusha. This Purusha is the jiva, the living self, with an ego, intelligence, and mind of its own, different from the real Self, the Purusha, who is undifferentiated and indivisible and described by Shankara as the Hiranyagarbha, the golden germ. 'I am,' this is the state of the Self. 'I am this and that' is the state of the Jiva, the living being or Viraj, the world, Purusha, or the Cosmic Being of the macrocosm.

2. so'bibhet, tasmad ekaki bibheti, sa hayam iksam cakre, yan mad anyan nasti, kasman nu bibhemiti, tata evasya bhayam viyay viyaya kasmad hy abhesyat, dvitiyad vai bhayam bhavati.

2. *He was afraid. Therefore, a person is afraid to be alone (even now). Then he thought to himself, "Since there is none else other than me, what should I fear?" With that, his fear left him, for what was there to fear? It is from duality (or the presence of another) that fear arises.*

Notes: The fear of death haunts every jiva. When a person overcomes the duality or the false notion of 'I am this and that' and realizes that he is the all-pervading, eternal, and indivisible Self (I am only), and there is nothing else, his fear vanishes.

3. sa vai naiva reme; tasmad ekaki na ramate; sa dvitiyam aicchat; sa haitavan asa yatha stri-pumamsau samparisvaktau; sa imam evatmanam dvedhapatayat, tatah patis ca patni cabhavatam; tasmat idam ardha-brgalam iva svah, iti ha smaha yajñavalkyah; tasmad ayam akasah striya puryata eva. tam samabhavat, tato manusya ajayanta.

3. *He felt no joy at all. Therefore, a person who is lonely does not experience joy. He desired to have a companion. He became as big as a man and woman in close embrace. He divided himself (his body) into two. From that manifested a husband and a wife. Hence, Yajnavalkya used to say, "This body is but one half of oneself, like one of the two shells of a split pea." Therefore, this space is filled by the wife. He became united with her. From that, human beings were born.*

Notes: According to Shankara, Viraj projected a new being with a large body who then divided itself into a man and a woman or Purusha and Prakriti. The body is one-half. The Self is the other half.

4. sa heyam iksam cakre, katham nu matmana eva janayitva sambhavati, hania tiro'saniti; sa gaur abhavat, rsabha itaras tam sam evabhavat, tato gavo' jayanta; vadavetarabhavat, asvavrsa itarah, gardhabhitara gardabha itarah, tam sam evabhavat, tata eka-sapham ajayata; ajetarabhavat, vasta itarah, avir itara, mesa itarah, tam sam evabhavat, tato'javayo' jayanta; evam eva yad idam kim ca mithunam, a-pipilikabhyah tat sarvam asrjata.

4. *She thought, "How can he be one with me when he produced me from himself? Therefore, I shall hide myself. She became a cow (to hide from him), the other (became) a bull and united with her. From that, cows were born. She became a mare, the other a stallion; she became a female ass, and the other a male ass. From that, one-hoofed animals were born. The one became a she-goat and the other a he-goat; the one*

became an ewe, the other became a ram, and from that, goats and sheep were born. Thus, he created everything, all that exists in pairs, down to the ants.

Notes: Purusha and Prakriti (Nature) manifest in creation in various forms. All duality and diversity manifest from their union or association only. It is wrong to believe that these two entities are actually gender-based. They exist in all, both in male and female bodies. Purusha is the Self, the consciousness; Prakriti is the body or the materiality. This is probably a description of how duality or the pairs of opposites manifested in creation, not just male and female entities.

5. so'vet, aham vava srstir asmi, aham hidam sarvam asrksiti; tatah srstir abhavat, srstyam hasyaitasyam bhavati ya evam veda.

5. He knew, "I, truly, am the creation. I have created all this. Thus, he became the creation. He who knows this as true also becomes (a creator) in this creation of him.

Notes: With the right knowledge, a person can become a creator like Viraj. He learns to project his thoughts and manifest reality. This may also mean with the knowledge of the Vedas and the Samans, he becomes effective as a priest or a sacrificer in manifesting results or achieving fulfillment of desires through sacrifices.

6. athety abhyamanthat, sa mukhac ca yoner hastabhyam cagnim asrjata, tasmad etad ubhayam alomakam antaratah, alomaka hi yonir antaratah, tad yad idam ahur amum yaja, amum yajety ekaikam devam, etasyaiva sa visrstih, esa u hy eva sarve devah. atha yat kim cedam ardram, tad retaso asrjata, tad u somah. etavad va idam sarvam annam caivannadas ca, soma evannam, agnir annadah. saisa brahmano'tisrstih, yac chreyaso devan asrjata: atha yan martyah sann amrtan asrjata, tasmad atisrstih. atisrstyam hasyaitasyam bhavati ya evam veda.

6. Then, with his hands, he rubbed his mouth back and forth and produced fire from the source. Hence, both these (back of the hands and mouth) are without hair on the inside. Even the source is without hair inside. When they say, "Sacrifice to this one, sacrifice to the other one," they are sacrificing but to one deity. They (the gods) are his creations and he alone is all gods. Further, all the liquid that is in the form of semen is produced by him only. That (semen) is Soma. All this is here is food and the eater of food. Soma is the food and fire is the eater of the food. This is the superior creation of a Brahmana, who created superior gods. Although a mortal, he created the immortals. Therefore, it is a superior creation. He who knows this as such becomes (a creator) in this super-creation of Viraj.

Notes: Viraj was the first Brahmana to manifest in creation. He is compared to a Brahmana (a pure being), and his bodily parts are compared to the gods and other beings. Yet they are all one because they are all part of Brahman only. That Brahmana (Viraj) performed a sacrifice with his bodily parts. He first produced fire, rubbing both his hands. Then, he performed the sacrifice. Through that self-sacrifice, he produced gods of heaven and gods of the earth (Brahmanas) out of himself. All these gods are but himself. The gods and Brahmanas emerged from his mouth (or speech), partaking in his nature or intelligence (semen). Thus, Viraj, as a Brahmana and a mortal, created immortals, the gods of heaven. Viraj (also called Isvara, Brahma, or Purusha) is a mortal because his form or materiality will be withdrawn eventually at the end of creation. "He rubbed his mouth back and forth with his hands" means either he produced fire from friction or put food in his mouth repeatedly to produce digestive fire from which was formed his divine nature, the semen. From that, gods and Brahmanas were produced. Food is also the source of creation and reproduction. Hence, the reference to food as the nourisher. In the body, food for the limbs comes from the digestive fire and, in creation, from the sacrificial fire. Hence, fire is described as the eater of food. This verse hints that in creation, the knowers of Brahman have a superior role as the creators and sustainers of the immortal gods in their bodies, and those who worship them must perform their obligatory duties to uphold them and the creation. Shankara commented that the reference to rubbing the mouth with hands was to describe how Viraj produced Brahmanas from his mouth.

7. taddhedam tarhy avyakrtam asit, tan nama-rupabhyam eva vyakriyata, asau nama, ayam idam rupa iti, tad idam apy etarhi nama-rupabhyam eva vyakriyate, asau nama, ayam idam rupa iti. sa esa iha pravista anakhagrebhyah yatha, ksurah ksuradhane' vahitah syat, visvam-bharo va visvambhara- kulaye, tam na pasyanti. a-krtsno hi sah, pranann eva prano nama bhavati, vadan vak, pasyams caksuh, srnvan srotram, manvano manah, tany asyaitani karma-namany eva. sa yo'ta ekaikam upaste, na sa veda, akrtsno hy eso'ta ekaikena bhavati, atmety evopasita, atra hi ete sarva ekam bhavanti. tad etat padaniyam asya sarvasya yad ayam atma, anena hy etat sarvam veda, yatha ha vai padenanuvindet. evam kirtim slokam vindate ya evam veda.

7. At that time, this body was undifferentiated. (When) it became differentiated into name and form; it was called (with) such and such name and such and such form. Hence, to this day, only when it is differentiated, all that is here is distinguished by such and such name and such and such form. He pervades the body up to the tip of the nails, just as a blade (remains) in the case up to the tip or fire in the firewood. He is not seen because they do not see him as a whole but only in parts, in the prana by the name prana, in speech by voice, in the eye by sight, in the ear by hearing, and in the mind by cognition. These are merely the names of his actions. Whoever meditates upon each of them individually does not know him for he remains incomplete in each of them that have one or the other (name and form). He should meditate upon the (whole) Self alone, wherein only all these (organs, names, and forms) become one. The Self is the basis of all these, and by it alone, one knows all these, just as one knows (an animal) through its footprints. He, who knows thus, finds name and fame.

Notes: The Self that is referenced here is not location-specific but pervades the whole body as its Lord and Enjoyer. It cannot be known or seen wholly because it is transcendental, hidden, and invisible. It is known only through the organs or parts by the actions he performs through them. In the body, it is associated with a name and form, which represents the whole instead of the parts. A person's identity (the Self) is the sum of all his or her aspects and bodily parts. You cannot identify him by his parts because, in them, he is incomplete. In the parts, you may see either a particular action or a specific form but not the whole person. To know a person or distinguish him from others, you must see him wholly as an individual being, having a distinct name and identity (self) of his own that separates him from the rest. In other words, individual parts in isolation do not become a person or distinguish him. To know him you must look at him wholly as a complete being (purna-purusha). In this verse, the Self is mixed up with a being's personality (world or Viraj) and represented as the feeling of "I am."

8. tad etat preyah putrat, preyo vittat, preyo'nyasmat sarvasmat, antarataram, yad ayam atma. sa yo'nyam atmanah priyam bruvanam bruyat, priyam rotsyatiti, isvaro ha tathaiva syat. atmanam eva priyam upasita, sa ya atmanam eva priyam upaste na hasya priyam pramayukam bhavati.

8. This Self, which is hidden within oneself, is dearer than a son, dearer than wealth and dearer than anything else. If one holds anything else other than the Self as dearer and if a person (who holds his Self as dearer) were to say to him that he will lose (what is dearer to him), very likely it will happen. (Therefore,) one should meditate upon his Self alone as dearer. He who worships his Self as dear, what he loves will not perish.

Note: The Self, Isvara, is the protector. One should take refuge in him, meditate on him as the highest and the most auspicious, and seek protection and support. A son ensures the continuity of the family lineage, safe passage to the ancestral world through rites and rituals, and possible rebirth in the same family. Isvara, the Supreme Lord, ensures liberation from the triple evils, death, darkness, and mortality, and passage to the immortal world. Hence, he is dearer than one's own son.

9. tad ahuh, yad brahma-vidyaya sarvam bhavisyanto manusya manyante, kim u tad brahmavet, yasmat tat sarvam abhavad iti.

9. They say, "If men think that by the knowledge of Brahman, they become all, what does that Brahman know by which It became all?"

Notes: It is true that Brahman is all. However, in meditation, one should think of Brahman as one and indivisible only. One should not focus on his parts or manifestations or identify themselves with his creation. This is explained in the next verse.

10. brahma va idam agra asit, tad atmanam evavet, aham brahmasmiti: tasmat tat sarvam abhavat, tad yo yo devanam pratyabubhyata, sa eva tad abhavat, tatha rsinam, tatha manusyanam. taddhaitat pasyan rsir vama-devah pratipede, aham manur abhavam suryas ceti, tad idam api etarhi ya evam veda, aham brahmasmiti sa idam sarvam bhavati; tasya ha na devas ca nabhutya isate, atma hy esam sa bhavati. atha yo anyam devatam upaste, anyo'sau anyo' ham asmiti, na sa veda; yatha pasur, evam sa devanam; yatha ha vai bahavah pasavo manusyam bhuñjyuh, evam ekaikah puruso devan bhunakti; ekasminn eva pasav adiyamane'priyam bhavati, kim u bahusu? tasmad esam tan na priyam yad etan manusya vidyuh.

10. In the beginning, this Self was indeed Brahman only. It knew inwardly as "I am Brahman." Therefore, it became all. Whoever among the gods knew it also became That (Brahman), and so were those among the seers and humans. Having realized it himself, sage Vamadeva made this utterance, "I am Manu, and I am the sun." It is true even now; whoever knows thus "I am Brahman," he become all this here. Even the gods cannot prevent him from becoming thus because he becomes their very Self. However, whoever worships another deity (other than the Self), thinking "He is another and I am another," he knows not. He is looked upon by the gods as an animal. Just as many animals serve each human being, each human being does serve the gods. If even one animal is taken away, it makes us unhappy; what can be said if many (are lost)? Therefore, the gods are not pleased if many human beings come to know this knowledge.

Notes: Gods do not like human beings who try to seek Brahman because they do not want to lose their patrons on earth. They are happy if human beings perform sacrifices and keep nourishing them, just as we are happy if our cattle do their job by providing milk, protecting our homes, or working in our farmlands. If we renounce the world and seek Brahman, the gods will not receive offerings from us. Therefore, they do not want us to renounce the world and know Brahman and will do everything in their capacity to prevent us from knowing him. However, they themselves, since they know Brahman, do not appreciate those who look upon Brahman with duality or consider his parts or manifestations as him and worship him accordingly. Only the enlightened one who thinks and knows that he is Brahman becomes Brahman, and even gods cannot prevent him from becoming That. This verse has echoes of the same teaching found in the Bhagavadgita: those who worship Me come to Me, and those who worship gods, demigods, etc., go to them.

11. brahma va idam agra asit, ekam eva; tad ekam san na vyabhavat. tac chreyo rūpam atyasrjata ksatram, yany etani devatra ksatrani, indro varunah somo rudrah parjanyo yamo mrityur isana iti. tasmat ksatrat param nasti, tasmat brahmanah ksatriyam adhastad upaste rajasūye, ksatra eva tad yaso dadhati; saisa ksatrasya yonir yad brahma. tasmad yady api raja paramatam gacchati, brahmaivantata upanisrayati svam yonim. ya u enam hinasti, svam sa yonim rcchati, sa papiyan bhavati, yatha sreyamsam himsitva.

11. Truly, in the beginning, this was Brahman, one only. Being alone, That one did not flourish. He created men of superior form having sovereign power (as rulers) and among gods those who have the sovereign power, namely Indra, Varuna, Soma, Rudra, Parjanya, Yama, Death, and Isana. Therefore (because they were the first created), there is none higher than the Kshatriyas. Therefore, (because they are superior), even the Brahmanas worship the Kshatriyas from a lower position in the Rajasuya Sacrifice. He has thus endowed the Kshatriyas with greatness. However, since Brahman is the source of the Kshatriyas, even if a king attains an exalted position, in the end he has to take shelter in his source, the Brahmana. He who harms the knower of Brahman injures his own source. He incurs great sin when he harms one who is superior.

Notes: This verse identifies Viraj, the First Purusha, who manifested from Brahman, as a Brahmana. He produced four classes of beings by producing fire and then performing a fire sacrifice using parts of himself. As declared in verse 6, he first produced gods and Brahmanas from mouth and intelligence. He produced the Kshatriyas of superior strength from his strength or virility. Since strength or physical prowess is superior to intelligence, the Kshatriyas in this world and the Kshatriya gods in heaven enjoy a superior status in all worldly matters. However, since Viraj was a Brahmana who created them, they owe their existence to a Brahmana only. Therefore, they must treat all the Brahmanas, the knowers of Brahman, with utmost respect. This respect is not just a formality but a recognition of the debt of gratitude that the Kshatriyas owe to the Brahmanas for their very existence. Otherwise, they will incur great sin. As described in the previous verses, a true Brahmana is the one who knows Brahman as himself and sees himself in everything and all aspects of creation. He represents Brahman's divine nature and superior intelligence. He should not be mistaken for an ignorant person born into a Brahmana family. For the true Brahmana, everything is Brahman or his very Self. Since he is all and present in all, anyone who hurts him also hurts himself. Therefore, the knower of Brahman is superior to all and should not be harmed or disrespected. A Brahmana is the source of Kshatriyas because Viraj (Brahma), a Brahmana, created them. Secondly, a Kshatriya becomes a king, wins wars, or produces progeny only with the cooperation of the Brahmanas, who perform sacrifices for him to please the gods and secure their blessings. Therefore, he owes them a debt of gratitude.

12. sa naiva vyabhavat, sa visam asrjata, yany etani devajatani ganasa akhyayante, vasavo rudra aditya visvedeva maruta iti.

12. Yet, he did not flourish. He created people of commonality (vis) and among gods those known as the gods of commonality, namely the Vasus, Rudras, Adityas, Visvadevas and Maruts.

Notes: Then, he produced Vaishyas and the gods of commonality, such as the Visvadevas, Maruts, Adityas, etc., to create wealth and prosperity. The Vaishyas are grouped with the groups of gods since they work in groups or with others to perform their duties, not by themselves. These gods are important for creating an ideal climate and environment for conducting trade and commerce, going on long voyages across the oceans, cultivating the farmlands, grazing cattle, and harvesting the produce to create wealth. It may be interesting to note that in the early Vedic conception, Vishnu, an Aditya, was worshipped as a god of commonality and identified with Vaishyas.

13. sa naiva vyabhavat, sa saudram varnam asrjata pusanam, iyam vai pusan, iyam hidam sarvam pusyati yad idam kim ca.

13. Still, He did not flourish. He created the varna (class) of Sudras as Pushan, the nourisher, for it nourishes everything that is here.

Notes: The Shudras are the people of the earth. Their god, Pushan, is the god of the earth (body) or the earth itself. He is the nourisher of all and is often equated with Shiva himself.

14. sa naiva vyabhavat. tat chreyo-rupam atyasrjata dharmam; tad etat ksatrasya ksatram yad dharmah, tasmad dharmad param nasti: atho abaliyan baliyamsam asamsate dharmena, yatha rajña evam. yo vai sa dharmah satyam vai tat; tasmat satyam vadantam ahuh, dharmam vadatiti, dharmam va vadantam, satyam vadatiti, etad hy evaitad ubhayam bhavati.

14. Yet he did not flourish. He further created that exceedingly great form, dharma. That dharma is the sovereign of even the sovereign Kshatriyas. Therefore, there is nothing higher than dharma. Hence, with the help of dharma even a weak person is able to command a strong person, as one does with the help of a king. Now, that which is dharma is nothing but truth. Therefore, they say about a person who speaks the truth, "He speaks dharma," or about a person who speaks dharma, "He speaks the truth." Indeed, both happen to be the same.

Notes: Dharma has many meanings, but primarily, it means obligatory duty. Truth is dharma. Law is dharma. Righteousness is dharma. Creation, preservation, and dissolution are God's eternal duties (dharma). As part of God's creation, the four classes of humans are expected to do their part and perform their obligatory duties derived from the Creator himself to ensure the order and regularity of the world. If they neglect their duties, they will not prosper and will incur sinful karma. For the world to prosper, all beings must abide by their nature and perform their duties. By adhering to his dharma (speaking truth and performing duties), even a weak man can defeat a strong man (who does not perform his duties).

15. tad etad brahma ksatram vit sudrah. tad agninaiva devesu brahmabhavat, brahmano manusyesu, ksatriyena ksatriyah, vaisyena vaisyah, sudrena sudrah; tasmad agnav eva devesu lokam icchante, brahmane manusyesu, etabhyam hi rupabhyam brahmabhavat. atha yo ha va asmal lokat svam lokam adrstva praiti, sa enam avidito na bhunakti, yatha vedo vananuktah anyad va karmakrtam. yad iha va apy anevamvid mahatpunyam karma karoti, taddhasyantatah ksiyata evaatmanam eva lokam upasita; sa ya atmanam eva lokam upaste, na hasya karma ksiyate, asmadd hy eva atmano yad yat kamayate tat tat srjate.

15. (Thus) these (four classes were created), Brahmana, Kshatriya, Vaisya and Sudra. Among the gods, Brahman manifested as fire and among men as Brahmana, among the Kshatriyas as Kshatriya, among the Vaisyas as Vaisya, and among the Sudras as Sudra. Therefore, people who desire to attain a place among gods and their world (do so) through fire only and among men through a Brahmana because Brahman is found in both these forms only. However, if anyone departs from this world without knowing his own world (his Self), since it is unknown does not protect him, just as the Vedas not recited or the deeds not performed do not (protect him). Even if a man performs many great, meritorious deeds without knowing (his Self) in the end, his actions are bound to diminish (in power). One should meditate upon oneself as one's (true) world. He who meditates upon his Self as his world, his actions do not diminish because whatever he desires, he creates out of himself.

Notes: A place in heaven among the gods is obtained by making offerings to fire or by generating fire (tapas) within oneself through austerities. A place among men means human birth. It is obtained by performing sacrificial ceremonies and obligatory duties for which the help of a Brahmana is required. While these two are good means to secure the next birth, they do not free one from rebirth or the mortal world. For that, knowledge of the Self is important. Whoever departs from here, knowing that his Self is his true world and identity, attains the immortal heaven and never returns.

16. atho ayam va atma sarvesam bhutanam lokah. sa yaj juhoti yad yajate, tena devanam lokah. atha yad anubrute, tena rsinam; atha yat pitrbhyo niprnati yat prajam icchate, tena pitrnam; atha yan manusyan vasayate, yad ebhyo'sanam dadati, tena manusyanam; atha yat pasubhyas trnodakam vindati, tena pasunam; yad asya grhesu svapada vayamsy apipilikabhya upajivanti, tena tesam lokah; yatha ha vai svaya lokayaristim icchet, evam haivam vide (sarvada) sarvani bhutany aristim icchanti. tad va etad viditam mimamsitam.

16. Now, this Self is verily the (inner) world of all beings. As far as man performs sacrifices and pours out libations, he enjoys the world of gods. As far as he masters the Vedas, he enjoys the world of the seers. As far as he makes offerings to his ancestors and desires children, he enjoys the world of ancestors. As far as he gives food and shelter to humans, he enjoys the world of humans. As far as he gives fodder and water to the animals, he enjoys the world of animals. As far as he allows beasts, birds, and even ants to feed in his house, he enjoys their world. Just as one wishes non-injury to oneself, all beings do wish him (non-injury) who knows it as so. This has been discussed and made clear in the Mimansa.

Notes: This verse refers to the five sacrifices (yajnas) to be performed by a householder as his daily obligatory duty. He who performs them sincerely enjoys the pleasures and blessings of these five worlds. Through the offerings, he becomes their object of enjoyment. They do not guarantee immortality, but surely a good next birth by earning pious karma and their blessings. If a person is good to all beings, from the lowest creatures to the highest gods, he is not going to be hurt by anyone. They are going to reciprocate his generosity and give him happiness. This is the conclusion. In support of this argument, the verse further quotes the Purva Mimansa Philosophy, which speaks about the consequences of performing rites and rituals.

17. atmaivedam agra asit, eka eva; so'kamayata, jaya me syat atha prajayeya; atha vittam me syad, atha karma kurviyeti. etavan vai kamah: necchams ca na ato bhuyo vindet. tasmad apy etarhy ekaki kamayate, jaya me syat, atha prajayeya, atha vittam me syad atha karma kurviyeti. sa yavad apy etesam ekaikam na prapnoti, a-krtsna eva tavan manyate. tasyo krtsnata: mana evasya atma, vag jaya, pranah praja, caksur manusam vittam, caksusa hi tad vindate, srotram daivam, srotrena hi tac chrnot, atmaivasya karma, atmana hi karma karoti. sa esa pankto yajñah, panktah pasuh, panktah purusah, panktam id-

am sarvam yad idam kim ca. tad idam sarvam apnoti, ya evam veda.

17. In the beginning, this was but the Self alone. He desired, "Let me have a wife, so that I may be born (through my descendants); and let me have wealth so that I may perform my obligatory duties." This much, indeed, is what one can desire. Even if he desires more, he cannot get more than this. Therefore, to this day, a person who is alone desires thus, "Let me have a wife so that I may be reborn. Let me have wealth so that I may perform my duties." As long as he does not obtain these, he considers himself incomplete. As to his completeness (it arises thus): the mind is his self, speech his wife, breath his progeny, eyes his worldly wealth for he obtains it through his eyes, ears his heavenly wealth for he obtains it through hearing (the Vedas), and with his body obligatory duties (karmakanda) for he performs his duties with his body only. Thus, fivefold is the sacrifice, fivefold is the animal, fivefold is the human being and fivefold is all this that exists here. He, who knows it as such, attains all this.

Notes: This verse suggests that a worldly person must be complete to perform sacrifices and earn the rewards that follow. To be complete, he must be a householder and must have a wife, at least. Having children is even better since they represent his lineage and ancestry and complete him further. Hence, like Viraj at the beginning of creation, a young Snataka (bachelor) desires to marry and have a wife to perform sacrifices and engage in the act of creation. However, when he does not have them, he can still aim for perfection or completeness by relying upon the organs in his body as his partners and practicing the fivefold sacrifices internally with his mind, speech, breath, eyes, and ears. He can perform his duties with his body using these five organs and enjoy the wealth of happiness and pious karma arising from them. Even if he does not actually perform any external sacrifices, his internal sacrifices also yield the same results since they are also performed using the same five parts of the body: the mind, speech, breath, eyes, and ears.

Fifth Brahmana

Seven Types of Food Created by Prajapati

1. yat saptannani medhaya tapasa janayat pita, ekam asya sadharanam, dve devan abhajayat; triny atmane' kuruta, pasubhya ekam prayacchat. tasmin sarvam pratisthitam, yac ca praniti yac ca na. kasmat tani na ksiyante adyamanani sarvada? yo vaitam aksitim veda, so'nnam atti pratikena; sa devan apigacchati, sa ūrjam upajivati. iti slokah.

1. When the father produced seven types of food through austerity, only one of them was common. He provided the gods with two. He made three for himself. One he gave to the animals. On that rests everything, whether it breathes or not. Then why do their numbers not decline even though they are always eaten? He who knows the cause of their imperishability eats food with great distinction. He goes to the gods and lives with great vigor. These are the verses.

Notes: The father refers to the householder or the head of the family who is ignorant of Brahman and bound to Samsara. He performs sacrifices due to desires and attachments in the pursuit of Dharma, Artha, Kama, and Moksha for his worldly enjoyment, treating the world as the object of his enjoyment. The gods and others who receive offerings from him treat him as the object of their enjoyment since he nourishes them. He makes these offerings to fulfill his desires. Therefore, he incurs karma and becomes bound. For the purposes of sacrifices, he invented seven types of food: one universal food for all, two for gods, three for himself, and one for the living and the nonliving. Everything is supported by the last one because animals are at the bottom of the food chain in the cosmic hierarchy. Humans depend upon animals for their nourishment and gods depend upon humans for their nourishment. The cause and effect or the karma produced by the sacrificial actions ensures that the food offered to the various beings is in constant supply.

2. "yat saptannani medhaya tapasa janayat pita" iti medhaya hi tapasajanayat pita. "ekam asya sadharanam" iti. idam evasya tat sadharanam annam, yad idam adyate. sa ya etad upaste na sa papmano vyavartate, misram hy etat. "dve devan abhajayat" iti, hutam ca prahutam ca; tasmad devebhyo juhvati ca pra ca juhvati, atho ahuh, darsapurnamasav iti; tasman nesti-yajukah syat. "pasubhya ekam prayacchat" iti. tat payah, pato hy evagre manusyas ca pasavas copajivanti. tasmat kumaram jatam ghrtam vai vagre pratilehayanti, stanam vanudhapayanti: atha vatsam jatam ahuh, "atrnada" iti; "tasmin sarvam pratisthitam yac ca praniti yac ca na" iti, payasi hidam sarvam pratisthitam, yac ca praniti yac ca na. tad yad idam ahuh samvatsaram payasa juhvad apa punarmrtyum jayatiti, na tatha vidyat. yad ahar eva juhoti, tad ahah punarmrtyum apajayaty evam vidvan; "sarvam hi devebhyo'nnadyam prayacchati." kasmat tani na ksiyante adyamanani sarvada "iti, puruso va aksitih, sa hidam annam punah punar janayate. "yo janayate. "yo vai tam aksitim veda" iti, puruso va aksitih, sa hidam annam dhiya dhiya janayate karmabhih, yaddhaitan na kuryat ksiyeta ha. "so'nnam atti pratikena" iti, mukham pratikam, mukhenety etat. sa devan apigacchati, sa urjam upajivati " iti prasamsa.

2. *"That the father produced seven types of food through his intelligence and austerity" means that the father indeed produced them with his intelligence and power of austerity. "One food was common" means*

that common food which is eaten by all this here. He who adores this common food is not free from sin because, truly, it is mixed. "He provided the gods with two" means they refer to burnt offerings (hutam) and oblations (prahutam). Therefore, the gods receive the offerings (hutam) and pourings (prahutam). Some, however, say they refer to the new moon and full moon sacrifices. Therefore, one should not perform sacrifices for material ends. "One he gave to the animals," that is milk, for, in the beginning, both humans and animals lived by milk only. Therefore, they first make a newborn baby lick clarified butter or press it to the (mother's) breast (for suckling). So also, they speak about a newborn calf as not yet eating grass. "On that rests everything, whether it breaths or not" means on milk rests everything that breathes or not. Regarding this, they say that by pouring offerings of milk in the fire for a year, one conquers further death. One should not think so. He who knows this conquers further death on the very day he makes the offering because he offers all his food to the gods. "Then why their numbers do not decline even though they are eaten always," means the person is imperishable and produces food again and again. "He who knows the cause of their imperishability," means the person is imperishable and produces the food through actions continuously. If he does not do it, his food will be exhausted. As for "he eats food with great distinction," it means his mouth (speech) becomes distinct, for by mouth only does one earn the distinction. "He goes to the gods and lives with great vigor," this is the praise or compliment.

Notes: This and the next verse describe the different types of offerings made and used by the head of the household or the sacrificer. However, we do not generally see this kind of explanation for the cryptic statements in the Upanishads. According to Shankara, intelligence and austerity (medha and tapas) used in this verse refer to the fivefold sacrifices performed internally with the mind, speech, breath, etc., and externally with the wife, children, etc. The first one he produced was annam, the cooked food made of rice, wheat, millet, barley, or any grain. It is the universal food used in every sacrifice and eaten by almost everyone, including gods, animals, birds, insects, worms, and even microorganisms. This universality of annam connects us all in the act of sacrifice and nourishment and establishes the concept of the universal family of God. The two foods he offered to gods refer to the burnt offerings or the solids (hutam) and the liquid offerings (prahutam) poured into the sacrificial fire. The one food he gave to the animals was milk. The newborn baby is mentioned in this verse because it also qualifies as an animal only since it is not yet initiated and becomes twice-born. Milk is the common offering in all the sacrifices associated with the conception and birth of the baby. Everything rests on milk because, without animals, our existence or the existence of gods is not possible. They nourish us, and we nourish the gods. The offerings thus made in the sacrifices produce more food as a consequence. Hence, the supply of food or offerings for the sacrifices, beings, or gods is never exhausted.

3. 'triny atmane'kuruta' iti, mano vacam pranam, tany atmane "kuruta": anyatra mana abhuvam nadarsam, anyatra mana abhuvam nasrausam iti, manasa hy'eva pasyati, manasa srnoti, kamah samkalpo vicikitsa, sraddha'sraddha, dhrtir adhrtir hrir dhir bhir ity etad sarvam mana eva. tasmad api prsthata upasprsto manasa vijanati; yah kas ca sabdo, vag eva sa; esa hi antam ayatta, esa hi na prano'panovyana udanah samano'na ity etat sarvam prana eva. etanmayo va ayam atma, van-mayah mano-mayah, prana-mayah.

3. *"Three he made for himself" means these: the mind, the speech, and the breath he made for himself. When my mind is elsewhere, I do not see. When my mind is elsewhere, I do not hear. It is in the mind one sees and hears. Desire, intention, doubt, faith, absence of faith, steadiness, unsteadiness, shame, intelligence, fear, all this is mind only. If one is touched on the back, one knows it with the mind. Whatever sound is there, that is speech only. Indeed, it lets us know the end of things, but not its own. Prana (inward breath), Apana (downward breath), Vyana (diffused breath), Udana (upward breath), and Samana (middle breath) - all these are breath (prana) only. This body is made up of speech, mind, and breath.*

Notes: He makes three offerings for himself, which means he made them to perform internal sacrifices for his enjoyment, for the gods, or for the Self in him. They are the mind (which includes his thoughts, desires, sensations, feelings, and other mental formations), speech, and breath. The mind is indiscernible and invisible, but its existence can be known through perceptions, desires, doubt, faith, steadiness, discernment, fear, etc. In the internal sacrifice, five types of offerings are made to the body through five types of breath. These refer to the five types of breath or the vital energy that circulates in the body: Prana, the incoming breath; Apana, the downward breath that goes out through the anus; Udana, the upward breath that escapes from the throat, mouth, or head; Samana, the breath (flatulence) that circulates in the middle of the body; and Vyana, the breath that permeates the whole body and keeps it intact. Although we translate Prana as breath, it is not just the air we breathe. It is a form of subtle energy that circulates in the whole creation in different forms and supports it. In the body also, it circulates through the five breath channels we mentioned before, in addition to millions of nerve channels (nadis). Moving thus, it carries the energy produced from the food (offerings) to the various organs in the body and keeps it nourished and invigorated.

4. trayo lokah eta eva, vag evayam lokah, mano'ntariksa lokah, prano'sau lokah.

4. *These are three worlds: speech is this world (bhur), mind is the midworld (bhuva), and prana is the heavenly world (suva).*

Notes: The middle world is the world of ancestors located on the moon, to which beings subject to rebirth go. The immortal world is the world to which liberated souls go after death. It is located in the sun. In the earliest Vedic cosmology, bhur, Bhuva, and Suva are equated with the earth, the region between the earth and the clouds, and the space above the clouds inhabited by morals, celestials, and gods, respectively.

5. trayo veda eta eva, vag eva rg vedah, mano yajur vedah pranah sama vedah.

5. The three Vedas are these only. Speech is the Rigveda, mind is the Yajurveda, and prana is the Samaveda.

Notes: The original Vedas were three. The comparison is apt. You need the power of speech to chant the hymns of the Rigveda, the power of breath to sing the Samans of the Samaveda, and the power of your mind to use the sacrificial formulas (Yajus) of the Yajurveda effectively.

6. devah pitaro manusya eta eva, vag eva devah, manah pitarah, prano manusyah.

6. These are the gods, the ancestors, and humans. Speech is gods, the mind is ancestors, and breath is humans.

Note: Speech is compared to gods because gods were produced from speech and intelligence. Mind is compared to ancestors because they live in our memory. Breath is compared to humans because we live by breath and live as long as we breathe.

7. pita mata praja eta eva, mana eva pita, van mata, pranah praja.

7. These are the father, mother, and offspring. The mind is the father; speech is the mother, and prana is the offspring.

Notes: It is true because in Vedic times, children acquired knowledge from their fathers, language from their mothers, and vital energy (prana) from both.

8. vijnatam vijijnasyam avijnatam eta eva; yat kim ca vijnatam, vacas tad rupam, vagg hi vijnata, vag enam tad bhutvavati.

8. These are the known, the knowable, and the unknown. What is known is a form of speech, for speech is the knower. By becoming that (known), speech protects.

Notes: We speak what we already know. Nothing is new about it. Whatever words we use in our speech are already spoken by others and well within our knowledge and awareness. Individually, we may not know certain words and expressions, but they are part of our culture and collective consciousness. Speech is, therefore, what is already known.

9. yat kim ca vijijnasyam, manasas tad rupam; mano hi vijnasyam, mana enam tad bhutvavati.

9. What is knowable is a form of the mind, for the mind is what is knowable. By becoming that (knowable), the mind protects.

Notes: The mind is an object of study and a repository of objective knowledge. By exploring it and knowing about it through meditation, observation, and contemplation, we can learn about ourselves. Hence, the mind is appropriately described here as that which is to be known.

10. yat kim cavijnatam, pranasya tad rupam; prano hy avijnatah, prana evam tad bhutvavati.

10. What is unknown is of the form of breath, for breath is the unknown. By becoming that (unknown), breath protects.

Notes: Breath is subtle, hidden, invisible, and imperceptible to the senses. It is often equated with the Self. Therefore, it is rightly described here as the unknown.

11. tasyai vacah prthivi sariram, jyoti-rupam ayam agnih; tad yavaty eva vak, tavati prthivi, tavan ayam agnih.

11. Of this speech, the earth is the body, and fire is its luminous form. As far as the speech goes, that far the earth and that far the fire.

Note: Speech resides in the body and has the form of breath (fire).

12. athaitasya manaso dyauh sariram, jyoti-rupam asav adityah, tad yavad eva manas, tavati dyauh, tavan asav adityah. tau mithunam samaitam: tatah prano ajayata sa indrah, sa eso'sapatnah: dvitiyo vai sapatnah: nasya sapatno bhavati, ya evam veda.

12. Of this mind, heaven is the body, and the sun is its luminous form. As far as the mind goes, so far goes heaven, and so far, the sun. The two joined together in an intercourse. From that, the breath was born. He is Indra; He is the Supreme Lord. He is without a rival. Verily, a second person is a rival. He who knows this has no rival.

13. athaitasya pranasyapah sariram, jyoti-rupam asau candrah, tad yavan eva pranah, tavatya apah, tavan asau candrah, ta ete sarva eva samah, sarve'nantah: sa yo haitan antavata upaste antavantam sa lokam jayati. atha yo haitan anantan upaste, anantam sa lokam jayati.

13. *Of this prana, water is the body, and the moon is its luminous form. As far as the breath goes, so far water and so far the moon. All these are equal and endless. Truly, he who worships them as finite wins a finite world. He who worships them as infinite attains the infinite world.*

14. sa esa samvatsarah prajapatih, sodasa-kalah; tasya ratraya eva pancadasa-kalah, dhruvaivasya sodasi kala. sa ratribhir eva ca puryate, apa ca ksiyate; so'mavasyam ratrim etaya sodasya kalaya sarvam idam pranabhrd anupravisya, tatah pratar jayate. tasmad etam ratrim prana-bhrtah pranam na vicchindyad api krkata sasya, etasya eva devataya apacityai.

14. *A year of Prajapati has sixteen parts. His nights have fifteen parts, and the sixteenth one is constant. He expands and contracts during the night. With his sixteenth part, on the new moon night, he enters all these living beings here that breathe and rises the next day morning. Therefore, for the sake of the deity, on that night, one should not take the life of living beings that breathe, not even that of a lizard.*

15. yo vai sa samvatsarah prajapatih sodasa-kalah, ayam eva sa yo'yam evam-vit purusah tasya, vittam eva pancadasakalah, atmaivasya sodasi kala, sa vittenaiva ca purayte apa caksiyate. tad etan nadhyam yad ayam atma, pradhir vittam. tasmad yady api sarvajyanim, jiyate, atmana cei jivati, pradhinagad ity evahuh.

15. *Truly, the person who knows this here is himself that Prajapati, whose year has sixteen parts. His wealth forms fifteen parts, and his body the sixteenth part. With regard to wealth alone, he expands and contracts. They are the spokes and his body the hub. Therefore, if a man loses everything but he himself lives, they say he has lost only the rim of his wheel.*

Notes: Wealth, in all of its forms, is compared to the waxing and waning moon during the 15 days of the fortnight. The body is compared to the constant, the full moon day.

16. atha trayo vava lokah, manusya-lokah, pitr-lokah. deva-loka iti. so'yam manusya-lokah putrenaiva jayyah, nanyena karmana. karmana pitr-lokah, vidyaya deva-lokah, deva loko vai lokanam sresthah: tasmad vidyam prasamsanti.

16. *Now, three are indeed the worlds: the world of humans, the world of ancestors, and the world of gods. This world of humans has to be won by the son alone, but not by any other actions, the world of ancestors by obligatory duties, and the world of gods by knowledge alone. The world of gods is truly the best of the worlds. Therefore, they praise knowledge.*

17. athatah samprattih. yada praisyan manyate, atha putram aha, tvam brahma tvam yajnah. tvam loka iti. sa putrah praty aha, aham brahma, aham yajnah, aham loka iti. yad vai kim canuktam, tasya sarvasya brahmety ekata. ye vai ke ca yajnah, tesam sarvesam yajna ity ekata; ye vai ke ca lokah, tesam sarvesam loka ity ekata; etavad va idam sarvam, etanma sarvam sann ayam ito'bhunajad iti, tasmat putram anusistham lokyam ahuh, tasmad enam anusasati, sa yadaivam vid asmal lokat praiti. athaibhir eva pranaih saha putram avisati, sa yady anena kim cid aksnaya krtam bhavati, tasmad enam sarvasmat putro muncati tasmat putro nama sa putrenaivasmiml loke pratisthati, athainam ete daivah prana amrta avisanti.

17. Now, therefore, the tradition - when a man thinks he is about to die, he says to his son, "You are Brahman, you are the sacrifice, and you are the world." The son answers, " I am Brahman, I am the sacrifice, I am the world." Truly, whatever has been learned, all that becomes one in Brahman. Truly, whatever sacrifices have been performed, they all become one in the (utterance of the word) sacrifice. All that exists here in this world becomes one in the (utterance of the word) world. All this, indeed, is this much. Being all this, let him protect me from this world, thus (thinks the father). Therefore, they call a son who is instructed in the Vedas as the obtainer of the world, and hence, he instructs him. When he who knows thus departs from this world, he enters into his son together with his breath. Whatever wrong deeds he may have performed, his son frees him from all that. Therefore, he is called a son. A father rests in this world through his son. Then, the divine, immortal breath enters into him.

Note: This explains why a dying father requires a son for safe passage to the next world. It is one of the earliest Vedic beliefs, suggesting how a father entrusts his duties to his son along with his faults and failures, cleanses himself of sinful karma with his help, and becomes a part of his speech, breath, etc., through transference, equating him with Brahman. The son's role in the transference of knowledge, speech, mind, and breath from father to son is of utmost importance in this belief system. How does he do that? He promises to take care of his omissions, failures, and mistakes in the performance of his duties by taking necessary corrective and expiatory actions. Wealth, sacrifices, wife (for she gives birth to the son), etc., are also useful to obtain the higher worlds, but not without a son who can compensate for his failures, omissions, and commissions, knows how to receive his knowledge, speech, mind, and breath into himself and grant him a safe passage.

18. prthivyai cainam agnes ca daivi vag avisati, sa vai daivi vag, yaya yad yad eva vadati, tad tad bhavati.

18. *From the earth and from fire, the divine speech enters into him. It is by that divine speech, indeed, whatever one says happens.*

19. divas cainam adityac ca daivam mana avisati, tad vai daivam mano yenanandy eva bhavati, atho na socati.

19. From the heaven and from the sun, the divine mind enters into him. It is by that divine mind one becomes happy and never grieves.

20. adbhyas cainam candramasas ca daivah prana avisati; sa vai daivah prano, yah samcarams casamcarams ca na vyathate, atho na risyati. sa evam-vit sarvesam bhutanam atma bhavati. yathaisa devata, evam sah. yathaitam devatam sarvani bhutany avanti, evam haivam-vidam sarvani bhutany avanti. yad u kim cemah prajah socanti, amaivasam tad bhavati, punyam evamum gacchati. na ha vai devan papam gacchati.

20. From water and the moon, the divine breath enters into him. Verily, it is the divine breath, which, whether moving or not moving, is neither disturbed nor injured. He who knows this becomes the Self of all beings. Just as this deity, so is he. Just as this deity is revered by all beings, so is he revered by them, who knows thus. Whatever grief the beings undergo, that remains within them, but whatever merit they have goes to him. Sin does not reach the gods.

Notes: The father, who his son has exonerated at the time of death by taking upon himself his karma, speech, mind, and breath, attains rebirth into the world of mortals through his son, the world of ancestors through sacrifices, and the world of gods through knowledge. When his prana joins the divine prana, he attains oneness with the Cosmic Being and becomes the Self of all. This does not happen because of his son, who can only grant him rebirth in the mortal world, sacrifices, which can only ensure him a place in the ancestral world, or knowledge, which can lead him to the world of gods. What can lead him to attain oneness with Brahman is the purity of his prana and when it unites seamlessly with the divine prana in the sun, the highest realm.

21. athato vrata-mimamsa. prajapatir ha karmani sasrje, tani srstani anyo'nyenaspardhanta. vadisyamy evaham iti vag dadhre; draksyamy aham iti caksuh; srosyamy aham iti srotram; evam anyani karmani yatha karma; tani mrtyuh sramo bhutva upayeme; tany apnot; tany aptva mrtyur avarundha; tasmat sramyaty eva vak, sramyati caksuh, sramyati srotram, athemam eva napnot yo'yam madhyamah pranah. tani jnatum dadhrire. ayam vai nah srestho yah samcarams casamcarams ca na vyathate, atho na risyati, hantasyaiva sarve rupam asameti: ta etasyaiva sarve rupam abhavan, tasmad eta etainakhyayante prana iti. tena ha vava tat kulam acaksate, yasmin kule bhavati

ya evam veda. ya u haivam vida spardhate, anususyati, anususya haivantato mriyate, iti adhyatmam.

21. *Now, a philosophical inquiry regarding the vows. Prajapati created the organs of action. After they were created, they developed differences among themselves. Speech vowed, "I will keep speaking." The eye, "I will keep seeing." The ear, "I will keep hearing." Thus, all the other organs vowed to do the same with regard to their functions. Then Death (Time) devised fatigue and took hold of them, and, having held them, it prevented them from doing their work. Therefore, speech, indeed, gets tired (with time); eyes get tired, and hearing gets tired. However, Death (Time) did not get hold of the middle breath. The organs wanted to know him and said, "This, verily, is the best among us. It is neither disturbed nor injured (by fatigue) when it is moving or not moving. Let us take up his form." They all assumed his form. Therefore, they are called after the name of the breath. In whatever family there is a man who knows this, his family is called after his name. And he who competes with him who knows this loses his strength, and after losing his strength, he dies in the end. This is with regard to the self (the body).*

Notes: When the Creator joined them to the body, the organs took the vow to perform their duties endlessly. However, due to Death, they were all subjected to fatigue due to aging, death, and decay, except the middle breath, which remained stable, tireless, and indestructible. Hence, seeing this, all the organs took refuge in breath and assumed his form to escape death, whereby they all came to be known as prana. At the time of death, all these organs join breath and leave the body for the mid-region, where they become dispersed and return to their respective spheres. For those who know this, their family names follow their names since they, too, become immortal and indestructible as their breath becomes one with the breath of Prajapati, the Creator. The breath here is a reference to the Self in the body, not to the prana or the vital energy that flows. In the early Vedic descriptions, breath represented the Self.

22. athadhidaivatam; jvalisyamy evaham ity agnir dadhre; tapsyamy aham ity adityah; bhasyamy aham iti candramah; evam anya devata yatha-devatam; sa yathaisam prananam madhyamah pranah, evam etasam devatanam vayuh, nimlocanti hy anya devatah, na vayuh. saisanastamita devata yad vayuh.

22. *Now, with reference to gods, fire vowed, "I will keep on burning." The sun, "I will keep on radiating heat." The moon, " I will keep on shining." The other gods also said the same according to their functions. Just as the middle breath among the breaths (in the body), so is*

Vayu (air) among the gods. Other gods have their low points, but not Vayu. Air is the deity that never rests.

Notes: All the organs in the body can be rested and allowed to overcome fatigue through sleep and rest, but one should never stop breathing in and out, for by that alone, Death can be prevented from invading the body and taking life. If prana (Vayu) becomes polluted or stops flowing, the world will come to an end.

23. athaisa sloko bhavati: yatas codeti suryah astam yatra ca gacchati iti pranad va esa udeti, prane'stam eti, tam devas cakrire dharmam sa evadya sa a svah. iti yad va ete'murhy adriyanta tad evapy adya kurvanti. tasmad ekam eva vratam caret, pranyac caiva, apanyac ca, nen ma papma mrtyur apnuvad iti; yady u caret samapipayiset teno. etasyai devatayai sayujyam salokatam jayati.

23. Now, there is this verse. From where the sun rises and in which it sets, that indeed is prana, from which it rises and into which it sets. Him the divinities regarded as the measure of duty -what he did that day, he did the next day also - and they followed it themselves. Thus, whatever functions they performed in the past, they perform even today. Therefore, let a man undertake one vow only. Breathing in and breathing out, let him think, "The sinful death should not get me." And when he takes the vow, let him observe it until the finish. With that, he attains union with that deity and a place in the same world as him.

Notes: One must follow Prana's example and perform one's duties tirelessly. Only then can one enter the highest world and attain immortality, becoming one with the Supreme Self.

Sixth Brahmana

Name, Form, and Action, The Threefold Diversity

1. trayam va idam, nama rupam karma; tesam namnam vag ity etad esam uktham, ato hi sarvani namany uttisthanti: etadesam sama; etadd hi sarvair namabhih samam; etad esambrahma, etadd hi etadd hi sarvani namani bibharti.

1. All this (creation) is threefold: name, form, and action. Of them, with regard to names, speech is the source because all names arise from speech only. It makes them similar; indeed, it is the same for all names. For them, it is their Brahman because it supports all names.

Notes: Name, form, and action represent the objective reality. Speech is Brahman for names only in the sense that it is their source and support.

Chapter 1

2. atha rupanam caksur ity etad esam uktham, ato hi sarvanirupany uttisthanti, etad esam sama, etadd hi sarvai rūpaihsamam, etad esam brahma; etadd hi sarvani rupanibibharti.

2. Now, with regard to forms, the eye is the source, for all forms arise from it only. It makes them similar; indeed, it is the same for all forms. For them, it is their Brahman because it supports all forms.

3. atha karmanam atmety etad esam uktham, ato hi sarvanikarmany uttisthanti, etad esam sama, etadd hi sarvaihkarmabhih samam, etad esam brahma, etadd hi sarvanikarmani bibharti. tad etad trayam sad ekam ayam atma, atma ekah sann etat trayam. tad etad amrtam satyenachannam, prano va amrtam, nama-rupe satyam; tabhyamayam pranas channah.

3. With regard to actions, the body is the source, for actions arise from it only. It makes them similar; indeed, it is the same for all actions. For them, it is their Brahman because it supports all actions. These three together are this one body. The body, although one, is these three. This immortal one is veiled by truth. Breath is immortal; name and form are truth. Breath is veiled by both of them.

Notes: Names, forms, and actions are chiefly responsible for all diversity and the continuation of mortal existence. Names arise from speech, forms from seeing, and actions from the body. They veil the Self, which is stated here as breath. These three are collectively identified with the body because they distinguish the body and give it a distinct identity. A person is known in this world by his name, form, and actions.

Chapter 2

First Brahmana

The Right and Wrong Knowledge of Brahman

1. Aum, drpta-balakir hanucano gargya asa, sa hovaca ajatasatrumkasyam, brahma te bravaniti, sa hovaca ajatasatruh, sahasram etasyam vaci dadmah. janakah, janaka iti vai janadhavantiti.

1. *Aum! The proud Balaki of the Gargya lineage was an interpreter. He said to Ajatasatru, (the king) of Kasi, "I will speak to you about Brahman." Ajatasatru said, "I will give you a thousand (cows) for this proposition. Others followed (with a similar proposal), saying, "O King, O King*

Notes: This verse mentions Balaki from a reputed Brahmana family as proud (drpta) because he was proud of his knowledge. Anuchanu means repeating what one learns from a teacher without understanding it. Balaki heard about Brahman from his teacher, but he did not truly understand what Brahman meant. Ajatasatru, the king of Kasi, had some knowledge of Brahman. He offered a thousand cows to Balakin for the proposal Balaki made to tell him about Brahman. According to Shankara, he did it to show his benevolence as a king, not because he was expecting Balaki to reveal any new knowledge that he did not know already. Others who saw it followed them, seeing that the King was benevolent and would give them similar gifts if they caught his attention.

2. sa hovaca gargyah, ya evasav aditye purusah, etam evahambrahmopasa iti. sa hovaca ajatsatruh; ma maitasmin samva-disthah atisthah sarvesam bhutanam murdha rajetiva aham etam upasa iti, sa ya etam upaste, atisthahsarvesam bhutanam murdha raja bhavati.

2. *Gargya said, "That person who is there in the sun, him I worship as Brahman." Ajatasatru said, "Please do not speak about him. I verily worship him as the all-surpassing and as the head and lord of all beings. He who worships him thus becomes all-surpassing, the head and lord of all beings."*

Notes: Ajatashatru did not accept Balaki's assertion. He said that Brahman was the highest of all. He could not be just in the sun or the sun only. He must be everywhere and beyond all. From here on, Balaki has been mentioned as Gargya. Probably, Balaki may be a nickname to indicate his immaturity or lack of knowledge.

3. sa hovaca gargyah: ya evasau candre purusah, etam evaham brahmopasa iti. sa hovaca ajatsatruh, ma maitasmin samva-

disthah. brhan paṇḍara-vasah somo rajeti va aham etam upasa iti. sa ya etam evam upaste, ahar ahar ha sutah prasuto bhavati, nasyannam ksiyate.

3. *Gargya said, "That person who is there in the moon, him I worship as Brahman." Ajatasatru said, "Please do not speak about him. I verily worship him as the great, white-robed king Soma. He who worships him thus for him Soma will pour forth abundantly during Suta and Prasuta pressings every day, and his food will never be in short supply.*

Notes: Suta and Prasuta refer to the extraction of Soma during the main and auxiliary Soma sacrifices performed in honor of Soma, the moon. Ajatashatru identified Brahman as the presiding deity of the Soma Sacrifice.

4. sa hovaca gargyah: ya evasau vidyuti purusah, etam evaham brahmopasa iti. sa hovaca ajatsatruh, ma maitasmin samvadisthah, tejasviti va aham etam upasa iti. sa ya etam evam upaste, tejasvi ha bhavati, tejasvini hasya praja bhavati.

4. *Gargya said," That person who is there in the lightning, him I worship as Brahman. Ajatasatru said, "Please do not speak about him. I verily worship him as the very dazzling. "He who worships him thus becomes very dazzling and his offspring too become dazzling.*

Notes: Brahman is not mere lighting but the light that dazzles in it.

5. sa hovaca gargyah, ya evayam akase purusah, etam evaham brahmopasa iti. sa hovaca ajatasatruh, ma maitasmin samvadisthah, purnam apravartiti va aham etam upasa iti, sa ya etam evam upaste, puryate prajaya pasubhih nasyasmal lokat prajodvartate.

4. *Gargya said, "That person who is there in the space, him I worship as Brahman. Ajatasatru said, "Please do not speak about him. I verily worship him as full and unmoving. He who worships him thus becomes full, with offspring and cattle, and his descendants will not disappear from this world.*

Notes: Brahman pervades the whole space without a second. Therefore, he is fixed and unmoving

6. sa hovaca gargyah, ya evayam vayau purusah, etam evaham brahmopasa iti. sa hovaca ajatasatruh, ma maitasmin samvadisthah indro vaikunthoparajita seneti va aham etam upasa iti, sa ya etam evam upaste, jisnur haparajisnur bhavaty anyatastya-jayi.

6. *Gargya said, "That person who is there in the air, him I worship as Brahman. Ajatasatru said, "Please do not speak about him. I verily*

worship him as the Lord of heaven, as the irresistible and as an invincible army. He who worships him thus becomes victorious and invincible and a conqueror of enemies.

7. sa hovaca gargyah, ya evayam agnau purusah, etam evaham brahmopasa iti. sa hovaca ajatasatruh, ma maitasmin samvadisthah, visasahir iti va aham etam upasa iti, sa ya etam evam upaste visasahir ha bhavati, visasahir hasya praja bhavati.

7. Gargya said, "That person who is there in the fire, him I worship as Brahman. Ajatasatru said, "Please do not speak about him. I verily worship him as very tolerant. He who worships him thus becomes very tolerant, and his progeny also become tolerant.

8. sa hovaca gargyah, ya evayam apsu purusah, etam evaham brahmopasa iti. sa hovaca ajatasatruh, ma maitasmin samvadisthah, pratirupa iti va aham etam upasa iti, sa ya etam evam upaste, pratirupam haivainam upagacchati, napratirupam, atho pratirupo'smaj jayate.

8. Gargya said, "That person who is there in the water, him I worship as Brahman. Ajatasatru said, "Please do not speak about him. I verily worship him as very agreeable. He who worships him thus has only agreeable things coming to him but not disagreeable ones, and from him descend children who are also agreeable.

Notes: Pratirupam means likeness, agreeable, reflection, suitable, etc. According to Shankara, it is dutiful adherence to the Smritis and Srutis. Perhaps, in a wider context, it is the quality of living in harmony with others and with the whole creation and flowing with the flow. Water has that quality.

9. sa hovaca gargyah, ya evayam adarse purusah, etam evaham brahmopasa iti. sa hovaca ajatasatruh, ma maitasmin samvadisthah. rocisnur iti va aham etam upasa iti. sa ya etam evam upaste rocisnur ha bhavati, rocisnur hasya praja bhavati, atho yaih samnigacchati, sarvams tan atirocate.

9. Gargya said, "That person who is there in the mirror, him I worship as Brahman. Ajatasatru said, "Please do not speak about him. I verily worship him as the bright one. He who worships him thus becomes bright, and his progeny also become bright. He outshines all those whom he meets.

Notes: The image that appears in a mirror has no light of its own. Brahman is self-illuminated and shines by himself.

10. sa hovaca gargyah; ya evayam yantam pascat sabdo'nudeti; etam evaham brahmopasa iti. sa hovaca ajatasatruh; ma maita-

smin samvadisthah, asur iti va aham etam upasa iti, sa ya etam evam upaste, sarvam haivasmiml loka ayur eti, nainam pura kalat prano jahati.

10. Gargya said, "That sound which follows a person when he walks, that I worship as Brahman. Ajatasatru said, "Please do not speak about that. I verily worship it as life. He who worships him thus attains a full lifespan in this world. Breath does not depart from him until his lifespan is full.

Notes: Ajatashatru said he worshipped Brahman as the spirit (asur) who supported the body and all its actions and functions, including breath.

11. sa hovaca gargyah, ya evayam diksu purusah, etam evaham brahmopasa iti. sa hovaca ajatsatruh, ma maitasmin samvadisthah, dvitiyo'napaga iti va aham etam upasa iti, sa ya etam evam upaste, dvitiyavan ha bhavati, nasmad ganas chidyate.

11. Gargya said, "That person who is in the quarters of the space, him I worship as Brahman. Ajatasatru said, "Please do not speak about him. I verily worship him as the second, from whom we are never separate. He who worships him thus always has a second, and his community is not separated from him.

Notes: 'The second' is probably the Purusha, who manifested from Brahman, or the embodied Self hidden in each jiva.

12. sa hovaca gargyah, ya evayam chayamayah purusah, etam evaham brahmopasa iti. sa hovaca ajatasatruh, ma maitasmin samvadisthah, mrtyur iti va aham etam upasa iti, sa ya etam evam upaste, sarvam haivasmiml loka ayur eti, naivam pura kalan mrtyur agacchati.

12. Gargya said, "That person who is there in the shadow, him I worship as Brahman. Ajatasatru said, "Please do not speak about him. I verily worship him as death. He who worships him as such attains a full lifespan, and death does not overtake him until he completes his full lifespan.

Notes: Brahma is not the shadow (darkness or ignorance), but the deity who is hidden in the shadow of ignorance as Death.

13. sa hovaca gargyah, ya evayam atmani purusah, etam evaham brahmopasa iti. sa hovaca ajatasatruh, ma maitasmin samvadisthah, atmanviti va aham etam upasa iti, sa ya etam evam upaste, atmanvi ha bhavati atmanvini hasya praja bhavati. sa ha tusnim asa gargyah.

13. Gargya said, "That person who is there in the Self, him I worship as Brahman. Ajatasatru said, "Please do not speak about him. I verily worship him as the one who holds the Self. He who worships him thus becomes a holder of the Self, and his progeny also become holders of their Selves. Gargya became silent.

Notes: Balaki mistook the person (ego) in the body for the Self. Ajatashatru corrected him, saying he worshipped him as the holder or possessor (atmanvin) of that person. It may also mean that Brahman is not the individual Self (Purusha) but the Supreme Self (Hiranyagarbha) who holds or contains all the individual Selves. Balaki became silent as he had nothing more to say when Ajatashatru refuted all his statements

14. sa hovaca ajatasatruh, etavan nu iti, etavad-dhiti; naitavata viditam bhavatiti: sa hovaca gargyah upa tvayaniti.

14. Ajatasatru said, "Is that all?"

"That is all."

"By knowing this much, he is not known."

Gargya said, "I approach you."

Notes: As per the Vedic tradition, if a Brahmana went to a Kshatriya and said," I approach you," it was to indicate that the Brahmana wanted to learn from the Kshatriya as a student. A Brahmana student under a Kshatriya teacher had fewer obligations and household duties. This subject will be dealt with again in the sixth chapter regarding an interesting conversation between Gautama and Pravahana Jaivali regarding the paths that beings follow after death.

15. sa hovaca ajatasatruh, pratilomam cai tad yad brahmanah ksatriyam upeyat, brahma me vaksyatiti, vy eva tvajnapayisyamiti; tam panav adayottasthau. tau ha purusam suptam ajagmatuh, tam etair namabhir amantrayam cakre, brhan pandara-vasah soma rajann iti: sa nottasthau; tam panina pesam bodhayam cakara, sa hottasthau.

15. Ajatasatru said, "It is against practice that a Brahmana should approach a Kshatriya thinking, 'He will teach me about Brahman.' However, I will teach you." Holding his hand, he rose. They came to a person who was asleep. He addressed him with these names, "Great, White Robed, King, Soma." That person did not wake up. He pushed him with his hand until he woke up. Then he stood up.

16. sa hovaca ajatasatruh, yatraisa etat supto'bhut, ya esa vijnanamayah, purusah, kvaisa tadabhut, kuta etad agad iti. tad u ha na mene gargyah.

16. *Ajatasatru said, "When this one went into sleep, where was that person who is filled with intelligent awareness? And from where did he come back?" Gargya did not know.*

Notes: Ajatashatru wanted to convey that when the being went to sleep, the person (ego) in him whom he thought was Brahman was temporarily dissolved into the space (the breath or the Self) within, and all his bodily functions were temporarily suspended. What kept him alive and what remained active or awake during that time was the Self. Hence, he was able to return from sleep.

17. sa hovaca ajatasatruh, yatraisa etat supto'bhut esa vijnana-mayah, vijnanamayah purusah, tad esam prananam vijnanena vijnanam adaya ya eso'ntar-hrdaya akasah tasmin chete, tani yada grhnati atha haitat purusah svapiti nama. tad grhita eva prano bhavati, grhita vak, grhitam caksuh, grhitam srotram, grhitam manah.

17. Ajatasatru said, "When this person, who is filled with intelligent awareness, fell asleep thus, with his awareness, he absorbs the awareness of the breaths (senses) and rests in the space within the heart. When this person withdraws the senses, he is said to be in self-induced sleep (svapiti). Then, breath is restrained, speech is restrained, the eye is restrained, the ear is restrained, and the mind is restrained.

Notes: The heart is where the Self or Brahman is located. He is described here as the space in the heart.

18. sa yatraitaya svapnayacarati, te hasya lokah: tad uta iva maharajo bhavati, uta iva maha-brahmanah, uta iva uccavacam nigacchati: sa yada maharajo, janapadan grhitva sve janapade yatha-kamam parivarteta, evam evaisa etat pranan grhitva sve sarire yatha-kamam parivartate.

18. When he moves around in a dream, these are his worlds. Then he becomes as if he were an emperor, as if he were a Brahmana, and enters, as if he were, into positions high and low. Just as a great king, taking his people, moves about in his kingdom as he desires, so does this person, taking his breaths (senses), wander around as he desires in his own body.

Notes: The Self is the dreamer. The dream is his projection. Yet, since he does not really participate in it and since the experiences or the dream worlds and situations he creates are illusory, he is untouched by them.

19. atha yada susupto bhavati, yada na kasya cana veda, hita nama nadyo dva-saptatih sahasrani hrdayat puritatam abhipratisthante, tabhih pratyavasrpya puritati sete, sa yatha kumaro

va maharajo va maha-brahmano vatighnim anandasya gatva sayita, evam evaisa etac chete.

19. Now, when he falls asleep - when he does not know anything- by the seventy-two thousand arteries called hita, which extend from the heart to the entire body, he travels back and rests in the body. Just as a boy, as an emperor, as a great Brahmana may rest, having attained the supreme bliss, so does he rest in the body.

Notes: This is the deep sleep state in which the ego, the mind, and intelligence become withdrawn, and the Self remains absorbed in the heart from where the hita nerve channels extend in all directions into the body. In this state also, as in dreams, the Self is untouched by what happens or does not happen.

20. sa yathornanabhis tantunoccaret, yathagneh ksudra visphulinga vyuccaranti, evam evasmad atmanah sarve pranah, sarve lokah, sarve devah. sarvani bhutani vyuccaranti: tasyopanisat, satyasya satyam iti prana vai satyam, tesam esa satyam.

20. Just as a spider moves along the thread, just as sparks fly from fire, so do move forth from this Self all the breaths (senses), all the worlds, all the deities, and all the beings. The secret instruction regarding that is that it is the truth of the truth. The breaths (senses) are the truth, and It (the Self) is their truth.

Notes: Tantunama is an epithet of Brahman and Vishnu. The spider symbolism is often used to describe him as Death (Kala) and the Creator. The spider net is compared to the whole creation as the web of Maya projected by him and to samsara, in which the jivas become caught, and he devours them according to their karma. In this, the whole body and creation are described as the spiderweb. What is the truth of truth? The truth is that all this creation is threefold: name, form, and actions. The truth of the truth is that Brahman is self-existent, without any support, dependence, or connection, by himself and absorbed within himself without a second, and all that manifests from him (the truth) depends upon him, but he is untouched by it.

Second Brahmana

Breath and Other Deities in the Body

1. yo ha vai sisum saadhanam sapratyadhanam sasthunam sadamam veda, sapta ha dvisato bhratrvyan avarunaddhi: ayam vava sisur yo'yam madhyamah pranah tasyaidam evadhanam, idam pratyadhanam, pranah sthuna, annam dama.

1. Truly, he who knows the newly born calf with his abode, his support, his anchor, and his rope destroys his seven hostile kinsmen. The middle

breath in the body is the calf; the body is its abode, the head is its support, strength is its anchor, and food is its rope.

Notes: The kinsmen of the person in the body are the organs of the body or those who are born with him. As Shankara said, some of them are friendly, and some are hostile. The seven hostile kinsmen are the eyes, the ears, the nose, the tongue, and the mouth. They are located in the head. The calf is the subtle body made of prana. They are hostile because they keep him distracted and prevent him from knowing himself. Food is its rope or the controller.

2. tam etah saptaksitaya upatisthante. tad ya ima aksan lohinyo rajayah, tabhir enam rudro'nvayattah; atha ya aksann apas tabhih parjanyah; ya kaninaka, taya adityah; yat krsnam, tena agnih; yat suklam, tena indrah; adharayainam vartanya prthivy anvayatta; dyaur uttaraya; nasyannam ksiyate ya evam veda.

2. The seven imperishable deities stand nearby and serve him. Through the red veins in the eye, Rudra acts in compliance. Now, through the water in the eye, Prajanya. Through the pupil, the sun. Through the black (pupil in the eye), fire. Through the white (of the eye), Indra. Through the lower eyelid, the earth acts in compliance. Through the upper eyelid, the heaven. He who knows this thus does not suffer from shortages of food.

Notes: The seven imperishable gods are listed here. They serve the vital energy, prana, by becoming its food. Prajanya is the rain god. Anvayatta means to act in harmony or as per the commands. Here, all the deities in the body act according to the wishes of the subtle body (the heaven), which is filled with prana.

3. tad esa sloko bhavati: arvagbilas camasa urdhvabudhnah, tasmin yaso nihitam visvarupam: tasyasata rsayah saptatire, vag astami brahmana samvidana iti. "arvagbilas camasa urdhvabudhnah" itidam tac chirah, esa hy arvagbilas camasa urdhvabudhnah, tasmin yaso nihitam visvarupam" iti, prana vai yaso nihitam visvarupam, pranan etad aha. "tasyasata rsayah saptatire" iti, prana va rsayah pranan etad aha. "vag astami brahmana samvidana" iti, vag astami brahmana samvitte.

3. Regarding this, there is the verse, "There is a bowl with its mouth below and bottom above. In it is hidden the glory of the universal form. On its rim sit the seven seers, and speech, by its association with Brahman, as the eighth. What is called "the bowl with its mouth below and bottom above" is the head, for it is the bowl with its mouth below and bulge at the top. This one, "In it is hidden the glory of the universal form," refers to breath (vital energy), for breath, indeed, is (the glory of the universal form). "On its rim sit the seven seers." Verily, the breaths (senses) are the seers. "Speech by its association with Brahman (the Vedas), is the eighth," for speech as the eighth communicated with Brahman (the Vedas).

Notes: Speech is Brahman because he is the source of all speech, especially the sacred hymns of Vedas. The seven sages represent the various types of knowledge stored in the mind by the activities of the senses. The knowledge of the Vedas or Brahman is the highest among them.

4. imav eva gotamabharadvajau, ayam eva gotamah, ayam bharadvajah; imav eva visvamitrajamadagni, ayam eva visvamitrah, ayam jamadagnih; imav eva vasistha kasyapau, ayam eva vasisthah, ayam kasyapah; vag evatrih, vaca hy annam adyate, attir ha vai namaitad yad atrir iti; sarvasyatta bhavati, sarvam asyannam bhavati, ya evam veda.

4. These two, indeed, are Gautama and Bharadvaja. This one, verily, is Gautama and this one is Bharadvaja. These two, indeed, are Visvamitra and Jamadagni. This one, verily, is Vishvamitra, and this one is Bharadvaja. These two, indeed, are Vashista and Kashyapa: this one, verily, is Vashishta, and this one is Kashyapa: The tongue is Atri. With the tongue, the food is eaten. Eating has the same name as this Atri. He who knows thus becomes the eater of all. For him, everything becomes his food.

Notes: Ajatasatru showed Balaki the parts of his body while naming them. He pointed to his right and left ears, calling them Gautama and Bharadvaja. Visvamitra and Jamadagni were his eyes. Vishvamitra and Bharadvaja were his nostrils. Whoever knows that Atri is the tongue and enjoyer of food never becomes the enjoyed or the object of enjoyment for the gods or the Lord of Death.

Third Brahmana

The Two Forms of Brahman

1. dve vava brahmano rupe, murtam caivamurtam ca, martyam camrtam ca, sthitam ca, yac ca, sac ca, tyac ca.

I. Two, indeed, are the forms of Brahman, the formed and the formless, the mortal and the immortal, the fixed and the not fixed, the being and that (which is true).

Notes: This verse describes the duality of Brahman's manifestations: the formed and the formless, the mortal and the immortal, the fixed and not fixed, and the being and the non-being. The fixed is indestructible, and the destructible because it is subject to change and impermanence.

2. tad etan murtam yad anyad vayos cantariksac ca, etanmartyam, etat sthitam, etat sat, tasyaitasya murtasya,etasya martyasya etasya sthitasya, etasya sata esa raso yaesa tapati, sato hy esa rasah.

2. The one with the form is other than the air and space. It is mortal; it is fixed; it is existence. The essence of this formed, this mortal, this fixed, and this being is that which radiates heat, for it is the essence of the being.

Notes: Those made of water, earth, and fire constitute the visible and formed objects. The ones made of air and space are invisible and formless. The formed ones radiate heat as their essence. Sata means a person or being whose father is Brahman.

3. athamurtam vayus cantariksam ca, etad amrtam etad yat,etat tyat, tasyaitasyamurtasya, etasyamrtasya, etasya yatahetasya tasyaisa raso ya esa etasmin maṇḍale purusah, tasyahy esa rasah, ity adhidaivatam.

3. Now, regarding the formless, it is the air and space. It is immortal; it is the moving (unfixed), and it is that (which is present). The essence of this formless, immortal, moving, and present one is the Person who is in the sphere of the sun, for he is the essence of that (which is present). This is with reference to the presiding gods.

Notes: The subtle body is neither immortal nor indestructible. It is not a part of the Self. It is still a body made up of air and space, hence invisible and subtle. It is indestructible only in the sense that it does not have a form, and you cannot break it or destroy it, just as you can break any material object or extinguish any form produced by fire. However, the subtle body may last longer since it remains as long as creation exists or the being attains liberation. Upon death, the subtle body leaves the gross body and travels to the next world. In liberation, it becomes dissolved in the Self.

4. athadhyatmam idam eva murtam yad anyat pranac ca yascayam antaratmann akasah, etan martyam, etat sthitam,etat sat, tasyaitasya murtasya, etasya martyasya, etasyasthitasya, etasya sata esa raso yac caksuh, sato hy esa rasah.

4. Now, regarding this body. Verily, the formed one is different from breath and from the space within the body. This is the mortal, this is the fixed one, and this is the being. The essence of this formed, this mortal, this fixed, and this being is the eye. It, indeed, is the essence of the being.

5. athamurtam pranas ca yas cayam antaratmann akasah; etad amrtam, etad yat, etat tyam, tasyaitasyamurtasya, etasya-

mrtasya, etasya yatah, etasya tyasyaisa raso yo'yamdak-sine"ksan purusah, tyasya hy esa rasah.

5. Now, the formless is breath and the space within the body. It is immortal, it is moving, and it is that (which is true). The essence of that which is formless, immortal, moving, and that (which is true) is this person in the right eye. It, indeed, is the essence of that (which is true).

Notes: According to this verse, the right eye is the abode of the subtle person in the body who is made up of the essence of air and ether or space.

6. tasya haitasya purusasya rupam yatha maharajanam vasah, yatha pandvavikam, yathendragopah, yathagnyarcih, yathapundarikam, yatha sakrdvidyuttam; sakrdvidyutteva ha vaasya srir bhavati, ya evam veda. athata adesah na iti na iti, na hy etasmad iti, na ity anyat param asti; atha namadheyamsatyasya satyam iti. prana vai satyam, tesam esasatyam.

6. The form of that Person is like a robe dyed with saffron, like the wool of a gray sheep, like the color of an insect called Indragopa, like the flame of fire, like the white lotus, or like the flash of a lightning. He who knows this thus attains brilliance like the flash of a lightning. Now, therefore, this instruction, "Not this, not this." Since there is nothing else higher than this, therefore, it is (understood) only by "Not this." Now, the name given to him is "The Truth of the Truth." Breath, indeed, is the Truth. He is the Truth of that (Truth).

Notes: You cannot understand the subtle body because it is beyond the senses. You cannot describe it because it does not have a specific form. You cannot say that it exactly is this or that because it is undefined. So, the only way you can understand it is by saying what it is not or by excluding all that you can touch and feel in your body, using the 'not this, not this' method. By keeping on saying, 'Not this mind, not this intelligence, not these senses, not these limbs, not this consciousness, etc.,' you will gradually exhaust all possibilities and enter the deep silence, where you may perhaps come face to face with the absolute reality of the Self, which is none of them.

Forth Brahmana

A Conversation Between Yajnavalkya and Maitreyi

1. maitreyi, iti hovaca yajnavalkyah, ud yasyan va are'ham asmat sthanad asmi; hanta hanta, te' naya katyayanyantam karavaniti.

1. "Maitreyi, my dear, said Yajnavalkya, "I am ready to leave this place· Let me make a settlement between you and Katyayani."

Chapter 2

Notes: Yajnavalkya proposed a settlement between his two wives because he decided to give up his family and worldly life, take the vows of renunciation, and retire to a forest or a secluded place. It meant he had to leave his two wives, too, and become a forest dweller. From this conversation, we may presume that Maitreyi was drawn to spirituality while his other wife, Katyayani, was a simple housewife.

2. sa hovaca maitreyi, yan nu ma iyam, bhagoh, sarva prthivi vittena purna syat, katham tenamrta syam iti. na, iti hovaca yajnavalkyah; yathaivopakaranavatam jivitam, tathaiva te jivitam syad amrtatvasya tu nasasti vitteneti.

2. Then Maitreyi said, "Indeed, my lord, if all the wealth of this earth is mine, shall I become immortal through that?" "No," said Yajnavalkya. "Your life will be just like that of wealthy people, but there is no hope of immortality through wealth."

Notes: This shows that Maitreyi already knew the futility of having all the wealth in the world. Yet, she seemed to have to have to start a conversation and provoke Yajnavalkya to respond. Maybe she wanted to accompany him to the forest and take up sannyasa.

3. sa hovaca maitreyi, yenaham namrta syam, kim aham tena kuryam, yad eva bhagavan veda tad eva me bruhiti.

3. Then Maitreyi said, "What shall I do with that by which I will not become immortal? Please tell me that only, godman, which you know (about immortality).

4. sa hovaca yajnavalkyah, priya bata are nah sati priyam bhasase; ehi, assva, vyakhyasyami te; vyacaksanasya tu me nididhyasasva iti.

4. Yajnavalkya said, "My dear, you have been dearer to me, and you spoke to me words that are even dearer. Come, sit here. I will explain it to you. As I speak, listen with utmost attention, restraining your mind and reflecting upon my words."

5. sa hovaca: na va are patyuh kamaya patih priyo bhavati, atmanas tu kamaya patih priyo bhavati: na va are jayayai kamaya jaya priya bhavati, atmanas tu kamaya jaya priya bhavati; na va are putranam kamaya putrah priya bhavanti, atmanas tu kamaya putrah priya bhavanti; na va are vittasya kamaya vittam priyam bhavati, atmanas tu kamaya vittam priyam bhavati; na va are Brahmanah kamaya brahma priyam bhavati, atmanas tu kamaya brahma priyam bhavati; na va are ksatrasya kamaya ksatram priyam bhavati atmanas tu kamaya ksatram priyam bhavati; na va are lokanam kamaya lokah priya bhavanti, atmanas tu kamaya lokah priya bhavanti; na va

are devanam kamaya devah priya bhavanti, atmanas tu kamaya devah priya bhavanti; na va are bhutanam kamaya bhutani priyani bhavanti, atmanas tu kamaya bhutani priyani bhavanti; na va are sarvasya kamaya sarvam priyam bhavati, atmanas tu kamaya sarvam priyam bhavati; atma va are drastavyah srotavyo mantavyo nididhyasitavyah: maitreyi atmano va are darsanena sravanena matya vijnanenedam sarvam viditam.

5. He said, "Truly, it is not because a husband is desirable that the husband becomes dearer, but because the Self is desirable, the husband becomes dearer. It is not because a wife is desirable that the wife becomes dearer, but because the Self is desirable, the wife becomes dearer. It is not because sons are desirable that the sons become dearer, but because the Self is desirable, the sons become dearer. It is not because wealth is desirable that wealth becomes dearer, but because the Self is desirable, wealth becomes dearer. It is not because a Brahmana is desirable that the Brahmana becomes dearer, but because the Self is desirable, the Brahmana becomes dearer. It is not because a Kshatriya is desirable that the Kshatriya becomes dearer, but because the Self is desirable, the Kshatriya becomes dearer. It is not because the worlds are desirable that the worlds become dearer, but because the Self is desirable, the worlds become dearer. It is not because gods are desirable that the gods become dearer, but because the Self is desirable, the gods become dearer. It is not because beings are desirable that the beings become dearer, but because the Self is desirable, the beings become dearer. It is not because all this is desirable that all this becomes dearer, but because the Self is desirable, all this becomes dearer. Indeed, the Self should be seen, heard, meditated upon, and concentrated upon. Truly, Maitreyi, by seeing, hearing, thinking, and discerning the Self within, all this is known.

Notes: The truly lovable and adorable aspect of our existence is the Self within, not the wealth of the world, nor the relationships, nor the social and moral values, nor the identities we build around our names and forms. All these go away at some stage, but the Self alone remains. You are the eternal Self, and if there is anything that you should care for and hold on to, it is the Self. Since this Self is present in all, if there is any reason one must love others or see themselves in them, it is because we are all united with the Supreme Reality through that Self, which exists in all of us and is the same in all. The outward differences are superficial. The hidden Self is the same in all.

6. brahma tam paradad yo'nyatratmano brahma veda. ksatram tam paradad yo'nyatratmanah ksatram veda. lokas tam paradur yo'nyatratmano lokan veda. devas tam paradur yo'nyatratmano

devan veda. bhutani tam paradur yo'nyatratmano bhutani veda. sarvam tam paradad yo'nyatratmano sarvam veda. idam brahma, idam ksatram, ime lokah, ime devah, imami bhutani, idam sarvam, yad ayam atma.

6. A Brahmana regards him as distant (or adverse) who thinks he (the Brahmana) is different from himself. A Kshatriya regards him as distant who thinks he is different from himself. The worlds regard him as distant who think they are different from himself. The gods regard him as distant who thinks they are different from himself. Beings regard him as distant who think they are different from himself. All this regards him as distant who thinks all this is different from himself. The Brahmana, the Kshatriya, the worlds, the gods, the beings, and all this are this Self only.

Notes: A Brahmana or a Kshatriya, well versed in the Vedas, thinks he is different because he considers him ignorant and deluded. If you think that the world is different from you, it remains different from you. If duality exists in your mind, you will experience duality everywhere and in relation to everything. However, you cannot just love everyone or identify with everyone based on a mere notion or assumption. You must be established in that Self with oneness. You have to become That. When you step into the core of that truth of yours, you will realize the universal nature of your existence and your oneness with it. When breath enters your body, for that fraction of a moment, it becomes yours. You cannot hold on to that forever. You have to renounce it the very moment it leaves your body. When it goes out, it becomes universal. The same is the case with everything that becomes a part of your life or consciousness. It comes and goes. Except that everything does not happen that quickly. That is what life is all about. When breath leaves the body, finally, an individual becomes a part of creation, earth to earth, fire to fire, water to water, space to space, breath to breath, and Self to itself.

7. sa yatha dundubher hanyamanasya na bahyan sabdan saknuyad grahanaya, dundubhes tu grahanena dundubhyaghatasya va sabdo grhitah.

7. Just as when a drum is beaten, one cannot distinguish its particular sound, but by seeing the drum or its bearer, the sound is grasped...

Notes: The sound of a drum is the same everywhere. Without knowing its source, we cannot distinguish it. We cannot distinguish the universality of things. We can distinguish them in relation to the things to which they belong. The same is the case with the all-pervading Self. We cannot distinguish it since pure consciousness, which is its essential nature, is universal and found everywhere. We can do so only when we find it in relation to the person or the being in whom it resides.

8. sa yatha sankhasya dhmayamanasya na bahyan sabdan saknuyad grahanaya, sankhasya tu grahaenan sankhadhmasya va sabdo grhitah.

8. Just as when a conch is blown, one cannot distinguish its particular sound, but by seeing the conch or the blower of the conch, the sound is grasped...

9. sa yatha vinayai vadyamanayai na bahyan sabdan saknuyad grahanaya, vinayai tu grahanena vinavadasya va sabdo grhitah.

9. Just as when a Vina (a musical instrument) is played, one cannot distinguish its particular sound, but by seeing the Vina or the player of the Vina, the sound is grasped...

10. sa yathardra-edhagner abhyahitat prthag dhuma viniscaranti, evam va are'sya mahato bhutasya nihsvasitam, etad yad rgvedo yajurvedah samavedo'tharvangirasa itihasah puranam vidya upanisadah slokah sūtrany anuvyakhyanani vyakhyanani: asyaivaitani sarvani nihsvasitani.

10. Just as different kinds of smoke arise from a fire kindled with damp wood, even so, my dear, the Rigveda, Yajurveda, Samaveda, Atharvailgirasa, history, Puranas, various branches of supreme knowledge, Upanishads, verses, aphorisms, explanations, and commentaries - all these are breathed out by this (Self) only.

11. sa yatha sarvasam apam samudra ekayanam, evam sarvesam sparsanam tvag ekayanam, evam sarvesam sarvesam gandhanam nasike ekayanam, evam sarvesam rasanam jihva ekayanam, evam sarvesam rupanam caksur ekayanam, evam sarvesam sarvesam sabdanam srotram ekayanam, evam sarvesam samkalpanam mana ekayanam, evam sarvasam vidyanam hrdayam ekayanam, evam sarvasam karmanam hastav ekayanam, evam sarvasam anandanam upastha ekayanam, evam sarvesam sarvesam visarganam payur ekayanam, evam sarvesam adhvanam padav ekayanam, evam sarvesam vedanam vag ekayanam.

11. Just as all the waters become one with the ocean, just as all forms of touch become one with the skin, just as all odors become one with the nose, just as all tastes become one with the tongue, just as all forms become one with the eyes, just as all sounds become one with the ears, just all intentions become one with the mind, just all types of supreme knowledge (Brahma-vidyas) become one with the heart, just as all actions become one with the hands, just as all forms of enjoyment become one with the reproductive organs, just as all forms of excretion become one in the anus, just as all movements become one in the feet, just as all the Vedas become one in the speech...

Notes: Just as all things arise from the same Self as different forms of the same vital breath (prana), all things also dissolve in the same Self in the ocean of its vital breath.

12. sa yatha saindhava-khilya udake prasta udakam evanuviliyeta, na hasya udgrahanayeva syat, yato yatas tv adadita lavanam eva, evam va ara idam mahad bhutam anantam aparam vijnanaghana eva; etebhyo bhutebhyah samutthaya, tany evanuvinasyati; na pretya samjnasti, iti are bravimi, iti hovaca yajnavalkyah.

12. Just as a lump of salt dropped into water is dissolved and no one can grasp it thereafter, but whenever one sips it, it tastes salty, so does, my dear, this great being, who is infinite, limitless, and filled with intelligence join with these beings and vanish into them. When he departs, there is no more intelligence. This is what I say, my dear," said Yajnavalkya.

Notes: Just as a lump of salt dissolves in water and disappears without a trace, the individuality of the jiva dissolves when he attains liberation. He becomes one with the essence of Brahman and becomes indistinguishable.

13. sa hovaca maitreyi, atraiva ma bhagavan amumuhat, na pretya samjnastiti. sa hovaca, na va are"ham moham bravimi, alam va are idam vijnanaya.

13. Then Maitreyi said, "Godman, indeed you have now put me in confusion. by saying that, 'when he departs, there is no more intelligence,'" Yajnavalkya said, "Certainly, I have not said anything confusing. This should be intelligent enough."

Notes: Maitreyi was confused because she was subject to duality and did not distinguish between the intelligence of the being and the pure intelligence of the Self. The former dissolves without a trace, leaving the Pure intelligence of the Self to shine alone. This is explained in the next verse by Yajnavalkya.

14. yatra hi dvaitam iva bhavati, tad itara itaram jighrati, tad itara itaram pasyati, tad itara itaram srnoti, tad itara itaram abhivadati, tad itara itaram manute, tad itara itaram vijanati. yatra tv asya sarvam atmaivabhut, tat kena kam jighret, tat kena kam pasyet, tat kena kam srnuyat, tat kena kam abhi-vadet, tat kena kam manvita, tat kena kam vijaniyat? yenedam sarvam vijanati, tam kena vijaniyat, vijnataram are kena vijaniyad iti.

14. When there is duality, then only one smells another; one sees another, one hears another, one speaks to another, one thinks of another, one knows another. Truly, when everything becomes the Self, then by what and whom one smells, by what and whom one sees, by what and whom one hears, by what and to whom one speaks, by what and about whom one thinks, and by what and whom one should know? By what all this is known, how can that be known? By what means, my dear, the knower can be known?

Notes: When the jiva attains liberation, and the individual Self disappears into Brahman, there is no seer and no seeing or the seen. Hence, nothing can be said with certainty about that indeterminate state

Fifth Brahmana

The Sweetness of God Inherent in Creation

1. iyam prthivi sarvesam bhutanam madhu, asyai prthivyai sarvani bhutani madhu; yas cayam asyam prthivyam tejomayo'mrtamayah purusah, yas cayam adhyatmam sariras tejomayo'mrtamayah purusah, ayam eva sa yo'yam atma, idam amrtam, idam brahma, idam sarvam.

1. This earth is the honey for all beings, and all beings are honey for this earth. This shining immortal person who is in this earth is also the shining, immortal person as the body itself in the body. He is indeed this Self. This is immortal, this is Brahman, this is all.

Notes: Honey means whatever is sweet and good and nourishes. It refers to Prana, the vital energy needed by the jivas to live. The earth is honey for all beings, meaning all beings derive their nourishment (food) from the earth. The earth is able to nourish because the same Brahman (the Cosmic Self) is hidden in it, just as he is hidden in the body of each being. He is the nourisher, the source of all nourishment, and also the ultimate enjoyer of all nourishment.

2. ima apah sarvesam bhutanam madhu, asam apam sarvani bhutani madhu, yas cayam asv apsu tejomayo'mrtamayah purusah, yas cayam adhyatmam raitasas tejomayo' mrtamayah purusaha; ayam eva sa yo'yam atma; idam amrtam, idam brahma, idam sarvam.

2. This water is the honey for all beings, and all beings are honey for this water. This shining immortal person who is in this water is also the shining, immortal person as the semen itself in the body. He is indeed this Self. This is immortal, this is Brahman, this is all.

Notes: Water represents all liquid substances in the body and the world, including the water present in the reproductive organs and materials. It is life-sustaining and life-nourishing.

3. ayam agnih, sarvesam bhutanam madhu; asyagneh sarvani bhutani madhu; yas cayam asminn agnau tejomayo'mrtamayah purusah, yas cayam adhyatmam van-mayas tejomayo'mrtamayah purusah, ayam eva sa yo'yam atma, idam amr-tam, idam brahma, idam sarvam.

3. *This fire is the honey for all beings, and all beings are honey for this fire. This shining immortal person who is in this fire is also the shining, immortal person as the speech itself in the body. He is indeed this Self. This is immortal, this is Brahman, this is all.*

Notes: Fire exists in the beings as speech, knowledge, and intelligence. This and the following verses in this section speak about one or more aspects of creation in the world and organs in the body and their connection to Brahman, the Self.

4. ayam vayuh sarvesam bhutanam madhu; asya vayoh sarvani bhutani madhu; yas cayam asmin vayau tejomayao'mrtamayah purusah, yas ayam adhyatmam pranas tejomayo'mrtamayah purusah, ayam eva sa yo'yam atma, idam amrtam, idam brahma, idam sarvam.

4. *This air is the honey for all beings, and all beings are honey for this air. This shining immortal person who is in this air is also the shining, immortal person as the breath itself in the body. He is indeed this Self. This is immortal, this is Brahman, this is all.*

5. ayam adityah sarvesam bhutanam madhu; asyadityasya sarvani bhutani madhu; yas cayam asminn aditye tejomayo'mrtamayah purusah, yas cayam adhyatmam caksusas tejomayo'mrtamayah purusah, ayam eva sa yo'yam atma, idam amrtam, idam brahma, idam sarvam.

5. *This sun is the honey for all beings, and all beings are honey for this sun. This shining immortal person who is in this sun is also the shining, immortal person as the eye itself in the body. He is indeed this Self. This is immortal, this is Brahman, this is all.*

6. ima disah sarvesam bhutanam madhu; asam disam sarvani bhutani madhu; yas cayam asu diksu tejomayo'mrtamayah purusah, yas cayam adhyatmam srotrah pratisrutkas tejomayo'mrtamayah purusah, ayam eva sa yo'yam atma, idam amrtam, idam brahma, idam sarvam.

6. *These quarters are the honey for all beings, and all beings are honey for these quarters. This shining immortal person who is in these quar-*

ters is also the shining, immortal person as the hearing of the ear itself in the body. He is indeed this Self. This is immortal, this is Brahman, this is all.

7. ayam candrah sarvesam bhutanam madhu; asya candrasya sarvani bhutani madhu; yas cayam asmims candre tejomayo'mrtamayah purusah, yas cayam adhyatmam manasas tejomayo'mrtamayah purusah, ayam eva sa yo'yam atma, idam amrtam, idam brahma, idam sarvam.

7. This moon is the honey for all beings, and all beings are honey for this earth. This shining immortal person who is in this moon is also the shining, immortal person as the mind itself in the body. He is indeed this Self. This is immortal, this is Brahman, this is all.

8. iyam vidyut sarvesam bhutanam madhu; asyai vidyutah sarvani bhutani madhu; yas cayam asyam vidyuti tejomayo'mrtamayah purusah, yas cayam adhyatmam taijasas tejomayo'mrtamayah purusah, ayam eva sa yo'yam atma, idam amrtam, idam brahma, idam sarvam.

8. This lightning is the honey for all beings, and all beings are honey for this lightning. This shining immortal person who is in this lightning is also the shining, immortal person as light itself in the body. He is indeed this Self. This is immortal, this is Brahman, this is all.

9. ayam stanayitnuh sarvesam bhutanam madhu; asya stanayitnoh sarvani bhutani madhu; yas cayam asmin stanayitnau tejomayo'mrtamayah purusah, yas cayam adhyatmam sabdah sauvaras tejomayo'mrtamayah purusah, ayam eva sa yo'yam atma, idam amrtam, idam brahma, idam sarvam.

9. This cloud is the honey for all beings, and all beings are honey for this cloud. This shining immortal person who is in this cloud is also the shining, immortal person as the sound itself of the voice in the body. He is indeed this Self. This is immortal, this is Brahman, this is all.

10. ayam akasah sarvesam bhutanam madhu; asyakasasya sarvani bhutani madhu; yas cayam asminn akase tejomayo'mrtamayah, purusah, yas cayam adhyatmam hrdyakasah tejomayo'mrtamayah purusah, ayam eva sa yo'yam atma, idam amrtam, idam brahma, idam sarvam.

10. This space is the honey for all beings, and all beings are honey for this space. This shining immortal person who is in this space is also the shining, immortal person as the space itself of the heart in the body. He is indeed this Self. This is immortal, this is Brahman, this is all.

11. ayam dharmah sarvesam bhutanam madhu; asya dharmasya sarvani bhutani madhu; yas cayam asmin dharme, tejomayo'mrtamayah purusah, yas cayam adhyatmam dharmas tejomayo'mrtamayah purusah, ayam eva sa yo'yam atma, idam amrtam, idam brahma, idam sarvam.

11. This Duty is the honey for all beings, and all beings are honey for this Duty. This shining immortal person who is in this Duty is also the shining, immortal person as the Duties themselves of the organs in the body. He is indeed this Self. This is immortal, this is Brahman, this is all.

12. idam satyam sarvesam bhutanam madhu; asya satyasya sarvani bhutani madhu; yas cayam asmin satye tejomayo'mrtamayah purusah, yas cayam adhyatmam satyas tejomayo'mrtamayah purusah, ayam eva sa yo'yam atma, idam amrtam, idam brahma, idam sarvam.

12. This Truth is the honey for all beings, and all beings are honey for this Truth. This shining immortal person who is in this Truth is also the shining, immortal person as truthfulness itself in the body. He is indeed this Self. This is immortal, this is Brahman, this is all.

13. idam manusam sarvesam bhutanam madhu; asya manusasya sarvani bhutani madhu; yas cayam asmin manuse tejoma-yo'mrtamayah purusah, yas cayam adhyatmam manusas tejomayo'mrtamayah purusah, ayam eva sa yo'yam atma, idam amrtam, idam brahma, idam sarvam.

13. This human being is the honey for all beings, and all beings are honey for this human being. This shining immortal person who is in this human being is also the shining, immortal person as the human being itself in the body. He is indeed this Self. This is immortal, this is Brahman, this is all.

14. ayam atma sarvesam bhutanam madhu; asyatmanah sarvani bhutani madhu; yas cayam asminn atmani tejomayo'mrtamayah purusah, yas cayam atma tejomayo' mrtamayah purusah, ayam eva sa yo'yam atma, idam amrtam, idam brahma, idam sarvam.

14. This inner Self (Atman) is the honey for all beings, and all beings are honey for this inner Self. This shining immortal person who is in this inner Self is also the shining, immortal person as individual Self itself in the body. He is indeed this Self. This is immortal, this is Brahman, this is all.

Chapter 2

15. sa va ayam atma sarvesam bhutanam adhipatih; sarvesam bhutunam raja; tad yatha ratha nabhau ca ratha-nemau carah sarve samarpitah evam evasminn atmani sarvani bhutani sarve devah sarve lokah sarve pranah sarva eta atmanah samarpitah.

15. Truly, this Self is the Lord of all beings and King among all beings. Just as the spokes of a chariot wheel are held together by the hub and by the rim of the chariot wheel, so are all beings, all gods, all worlds, all breaths, and all these are held together by this Self.

16. idam vai tan madhu dadhyann atharvano'svibhyam uvaca. tad etad rsih pasyann avocat: tad vam nara sanaye damsa ugram. avis krnomi, tanyatur na vrstim. dadhyann ha yan madhv atharvano vam. asvasya sirsna pra yad im uvaca iti.

16. This, truly, is the honey that Dadhyac Atharvana declared to the two Asvins. Seeing this, the seer said, O Asvins in human form, that terrible deed of yours which you did out of greed, I will reveal just as the clouds declare the coming of the rain and just as Dadhyan declared to you from the Atharvaveda through the head of a horse.

17. idam vai tan madhu dadhyann atharvano'svibhyam uvaca. tad etad rsih etad-rsih pasyann avocat: atharvanayasvina dadhice asvyam sirah praty airayatam. sa vam madhu pra vocad rtayan, tvastram yad dasrav api kaksyam vam iti.

17. This, truly, is the honey that Dadhyac Atharvana declared to the two Asvins. Seeing this, the seer said, O Asvins, you, the terrible ones, you set the head of a horse upon the Dadhyan, with the help of the verses from the Atharvaveda. To keep his promise, he taught you the honey of Tvastri, which is your secret.

18. idam vai tan madhu dadhyann atharvano 'svibhyam uvaca, tad etad rsih pasyann avocat: puras cakre dvipadah, puras cakre catuspadah. purah sa paksi bhutva purah purusa avisat iti. sa va ayam purusah sarvasu pursu purisayah, nainena kim ca nanavrtam, nainena kim ca nasamvrtam.

18. This, indeed, is that honey that Dadhyac Atharvana declared to the two Asvins. Seeing this, the seer said, "He made bodies with two legs and bodies with four legs. Having become a bird, he, the person, entered the bodies. This one alone is the person who dwells in all the bodies. There is nothing that he does not cover and that he does not pervade.

19. idam vai tan madhu dadhyann atharvano' svibhyam uvaca, tad etad rsih pasyann avocat: rupam rupam pratirupo babhuva, tad asya rupam praticaksanaya; indro mayabhih puru-rupa iyate. yukta hy asya harayah sata dasa iti. ayam vai harayah,

ayam vai dasa ca sahasrani bahuni canantani ca, tad etad brahmapurvam, anaparam, anantaram, abahyam, ayam atma brahma sarvanubhuh, ity anusasanam.

19. This, indeed, is that honey that Dadhyac Atharvana declared to the two Asvins. Seeing this, the seer said, "He assumed forms according to each form. This form of him was meant to reveal his true form. He is the Lord of heaven, who goes by many forms with his magic (maya). To him are yoked the horses, hundreds (arteries), and ten (senses). He is also the horse. He alone is tens and thousands, many and numerous. This Brahman is without a back and without a front, without an inside and without an outside. This Self is Brahman, the enjoyer of all. This is the teaching.

Notes: The story of sage Dadhyac or Dadhachi and the twin Asvins is mentioned here to extol the importance of this knowledge.

Sixth Brahmana

The Line of Teachers and Students

Editor's Note: This Brahmana contains a long line of teachers who were instrumental in transmitting the knowledge of the first two chapters, known as Madhukanda. The Sanskrit verses for this section are omitted to avoid redundancy since they contain the same names. Some of the names are repetitive, but they are different persons and probably lived in different times.

1. Now, the line of teachers: Pautimasya from Gaupavana. Gaupavana from Pautimasya. Pautimasya from Gaupavana. Gaupavana from Kausika. Kausika from Kaundinya. Kaundinya from Sandilya. Sandilya from Kausika and Gautama. Gautama...

2. From Agnivesya. Agnivesya from Sandilya and Anabhimlata. Anabhimlata from Anabhimlata. Anabhimlata from Anabhimlata. Anabhimlata from Gautama. Gautama from Saitava and Pracinayogya. Saitava and Pracinayogya from Parasarya. ParaSarya from Bharadvaja. Bharadvaja from Bharadvaja and Gautama. Gautama from Bharadvaja. Bharadvaja from Parasarya. Parasarya from Baijavapayana. Baijavapayana from Kausikayani. Kausikayani...

3. From Ghrtakausika. Ghrtakausika from Parasaryayana. Parasaryayana from Parasarya. Parasarya from Jatukarnya. Jatukarnya from Asurayana and Yaska. Asurayana from Traivani. Traivani from Aupajandhani. Aupajandhani from Asuri. Asuri from Bharadvaja. Bharadvaja from Atreya. Atreya from Manti. Manti from Gautama. Gautama from another Gautama. Gautama from Vatsya. Vatsya from Sandilya. Sandilya from Kaisorya Kapya. Kapya from Kumaraharita. Kumaraharita from Galava. Galava from Vidarbhikaundinya. Vidar-

bhikaundinya from Vatsanapat Babhrava. Babhrava from Pathin Saubhara. Saubhara from Ayasya Angirasa. Ayasya Angirasa from Abhuti Tvastra. Tvastra from Visvarupa Tvastra. Visvarupa Tvastra from the Asvins. Asvins from Dadhyac Atharvana. Dadhyac Atharvana from Atharvan Daiva. Atharvan Daiva from Mrtyu Pradhvamsana. Mrtyu Pradhvamsana from Pradhvamsana. Pradhvamsana from Ekarsi. Ekarsi from Viprachitti. Viprachitti from Vyasti. Vyasti from Sanaru. Sanaru from Sanatana. Sanatana from Sanaga. Sanaga from Paramesthin. Paramesthin from Brahma. Brahma is self-born. Salutation to Brahma.

Notes: Brahma is the source of all knowledge. Brahma imparted the knowledge first to his mind-born sons and then passed it down to others in the line. According to Shankara, this list refers to the long line (vamsa) of teachers of the first two chapters. It is called vamsa because it resembles a bamboo stalk, with sections (as in a bamboo stalk) starting from the top and continuing up to the root.

Chapter 3

First Brahmana

Yajnavalkya on Sacrificial Rites

1. aum, janako ha vaideho bahu-daksinena yajneneje. tatra ha kurupancalanam brahmana abhisameta babhuvuh. tasya ha janakasya vaidehasya vijijnasa babhuva: kah svid esam brahmananam anucanatama iti. sa ha gavam sahasram avarurodha. dasa dasa pada ekaikasyah srngayor abaddha babhuvuh.

1. Aum. Janaka, (the king of) Videha, in order to distribute many gifts, performed a sacrifice. Therefore, many Brahmanas from Kuru and Panchala assembled there. On that occasion, Janaka of Videha developed a curiosity to know which of the Brahmanas was the most conversant with the scriptures. He gathered a thousand cows with ten pads (gold coins) fastened to each horn.

2. tan hovaca: brahmana bhagavantah, yo vo brahmisthah, sa eta ga udajatam iti. te ha brahmana na dadhrsuh. atha ha yajnavalkyah svam eva brahmacarinam uvaca: etah, saumya, udaja, samasrava iti. ta hodacakara, te ha brahmanas cukrudhuh: katham nu no brahmistho bruviteti. atha ha janakasya vaidehasya hotasvalo babhuva: sa hainam papraccha, tvam nu khalu nah, yajnavalkya, brahmistho'siti. sa hovaca: namo vayam brahmisthaya kurmah; gokama eva vayam sma iti. tam ha tata eva prastum dadhre hotasvalah.

He said to them, "Godly Brahmanas, whoever is the wisest among the Brahmanas, can come and claim these cows. The Brahmanas did not dare. Then Yajnavalkya said thus to his pupil, "Samsravas, my dear, take them away." He took them away. The Brahmanas were angry, "How could he declare himself as the wisest among the Brahmanas?" Now, in the court of Janaka of Videha, there was a Hotri priest named Asvala. He asked him, "Yajnavalkya, are you really the wisest among the Brahmanas?" Yajnavalkya replied, "I bow to the wisest Brahmana, but I just desired to have the cows." Then, Asvala decided to question him.

Notes: Yajnavalkya is one of the most inspiring and interesting teachers of the Upanishads. He is probably as significant from a historical perspective to the knowledge of the Self as Shankaracharya was to the cause of Vedanta. Unfortunately, not much academic research has been done about him, after whom this section (munikhanda) was named. Therefore, very few people even know about him. This section clearly proves his erudition and knowledge of the

Vedas. Wise as he was, he did not want to offend anyone by claiming the cows. Hence, he humbly said that he claimed the cows because he wanted them, not because he was the most knowledgeable. In the past, gifts were the means by which Kings and influential people acquired knowledge. In the previous section, King Ajatashatru offered cows to Balaki, and here, King Janaka. Here, Yajnavalkya was humble enough to say that he took the cows because he needed them, not because he was proud of his knowledge.

3. yajnavalkya, iti hovaca. yad idam sarvam mrtyunaptam, sarvam mrtyunabhipannam, kena yajamano mrtyor aptim atimucyata iti: hotra rtvija, agnina, vaca: vag vai yajnasya hota, tad yeyam vak. so'yam agnih, sa hota, sa muktih, satimuktih.

3. *"Yajnavalkya," he said, "since everything here is seized by death and everything is overtaken by death, by what means should the host of a sacrifice go beyond death?" "With the help of a Hotri priest, with speech, and with fire, Truly speaking, speech is the Hotri priest of a sacrifice. That which is speech is this fire. This is the Hotri priest. This is liberation. This is the highest liberation."*

Notes: Going beyond death does not mean liberation or becoming immortal. It is simply leaving this mortal world upon death and going to heaven. Yajnavalkya replied that by performing sacrifices with speech as a Hotri priest, one could (temporarily) leave this world and escape from death.

4. yajnavalkya, iti hovaca. yad idam sarvam ahoratrabhyam aptam, sarvam ahoratrabhyam abhipannam, kena yajamano'horatrayor aptim atimucyata iti. adhvaryuna rtvija, caksusa adityena, caksur vai yajnasya adhvaryuh, tad yad idam caksuh, so'sav adityah; so'dhvaryuh, sa muktih, satimuktih.

4. *"Yajnavalkya," he said, "since everything here is seized by day and night and everything is overtaken by day and night, by what means should the host of a sacrifice transcend day and night?" "With the help of an Adhvaryu priest, with the sight, and with the sun, Truly speaking, the eye is the Adhavaryu priest of a sacrifice. That which is the eye is the sun above. This is the Adhvaryu priest. This is liberation. This is the highest liberation."*

Notes: Time is another name for Death (Kala). One can escape from the earth's time, which is shorter than that of heaven, by worshipping the sun, the presiding deity. Adhvaryu priests build altars for the sacrifices and act as the officiating priests. They also specialize in chanting the mystic hymns (Yajus) of the Yajurveda to ward off death or adversity.

5. yajnavalkya, iti hovaca, yad idam sarvam purva-paksaaparapaksabhyam aptam, sarvam purvapaksaaparapaksabhyam abhipannam. kena yajamanah purvapaksa-aparapaksayor ap-tim

atimucyata iti: udgatra rtvija, vayuna, pranena, prano vai yajnasya udgata, tad yo'yam pranah. sa vayuh, sa udgata, sa muktih satimuktih.

5. *"Yajnavalkya," he said, "since everything here is seized by the bright and dark fortnights and everything is overtaken by the bright and dark fortnights, by what means should the host of a sacrifice transcend the bright and dark fortnights?" "With the help of an Udgatri priest, with air and with breath. Truly speaking, breath is the Udgatri priest of a sacrifice. That which is the breath is the air. This is the Udgatri priest. This is liberation. This is the highest liberation."*

Notes: One can escape from impermanence, as represented by the waxing and waning moon, by worshipping and sacrificing to air (Vayu) or breath (prana), acting as the Samans as a Udgatri priest.

6. yajnavalkya, iti hovaca, yad idam antariksam anarambanam iva kenakramena yajamanah svargam lokam akramata iti: brahmana rtvija, manasa, candrena; mano vai yajnasya brahma, tad yad idam manah, so'sau candrah, sa brahma, sa muktih, satimuktih ity atimoksah, atha sampadah.

6. *"Yajnavalkya," he said, "since the mid-region here is without support, by what means does the host of a sacrifice ascend to heaven?" With the help of a Brahman priest, with the mind, with the moon. Truly speaking, the mind is the Brahman of the sacrifice. That which is mind is the moon up there. This is Brahman. This is liberation. This is the highest liberation. This is the final liberation. Now, as to the gains of sacrifice.*

Notes: Brahman is without support. With the help of a Brahman priest (meaning by meditating on Brahman silently like a Brahman priest who remains passive and supervises the sacrifice), the performer or the host of the (internal) sacrifice can become self-supporting, independent, or without any external support. This is the highest liberation. Other liberations from Death, Time, etc., are temporary.

7. yajnavalkya, iti hovaca, katibhir ayam adya rgbhir hotasmin yajne karisyatiti: tisrbhir iti: katamas tas tisra iti. puro'nuvakya ca yajya ca sasyaiva trtiya. kim tabhir jayatiti: yat kim cedam pranabhrd iti.

7. *"Yajnavalkya," he said, "How many Riks will the Hotri priest use today for the sacrifice?" "Three." "What are the three?" "The beginning hymn Anuvakya, the sacrificial hymn Yajya and the third acclamatory hymn Sasya." "What does one gain through them?" "Whatever that breathes here."*

Notes: Anuvakyas are the preliminary hymns of the Rigveda, sung before a sacrifice. Yajyas are sung during the sacrifice when offerings are poured into the sacrificial fire. Sasya are eulogistic hymns sung in the end. What does he win by them? Progeny, relations, and cattle. Asvala tested here Yajnavalkya's knowledge of the sacrifices.

8. yajnavalkya, iti hovaca, katy ayam adyadhvaryur asmin yajna ahutir hosyatiti: tisra iti: katamas tas tisra iti: ya huta ujjvalanti, ya huta atinedante, ya huta adhiserate: kim tabhir jayatiti: ya huta ujjvalanti deva-lokam eva tabhir jayati, dipyata iva hi deva-lokah; ya huta atinedante, pitr- lokam eva tabhir jayati, ativa hi pitr-lokah; ya huta adhiserate, manusya-lokam eva tabhir jayati, adha iva hi manusya-lokah.

8. *"Yajnavalkya," he said, "How many types of oblations will an Adhvaryu priest burn in the sacrifice today?" "Three" "What are the three?" "Those offerings that burn brightly; those offerings that burn with great noise; and those offerings that sink below." "What does one gain through them?" "Those offerings that burn brightly win the world of immortal gods, for this world shines (brightly like them); those offerings that burn with great noise win the world of ancestors for this world is full of noise; and those offering that sink below win the world of humans for this world, indeed, is down below only.*

Notes: By making these offerings, the worshipper ensures that he will obtain at least one of these worlds and does not fall into the underworld

9. yajnavalkya, iti hovaca, katibhir ayam adya brahma yajnam daksinato devatabhir gopayatiti: ekayeti: katama saiketi: mana eveti, anantam vai manah ananta visve-devah, anantam eva sa tena lokam jayati.

9. *"Yajnavalkya," he said, "with how many gods does this Brahmana priest on the right protect the sacrifice today?" "With one." "Who is that one?" "The mind only. Truly, the mind is infinite, and infinite are the universal deities. An infinite world he gains by worshipping them in the mind."*

Notes: The Brahman priest performs the sacrifice silently with his mind. Other priests, the Hotris, Adhvaryus, Udgatris, etc., do it with speech and breath. Therefore, he relies upon one god, Indra, the presiding deity of the mind and the lord of the senses.

10. yajnavalkya, iti hovaca, katy ayam adyodgatasmin yajne stotriyah stosyatiti: tisra iti: katamas tas tisra iti: puro'nuvakya ca yajya ca sasyaiva trtiya: katamas ta ya adhyatmam iti: prana eva puro'nuvakya, apano yajya, vyanah sasya: kim tabhir jayatiti: prthivi-lokam eva puro'nuvakyaya jayati, antariksa-lokam yajyaya, dyu-lokam sasyaya. tato ha hotasvala upararama.

10. "Yajnavalkya," he said, "how many hymns of praise will the Udgatir priest chant today in the sacrifice?" "Three." "What are the three?" "The preliminary hymn Anuvakya, the sacrificial hymn Yajya, and the third acclamatory hymn Sasya." "Which of them pertains to the body?" "Incoming breath (Prana) is the beginning hymn, the downward breath (Apana) is the sacrificial hymn, and the diffused breath (Yyana) is the acclamatory hymn." "What does he gain by them?" "With the preliminary hymn, he wins the earth; with the sacrificial hymns, he wins the mid-region; and with the acclamatory hymn, he wins the heaven, Dyau." With that, the Hotri priest, Asvala, remained silent.

Notes: Asvala fell silent as he realized that Yajnavalkya was indeed well-informed and well-versed in the Vedas, sacrifices, Brahman, and liberation.

Second Brahmana

Yajnavalkya on Senses and Sense Objects

1. atha hainam jaratkarava artabhagah papraccha: yajnavalkya iti hovaca, kati grahah katy atigraha iti. astau grahah astav atigraha iti. ye te'stau grahah astav atigrahah, katame ta iti.

1. Then Jaratkarava Artabhagah asked him. "Yajnavalkya," he said, "how many are the grasping deities, and how many are the overseeing grasping deities? "There are eight grasping deities and eight overseeing grasping deities." "Which are the eight grasping deities and the eight overseeing grasping deities?"

Notes: After Asvala, Jaratkarava Artabhagah stood up to test him. He asked him about the grahas, the grasping organs (the senses), and their presiding deities (atigrahas). The senses are called grahas because they grasp sense objects. Their atigrahas are the subtle senses that enjoy the things they grasp. For them, the senses are the objects of enjoyment.

2. prano vai grahah, so'panenatigrahena grhitah, apanena hi gandhan jighrati.

2. The nose (prana), indeed, is a grasping deity. It is further grasped by Apana, the downward breath, its overseeing grasping deity. Through Apana, only one smells the odors.

3. vag vai grahah, sa namnatigrahena grihitah, grhitah, vaca hi namany abhivadati.

3. Speech, indeed, is a grasping deity. It is further grasped by Name, its overseeing grasping deity. By speech only, names are uttered.

4. jihva vai grahah, sa rasenatigrahena grhitah, jihvaya hi rasan vijanati.

4. The tongue, indeed, is a grasping deity. It is further grasped by taste, its overseeing grasping deity. With the tongue only, tastes are known.

5. caksur vai grahah, sa rupenatigrahena grhitah, caksusa hi rupani pasyati.

5. The eye, indeed, is a grasping deity. It is further grasped by Form, its overseeing grasping deity. With the eyes, forms are perceived.

6. srotram vai grahah, sa sabdenatigrahena grhitah, srotena hi sabdan srnoti.

6. The ear, indeed, is a grasping deity. It is further grasped by Sound, its overseeing grasping deity. With the ears, sounds are heard.

7. mano vai grahah, sa kamenatigrahena grhitah, manasa hi kaman kamayate.

7. The mind, indeed, is a grasping deity. It is further grasped by Desire, its overseeing grasping deity. With the mind, desires are sought.

8. hastau vai grahah, sa karmanatigrahena grhitah, hastabhyam hi karma karoti.

8. The hands, indeed, are grasping deities. They are further grasped by Duty, their overseeing grasping deity. With the hands, duty is performed.

9. tvag vai grahah, sa sparsenatigrahena grhitah, tvaca hi sparsan vedayate: ity ete'stau grahah, astav atigrahah.

9. The skin, indeed, is a grasping deity. It is further grasped by Touch, its overseeing grasping deity. With the skin, touch is perceived. These are the grasping deities and the eight overseeing grasping deities.

10. yajnavalkya iti hovaca, yad idam sarvam mrtyor annam, ka svit sa devata, yasya mrtyur annam iti: agnir vai mrtyuh, so' pam annam, apa punar mrtyum jayati.

10. "Yajnavalkya," he said, "all this here is food for Death. Who is that deity for whom death is the food?" "To fire, indeed, is Death. It is food for water. With water, one conquers the recurring death.

Notes: Fire destroys everything, even food. Hence, it is Death. Water douses fire and rejuvenates and regenerates life. Hence, it is life-giving and protects the jivas from fire and death.

Chapter 3

11. yajnavalkya, iti hovaca, yatrayam puruso mriyate, ud asmat pranah kramanty aho neti. na iti hovaca yajnavalkyah, atraiva samavaniyante, sa ucchvayati, adhmayati, admnato mrtah sete.

11. Yajnavalkya," he said, "when a person dies, whether his breaths (senses) go up with him or not?" "No," replied Yajnavalkya, "they remain inside only. The body bloats and remains bloated in the mortal state.

Notes: The sense organs do not accompany the departed person. Only their presiding deities accompany him up to the mid-region and return to their respective abodes. Shankara gave a different explanation, suggesting that they do not accompany a liberated person. It may be recalled that in a previous section, we learned that the senses became immortal by taking refuge in the breath, the Lord of the organs.

12. yajnavalkya, iti hovaca, yatrayam puruso mriyate, kim enam na jahatiti: nama iti, anantam vai nama, ananta visve-devah, anantam eva sa tena lokam jayati.

12. "Yajnavalkya," he said, "when a person dies, what does not leave him?" "Name. Name, indeed, is infinite, like the universal deities who are infinite. Infinite, indeed, is he, like them, who wins this world.

Notes: In this context, nama means the name one earns through his deeds, not the physical name. The names of most people are forgotten after they die, but the one who conquers this world through his extraordinary deeds is remembered for a long and sometimes even worshipped as a deity.

13. yajnavalkya, iti hovaca, yatrasya purusasya mrtasyagnim vag apyeti, vatam pranah, caksur adityam, manas candram, disah srotram, prthivim sariram, akasam atma, osadhir lomani, vanaspatin kesah, apsu lohitam ca retas ca nidhiyate, kvayam tada puruso bhavatiti. ahara, somya, hastam, artabhaga; avam evaitasya vedisyavah, na nav etat sajana iti. tau hotkramya, mantrayam cakrate: tau ha yad ucatuh, karma haiva tad ucatuh, atha yat prasasamsatuh karma haiva tat prasasamsatuh: punyo vai punyena karmana bhavati, papah papeneti. tato ha jarat-karava artabhaga upararama.

13. "Yajnavalkya," he said, "when the speech of a person, who dies, is merged in fire, his breath in the air, eye in the sun, mind in the moon, ear in the quarters, body in the earth, the space inside the body in the space outside the body, the hair on the body in the plants, hair on the head in the trees, and when the blood and semen are deposited in the water, then what becomes of this person? "Give me your hand, Artabhaga, my dear. We will know this between our two, but not in the presence of these people." The two went out and talked about it. What they discussed was about actions, and what they praised was actions. Truly, one becomes virtuous by virtuous actions and sinful by sinful actions. After that, Jaratkarava Artabhagah kept silent.

Notes: Yajnavalkya did not reveal the answer in public but talked about it privately with Arthabhaga because certain spiritual matters were considered the utmost secret and not revealed to everyone. Today, many of these subjects are public knowledge, but in Vedic times, some secrets were revealed selectively because of the instruction, which is also found in the Bhagavadgita, that certain teachings should be taught only to the most qualified and virtuous ones.

Third Brahmana

Yajnavalkya on Where Horse Sacrificers Go

1. atha hainam bhujyur lahyayanih papraccha: yajnavalkya, iti hovaca, madresu carakah paryavrajama, te patancalasya kapyasya grhan aima; tasyasid duhita gandharvagrhita; tam aprcchama ko'siti, so'bravit sudhanvangirasa iti, tam yada lokanam antan aprcchama, athainam abruma, kva pariksita abhavann iti, kva pariksita abhavan, sa tva prechami, yajnavalkya, kva pariksita abhavann iti.

1. Then Bhujyu, the grandson of Lahyayani, asked him. "Yajnavalkya," he said, "we went to Madra while wandering around as Parivrajakas and arrived at the house of Patancala Kapya. His daughter was suffering from a possession by a Gandharva. We asked him, "Who are you?" He said, "I am Sudhanvan, of the lineage of Angiras." We asked him about the limits of the world. We also asked him, "What had happened to Pariksit, and what had happened to the descendants of Pariksit? Yajnavalkya, what had become of the descendants of Pariksit?"

Notes: Parivrajakas were homeless, wandering ascetics or students of ancient India who are mentioned in several Hindu, Buddhist and Jain texts. Gandharvas are a class of celestial beings. The people of the Gandhara region were also known as Gandharvas. Takshasila was a prominent religious center and capital of this region. Pariksit was the son of Abhimanyu, the grandson of Arjuna, the successor of Yudhistir of the Mahabharata, and the only surviving descendent of the Pandavas after the Kurukshetra war. According to the legends, he ascended the throne of the Kuru empire at Takshasila. After his untimely demise due to a curse, he was succeeded by his son, Janamejaya. The Gandharva in this story was a ghost or spirit. Parikshit, in this context, stands for a deceased person. The question asked was what happens to people who die suddenly, like Pariksit.

2. sa hovaca, uvaca vai sah agacchan vai te tad yatrasvamedhayajino gacchantiti. kva nv asva-medha-yajino gacchantiti. dvat-

rimsatam vai deva-ratha-ahnyany ayam lokah, tam samantam prthivi dvis tavat paryeti; tam samantam prthivim dvis tavat samudrah paryeti, tad yavati ksurasya dhara, yavad va maksi-kayah pattram, tavan antarenakasah; tan indrah suparno bhutva vayave prayacchat, tan vayur atmani dhitva tatraga-mayad, yatrasva-medha-yajino'bhavann iti; evam iva vai sa vayum eva prasasamsa, tasmad vayur eva vyastih, vayuh sa-mastih: apa punar mrtyum jayati, ya evam veda. tato ha bhujyur lahyayanir upararama.

2. Yajnavalkya said, "The Gandharva obviously told you that they went where the performers of horse sacrifice usually go." "And where do the performers of horse sacrifice go?" "Thirty-two times the distance covered by the chariot of the sun in a day is the extent of this world. Surrounding it, twice that area, is the earth. Surrounding the earth, twice that area, is the ocean. Now, as much as the edge of a barber's knife or the wing of a mosquito is the opening between the two halves of the skull. Through that, by becoming a bird, Indra delivers them to the air, which rules the mid-region. Holding them in itself, the air takes them to the place where the performers of horse sacrifice are present. Hence, he did, indeed, praise the air only. Therefore, air is the separator of beings, and air is the unifier of beings. He who knows this as such conquers further death. After that Bhujya Lahyayani, remained silent.*

Notes: The departing soul and the breaths are delivered by the mind (Indra) to Vayu, who presides over the mid-region. From there, the Self leaves the breaths behind and travels to the world of ancestors, a realm where the souls of deceased family members reside and where the performers of sacrifices go. Parikshit, being a king, must have performed horse sacrifice. Therefore, he was qualified to ascend to the region where the horse sacrificers went. Breath separates the Self from the body at the time of death. It again unifies him with his ancestors by facilitating his journey to the ancestral heaven through the mid-region. Breath in this context refers to the element Air, the god Vayu, who is the lord of the mid-region, the breaths in the body, and the departing Self. As we said before, in the early Vedic literature, breath was synonymous with the Self. Hence, Yajnavalkya equated the subtle body made of breath and space as the subtle body. In the later description, we find the subtle body consisting of the breath, mental, intelligence, and bliss bodies as distinct from the Self. The Self is immaterial and has no association with any elements or tattvas.

Fourth Brahmana

Yajnavalkya on the Unknowability of Self

1. atha hainam usastas cakrayanah papraccha: yajnavalkya, itihovaca, yat saksad aparoksad brahma, ya atma sarvantarah,

tam me vyacaksveti. esa ta atma sarvantarah. katamahyajnavalkya, sarvantarah. yah pranena praniti, sa ta atmasarvantarah, yo'panenapaniti sa ta atma sarvantarah, yovyanena vyaniti sa ta atma sarvantarah; ya udanena udaniti,sa ta atma sarvantarah, esa ta atma sarvantarah.

1. Then Usasta Cakrayana asked him. "Yajnavalkya," he said, "He who is evidently present but imperceptible, and who is the Self within all, please explain that Brahman to me." "This is your Self, which is within all." "Which Self, Yajnavalkya, is within all?" "He who breathes the incoming breath is your Self, who is in all. He who breathes down the downward breath is your Self, who is in all. He who breathes, spreading the diffused breath, is your Self, who is in all. He, who breathes upward with the upwards breath, is your Self, who is in all. He, indeed, is your Self, who is in all.

Notes: Usasta wanted Yajnavalkya to identify the Self in the body clearly and perceptibly without using metaphors or analogies. Yajnavalkya told him that the person who breathed in the body and was responsible for its circulation in different directions was indeed the Self or Brahman.

2. sa hovaca usastas cakrayanah: yatha vibruyad, asau gauh,asav asva iti, evam evaitad vyapadistam bhavati, yad evasaksad aparoksad brahma ya atma sarvantarah tam mevyacaksva iti: esa ta atma sarvantarah. katamahyajnavalkya, sarvantarah. na drster drastaram pasyeh, nasruter srotaram srnuyah, na mater mantaram manvithah, navijnater vijnataram vijaniyah, esa ta atma sarvantarah, ato'nyad artam. tato ha usastas cakrayana upararama.

2. Usasta Cakrayana said, "You have explained to me, just as one might say, 'This is the cow, and this is the horse.' He who is evidently present but imperceptible, and who is the Self within all, please explain that Brahman to me." "This is your Self, which is within all." "Which Self, Yajnavalkya, is within all?" "You cannot see the seer of your seeing. You cannot hear the hearer of your hearing. You cannot think the thinker of your thinking. You cannot know the knower of your knowing. This is your Self, who is within all. Everything else is evil. Thereupon, Usasta Cakrayana remained silent.

Notes: The Self is the subject, not the object of the senses, the mind, intelligence, gods, or anything else. Hence, no one can know him objectively.

Chapter 3
Fifth Brahmana

Yajnavalkya on Renunciation and Liberation

1. atha hainam kaholah kausitakeyah papraccha: yajnavalkya, iti hovaca, yad eva saksad aparoksad brahma, ya atma sarvantarah, tam tam me vyacaksva iti. esa ta atma sarvantarah-katamah, yajnavalkya, sarvantarah. yo'sanayapipase sokam moham jaram mrtyum atyeti. etam vai tam atmanam viditva, brahmanah putraisanayas ca vittaisanayas ca lokaisanayas ca vyutthaya, atha bhiksacaryam caranti. ya hy eva putraisana sa vittaisana ya vittaisana sa lokaisana, ubhe hy ete esane eva bhavatah; tasmad brahmanah, pandityam nirvidya balyena tisthaset; balyam ca pandityam ca nirvidya, atha munih; amaunam ca maunam ca nirvidya, atha brahmanah. sa brahmanah kena syat. yena syat tena idrsa eva ato'nyad artam. tato ha kaholah kausitakeya upararama.

1. Then Kahola Kausitakeya asked him. Yajnavalkya," he said, "He who is evidently present but imperceptible, and who is the Self within all, please explain that Brahman to me." "This is your Self, which is within all." "Which Self, Yajnavalkya, is within all?" "That which is beyond hunger, thirst, sorrow, delusion, old age, and death. Knowing this very Self, the Brahmanas renounce their desire for sons, for wealth, and for the world and wander around begging for alms. Indeed, that which is the desire for sons is the desire for wealth, and that which is the desire for wealth is the desire for the world. Both these, indeed, are desires only. Therefore, let a Brahmana, having become a scholar, live by unlearning what he learns in his childhood. Having lived by unlearning what has been learned in his childhood, he should become an ascetic, the silent one (muni). Through recitation, through silence, and through unlearning or detachment from the learned knowledge, thus he should become the knower of Brahman." "How does that knower of Brahman behave?" "Howsoever he may behave, he remains as such. Everything else is afflicted with suffering." Thereupon Kahola Kausitakeya remained silent.

Notes: Nirvidya means unlearning or giving up what has been learned in childhood. Pandityam is a reference to the mechanical knowledge of the rites and rituals (karma kanda) one learns from a guru as a student. The pursuer of Brahman, who takes the vows of renunciation, must renounce all forms of ignorance and lower knowledge (avidya) acquired through study, learning, and observation (or the mind, intellect, and senses) and rely solely upon self-knowledge (jnana kanda) to know the Self. Some translate nirvidya as detachment. However, unlearning or unconditioning is more apt since the mind and all accumulated knowledge are obstacles in the pursuit of liberation or self-knowledge. Only when the mind is emptied of all the accumulated knowledge and silenced does one truly become the silent one (muni).

Sixth Brahmana

Yajnavalkya on the Worlds and Their Support

1. atha hainam gargi vacaknavi papraccha, yagnavalkya, iti hovaca, yad idam sarvam apsv otam ca protam ca, kasmin nu khalv apa otas ca protas ceti. vayau, gargi, iti. kasmin nu khalu vayur, otas ca protas ceti. antariksa-lokesu, gargi, iti. kasmin nu khalv antariksa-loka otas ca protas ceti, gandharva-lokesu gargi, iti. kasmin nu khalu gandharva-loka otas ca protas ceti. aditya-lokesu, gargi, iti. kasmin nu khalv aditya-loka otas ca protas ceti. candra-lokesu, gargi, iti. kasmin nu khalu candra-loka otas ca protas ceti. naksatralokesu, gargi, iti. kasmin nu khalu naksatra-loka otas ca protas ceti. deva-lokesu, gargi, iti. kasmin nu khalu devaloka otas ca protas ceti. indra-lokesu, gargi, iti. kasmin nu khalu indra-loka otas ca protas ceti. brahma-lokesu, gargi, iti. kasmin nu khalu brahma-loka otas ca protas ceti. sa hovaca, gargi matipraksih, ma te murdha vyapaptat, anatiprasnyam vai devatam atiprechasi, gargi, matipraksir iti. tato ha gargi vacaknavy upararama.

1. Then Gargi Vacaknavi asked him. Yajnavalkya," she said, "All this here is woven, like warp and woof, with water; with what then is water woven like warp and woof?

"With air, O Gargi."

"With what then is air woven, like warp and woof?"

"With the mid-region, O Gargi,"

"With what then is the mid-region woven, like warp and woof?"

"With the world of Gandharvas, O Gargi."

"With what then is the world of Gandharvas woven, like warp and woof?"

"With the world of the Aditya, O Gargi."

"With what then is woven the world of Aditya, like warp and woof?"

"With the world in the moon, O Gargi."

"With what then is woven the world in the moon, like warp and woof?"

"With the world of stars, O Gargi."

"With what then is woven the world of stars, like warp and woof?"

"The world of gods, O Gargi."

"With what then is woven the world of gods, like warp and woof?"

"With the world of Indra, O Gargi."

"With what then is woven the world of Indra, like warp and woof?"

"With the world of Prajapati, O Gargi."

"With what then is woven the world of Prajapati, like warp and woof?"

"With the world of Brahma, O Gargi."

"With what then is woven the world of Brahma, like warp and woof?"

He said, "Gargi, do not ask me too many questions. Otherwise, you will lose your mind. In fact, you are asking me too many questions about a deity about whom we should not ask too much. Do not ask too much, O Gargi."

After that, Gargi Vacaknavi remained silent.

Notes: Warp and woof (otam protam) mean support, foundation, base, etc., or whatever that pervades something like an invisible cloth or base. For example, the skeleton in the body is its support. The world of Brahma is the final support for all the worlds and spheres or deities preceding him in this verse. Yajnavalkya declined to describe the foundation of Brahma.

Seventh Brahmana

Yajnavalkya on the Inner Controller

1. atha hainam uddalaka arunih papraccha: yajnavalkya, iti hovaca madresv avasama, patancalasya kapyasya grhesu, yajnam adhiyanah. tasyasid bharya gandharva-grhita, tam aprcchama, ko'siti: so'bravit, kabandha atharvana iti. so'bravit patancalam kapyam yajnikams ca; vettha nu tvam, kapya, tat sutram yasminn (v: yena) ayam ca lokah, paras ca lokah, sarvani ca bhutani samdrbdhani, bhavantiti. so'bravit patancalah kapyam yajnikams ca. vettha nu tvam, kapya, tam antaryaminam, ya imam ca lokam param ca lokam sarvani ca bhutani yo'ntaro yamayatiti. so'bravit patancalah kapyah naham tam, bhagavan, vedeti. so'bravit patancalam kapyam yajnikams ca, yo vai tat, kapya, sutram vidyat, tam cantaryaminam iti, sa brahma-vit, sa loka-vit, sa deva-vit, sa veda-vit, sa bhuta-vit, sa atma-vit, sa sarva-vit, iti tebhyo'bravit tad aham veda; tac cet tvam, yajnavalkya, sutram avidvams tam cantaryaminam brahmagavir udajase, murdha te vipatisyatiti. veda va aham,

Chapter 3

gautama, tat sutram tam cantaryaminam iti. yo va idam kas cid bruyat, veda vedeti: yatha vettha, tatha bruhiti.

1. Then Uddalaka, Aruni, asked him. "Yajnavalkya," he said, "We lived in Madra, in the house of Patancala Kapya (descendant of Kapi), studying the knowledge of the sacrifices. His wife was possessed by a Gandharva. We asked him who he was. He said, 'I am Kabandha Atharvana.' He said to Patancala Kapya and those who were learning the knowledge of sacrifices, 'Kapya, do you know that thread by which this life, the next life, and all the beings are strung together?' Patancala Kapya said, 'I do not know Godman.' He said to Patancala Kapya and the students, 'Kapya, do you know that inner controller who controls from within this world and the next and all the beings?' Patancala Kapya said, 'I do not know him, Godman.' He said to Patancala Kapya and the students, 'Kapya, he who knows that thread and that inner controller, indeed knows Brahman, knows the worlds, knows the gods, knows the Vedas, knows the beings, knows the Self, and knows everything.' Thus, he explained it all to them. I know it. If you, Yajnavalkya, do not know that thread and that inner control and still take away the cows that belong only to the knowers of Brahman, you will lose your head (mind)." "I know, O Gautama, that thread and that inner controller." Anyone can say, "I know, I know." "Tell us what you know."

2. sa hovaca vayur vai, gautama, tat sutram; vayuna vai, gautama, sutrenayam ca lokah paras ca lokah sarvani ca bhutani samdrbdhani bhavanti, tasmad vai, gautama, purusam pretam ahuh vyasramsisatasyanganiti; vayuna hi, gautama, sutrena samdrbdhani bhavantiti. evam etat, yajnavalkya, antaryaminam bruhiti.

2. He said, "Vayu, indeed, is that thread, O Gautama. By the thread of air only, O Gautama, this world and the next world and all the beings are strung together. Therefore, O Gautama, when a person dies, they say his limbs have been loosened, for by thread of air only, O Gautama, they are held together." "That is true, Yajnavalkya. Now, describe the internal controller."

3. yah prthivyam tisthan prthivya antarah, yam prthivi na veda, yasya prthivi sariram, yah prthivim antaro yamayati, esa ta atmantaryamy amrtah.

3. "He who is seated in the earth and is inside the earth, but whom the earth does not know, whose body is the earth, who controls the earth from within, is your Self, inner controller and immortal."

Chapter 3

4. yo'psu tisthann, adbhyo'ntarah, yam apo na viduh, yasyapah, sariram, yo'po'ntaro yamayati, esa ta atmantaryamy amrtah.

4. "He who is seated in the waters and is inside the water, whom the water does not know, whose body is the water and who controls water from within, is your Self, inner controller and immortal."

5. yo'gnau tisthann, agner antarah, yam agnir na veda, yasyagnih sariram, yo'gnim antaro yamayati, esa ta amrtah.

5. "He who is seated in the fire and is inside the fire, whom fire does not know, whose body is the fire and who controls the fire from within, is your Self, inner controller and immortal."

6. yo'ntarikse tisthann antariksad antarah, yam antariksam na veda, yasyantariksam sariram, yo'ntariksam antaro yamayati, esa ta atmantaryamy amrtah.

6. "He who is seated in the mid-region and is inside the mid-region whom the mid-region does not know, whose body is the mid-region and who controls the mid-region from within, is your Self, inner controller and immortal."

7. yo vayau tisthann vayor antarah, yam vayur na veda, yasya vayuh sariram, yo vayum antaro yamayati, esa ta atmantaryamy amrtah.

7. "He who is seated in the air and is inside the air, whom the air does not know, whose body is the air and who controls the air from within, is your Self, inner controller and immortal."

8. yo divi tisthan divo'ntarah, yam dyaur na veda, yasya dyauh sariram, yo divam antaro yamayati, esa ta atmantaryamy amrtah.

8. "He who is seated in the heaven and is inside the heaven, whom the heaven does not know, whose body is the heaven and who controls the heaven from within, is your Self, inner controller and immortal."

9. ya aditye tisthann adityad antarah, yam adityo na veda, yasyadityah sariram, ya adityam antaro yamayati, esa ta atmantaryamy amrtah.

9. "He who is seated in the sun and is inside the sun, whom the sun does not know, whose body is the sun and who controls the sun from within, is your Self, inner controller and immortal."

10. yo diksu tisthan, digbhyo'ntarah, yam diso na viduh, yasya disah sariram, yo diso antaro yamayati, esa ta atmantaryamy amrtah.

10. "He who is seated in the quarters and is inside the quarters, whom the quarters do not know, whose body is the quarters and who controls the quarters from within, is your Self, inner controller and immortal."

11. yas candra-tarake tisthams candra-tarakad antarah, yam candra-tarakam na veda, yasya candra-tarakam sariram yas candra-tarakam antaro yamayati, esa ta atmantaryamy amrtah.

11. "He who is seated in the moon and the stars, whom the moon and the stars do not know, whose body is the moon and stars and who controls the moon and stars from within, is your Self, inner controller and immortal."

12. ya akase tisthan akasad antarah, yam akaso na veda, yasyakasah sariram, ya akasam antaro yamayati, esa ta atmantaryamy amrtah.

12. "He who is seated in space and is inside space, whom the space does not know, whose body is space and who controls space from within, is your Self, inner controller and immortal."

13. yas tamasi tisthams tamaso'ntarah, yam tamo na veda yasya tamah sariram, yas tamo'ntaro yamayati, esa ta atmantaryamy amrtah.

13. "He who is seated in the darkness and is inside the darkness, whom the darkness does not know, whose body is the darkness and who controls the darkness from within, is your Self, inner controller and immortal."

14. yas tejasi tisthams tejaso'ntarah, yam tejo na veda, yasya tejah sariram, yas tejo'ntaro yamayati, esa ta atmantaryamy amrtah ity adhidaivatam, athadhibhutam.

14. "He who is seated in the light and is inside the light, whom the light does not know, whose body is the light and who controls light from within, is your Self, inner controller and immortal."

15. yah sarvesu bhutesu tisthan, sarvebhyo bhutebhyo'ntarah, yam sarvani bhutani na viduh, yasya sarvani bhutani sariram, yah sarvani bhutani antaro yamayati, esa ta atmantaryamy amrtah, amrtah. ity adhibhutam;athadhyatmam.

15. "He who is seated above all beings and is inside all beings, whom all these beings do not know, whose body is the beings and who controls all the beings from within, is your Self, inner controller and immortal."

Chapter 3

16. yah prane tisthan pranad antarah, yam prano na veda, yasya pranah, sariram, yah pranam antaro yamayati, esa ta atmantaryamy amrtah.

16. *"He who is seated in the breath and is inside the breath, whom the breath does not know, whose body is the breath and who controls the breathing from within, is your Self, inner controller and immortal."*

17. yo vaci tisthan vaco'ntarah, yam van na veda, yasya vak sariram yo vacam antaro yamayati, esa ta atmantaryamy amrtah.

17. *"He who is seated in the speech and is inside the speech, whom the speech does not know, whose body is the speech and who controls the speech from within, is your Self, inner controller and immortal."*

18. yas caksusi tisthams caksuso'ntarah, yam caksur na veda, yasya caksuh sariram, yas caksur antaro yamayati, esa ta atmantaryamy amrtah.

18. *"He who is seated in the eye and is inside the eye, whom the eye does not know, whose body is the eye and who controls the eye from within, is your Self, inner controller and immortal."*

19. yah srotre tisthan srotrad antarah, yam srotram na veda, yasya srotram sariram, yah srotram antaro yamayati, esa ta atmantaryamy amrtah.

19. *"He who is seated in the ear and is inside the ear, whom the ear does not know, whose body is the ear and who controls the ear from within, is your Self, inner controller and immortal."*

20. yo manasi tisthan manaso'ntarah, yam mano na veda, yasya manah sariram, yo mano'ntaro yamayati, esa ta atmantaryamy amrtah.

20. *"He who is seated in the mind and is inside the mind, whom the nose does not know, whose body is the nose and who controls the nose from within, is your Self, inner controller and immortal."*

21. yas tvaci tisthams tvaco'ntarah, yam tvan na veda, yasya tvak sariram, yas tvacam antaro yamayati, esa ta atmantaryamy amrtah.

21. *"He who is seated in the skin and is inside the skin, whom the skin does not know, whose body is the skin and who controls the skin from within, is your Self, inner controller and immortal."*

22. yo vijnane tisthan, vijnanad antarah, yam vijnanam na veda, yasya vijnanam sariram, sariram, yo vijnanam antaro yamayati, esa ta atmantaryamy amrtah.

22. *"He who is seated in the intelligence and is inside the intelligence, whom the intelligence does not know, whose body is the intelligence and who controls the intelligence from within, is your Self, inner controller and immortal."*

23. yo retasi tisthan retaso'ntarah, yam reto na veda, yasya retah sariram, yo reto'ntaro yamayati, esa ta atmantaryamy amrtah; adrsto drasta, asrutah srota, amato manta, avijnato vijnata. nanyo'to'sti drasta, nanyo'to'sti srota, nanyo'to'sti manta, nanyo'to'sti vijnata; esa ta atmantaryamy amrtah; ato'nyad artam. tato hoddalaka arunir upararama. iti samaptam brahmanam.

23. *"He who is seated in the semen and is inside the semen, whom the semen does not know, whose body is the semen and who controls the semen from within, is your Self, inner controller and immortal. He is not seen but is the seer. He is not heard but is the listener. He is not grasped by the mind but is the thinker. He is not known but is the knower. There is no witness except him, no other listener except him, no other thinker except him, and no other knower except him. He is your Self, the inner controller, the immortal. Everything else is afflicted with suffering." After that, Uddalaka Aruni remained silent.*

Notes: The sum of these teachings is that the Self or Brahman is the ultimate support, connecting thread, controller, and subject of all that moves and moves not within the body, all the worlds, and the whole creation. He is seated in all beings and manifestations as their very support.

Eighth Brahmana

Yajnavalkya on Imperishable, Unseen Brahman

1. atha ha vacaknavy uvaca, brahmana bhagavantah, hanta, aham imam dvau prasnau praksyami; tau cen me vaksyati, na vai jatu yusmakam imam kas cid brahmodyam jeteti. prccha gargiti.

I. Then Vacaknavi said, "Godly Brahmanas, I shall ask him two questions. If he answers them to me, none of you can ever beat him in a debate about Brahman." "Ask, O Gargi."

2. sa hovaca: aham vai tva, yajnavalkya, yatha kasyo va vaideho va ugra-putrah, ujjyam dhanur adhijyam krtva, dvau banavantau sapatna-ativyadhinau haste krtva upottisthet,

Chapter 3

evam evaham tva dvabhyam prasnabhyam upodastham, tau me bruhiti. prccha, gargi, iti.

2. She said, "Now I have these two questions to ask. O Yajnavalkya, just as the angry son of the king of Kasi or of Videha might rise against you, having strung or unstrung his bow and holding two pointed and foe-piercing arrows, so do I have risen against you with these two questions, Answer me these." "Ask, O Gargi."

3. sa hovaca: yad urdhvam, yajnavalkya, divah, yad avak prthivyah, yad antara dyavaprthivi ime, yad bhutam ca bhavac ca bhavisyac cety acaksate; kasmims tad otam ca protam ceti.

3. She said, "That which, O Yajnavalkya, is above the heaven and that which is below the earth, that which is between the two, the heaven and the earth, and that Being which they say was, is and will be, please tell me in what is it woven like warp and woof?

4. sa hovaca: yad urdhvam, gargi, divah, yad avak prthivyah, yad antara dyavaprthivi ime, yad bhutam ca bhavac ca bhavisyac cety acaksate; akase tad otam ca protam ceti.

4. He said, "That, O Gargi, which is above the heaven and that which is below the earth, and that which is between these two, the heaven and earth, and which they say was, is and will be, is pervaded by space, like warp and woof."

5. sa hovaca: namas te'stu, yajnavalkya, yo ma etam vyavocah: aparasmai dharayasveti. prccha, gargi, iti.

5. She said, "Salutations to you, Yajnavalkya, who answered this question of mine. Now, be prepared for the next question." "Ask, O Gargi."

6. sa hovaca: yad urdhvam, yajnavalkya, divah, yad avak prthivyah, yad antara dyava-prthivi ime, yad bhutam ca bhavac ca bhavisyac cety acaksate: kasmims tad otam ca protam ceti.

6. She said, "That which, O Yajnavalkya, is above the heaven and that which is below the earth, that which is between the two, the heaven and the earth, and that Being which they say was, is and will be, please tell me in what is it woven like warp and woof?"

7. sa hovaca: yad urdhvam, gargi, divah, yad avak prthivyah, yad antara dyavaprthivi ime, yad bhutam ca bhavac ca bhavisyac cety acaksate akasa eva tad otam ca protam ceti; kasmin nu khalv akasa otas ca protas ceti.

7. He said, "That, O Gargi, which is above the heaven and that which is below the earth, and that which is between these two, the heaven and

earth, and which they say was, is and will be, is pervaded by space, like warp and woof." "In what is it woven like warp and woof?"

Notes: Yajnavalkya already answered that both heaven and earth existed in space and were pervaded by space. But Gargi repeated the question to find out whether Yajnavalkya would answer differently or not answer her question at all. Yajnavalkya did not want to give a different reply. At the same time, he did not want to remain silent and thereby appear to others as if he did not know the answer. So, he repeated the same answer to convey that he was certain of what he said before.

8. sa hovaca: etad vai tad aksaram, gargi, brahmana abhivadanti, asthulam, ananu, ahrasvam, adirgham, alohitam, asneham, acchayam, atamah, avayv anakasam, asangam, arasam, agandham, acaksuskam, asrotram, avak, amanah, atejaskam, apranam, amukham, amatram, anantaram, abahyam; na tad asnati kim cana, na tad asnati kas cana.

8. He said, "O Gargi, the Brahmanas, the knowers of Brahman, say That is imperishable one, not gross, not minute, not short, not long, not red in color, not binding, not darkness, not air, not space, unassociated, without taste, without smell, without eyes, without ears, without voice, without mind, without brilliance, without breath, without face, without measure, and without an interior or exterior. It does not eat, and it cannot be eaten.

Notes: The meaning of this is: Hidden within space which pervades above, below and everywhere is That (tad) which is indescribably and indeterminate. He used the 'not t this, not this' analogy to describe Brahman and precluded the possibility of further questioning by Gargi.

9. etasya va aksarasya prasasane, gargi, suryacandramasau vidhrtau tisthatah; etasya va aksarasya prasasane, gargi, dyavaprithivyau vidhrte tisthatah; etasya va aksarasya prasa-sane, gargi, nimesa, muhurta, ahoratrany, ardhamasa, masa, rtavah, samvatsara iti. vidhrtas tisthanti; etasya va aksarasya prasasane, gargi, pracyo'nya nadyah syandante svetebhyah parvatebhyah, praticyo'nyah, yam yam ca disam anu; etasya va aksarasya prasasane, gargi, dadato manusyah prasamsanti; yajamanam devah, darvim pitaro "nvayattah.

9. By the command of this imperishable one only, O Gargi, the sun and the moon are held firmly in their positions. By the command of this imperishable one only, O Gargi, the heaven and the earth are held firmly in their positions. By the command of this imperishable one only, O Gargi, moments, hours, days and nights, fortnights, months, seasons, and the year stand in their positions. By the command of this imperish-

able one only, O Gargi, some rivers flow eastwards from the snowy mountains, others flow westward, and still some other in other directions. By the command of this imperishable one only, O Gargi, people praise those who give charity, the gods (praise) those who host sacrifices, and the forefathers (praise) those who wish for offspring.

Notes: Brahman not only exists in all and supports all but also the mighty Lord and Controller of all. He supports from within and rules from above.

10. yo va etad aksaram, gargi, aviditvasmiml loke juhoti, yajate, tapas tapyate, bahuni, varsa-sahasrany antavad evasya tad bhavati; yo va etad aksaram, gargi, aviditvasmal lokat praiti, sa krpanah; atha ya etad aksaram, gargi, viditvasmal lokat praiti, sa brahmanah.

10. Whoever, O Gargi, in this world, without knowing the imperishable, pours oblations into fire, performs sacrifices, and undergoes penances even for a thousand years, he will find that his works are finite. Whoever, O Gargi, departs from this world without knowing the imperishable deserves our sympathy. However, whoever, O Gargi, departs from here knowing the imperishable becomes a knower of Brahman.

Notes: For liberation, the knowledge of Brahman or the Self is absolutely necessary. Otherwise, one remains bound to samsara.

11. tad va etad aksaram, gargi, adrstam drastr, asrutam, srotr, amatam mantr, avijnatam vijnatr, nanyad ato'sti drastr, nanyad ato'sti srotr, nanyad ato'sti mantr, nanyad ato'sti vijnatr; etasmin nu khalv aksare, gargi, akasa otas ca protas ca.

11. That imperishable one, O Gargi, is not seen but is the seer, not heard, but is the hearer, unthought but is the thinker, and unknown but is the knower. There is no other seer but this; no other listener but this; no other thinker but this; and no other knower but this. By this imperishable one only, O Gargi, the space is woven like warp and woof.

12. sa hovaca; brahmana bhagavantah, tad eva bahu manyedhvam yad asman namaskarena mucyedhvam; na vai jatu yusmakam imam kascid brahmodyam jeteti. tato ha vacaknavy upararama. Iti astamam brahmanam

12. She said, "Godly Brahmanas, you may consider it a great blessing if you can get away from him with a salutation. No one can surpass him in any debate about Brahman." After that, (Gargi) Vacaknavi remained silent.

Chapter 3
Nineth Brahmana

Yajnavalkya on Many Gods and One God

1. atha hainam vidagdhah sakalyah papraccha: katy devah, yajnavalkya, iti. sa haitayaiva nivida pratipede, yavanto vaisvadevasya nividy ucyante; trayas ca tri ca sata, trayas ca tri ca sahasreti. aum iti. hovaca, katy eva devah, yajnavalkya, iti. trayas trimsad iti. aum iti. hovaca, katy eva devah, yajnavalkya, iti. sad iti. aum iti. hovaca, katy eva devah, yajnavalkya, iti. traya iti. aum iti. hovaca, katy eva devah, yajnavalkya, iti. drav iti. aum iti. hovaca, katy eva devah, yajnavalkya, iti. adhyardha iti. aum iti. hovaca, katy eva devah, yajnavalkya, iti. eka iti, aum iti, hovaca katame te trayas ca tri ca sahasreti.

I. Then Vidagdha Sakalya, asked him. "How many gods are there, Yajnavalkya?"

Yajnavalkya replied, according to the names mentioned in Nivid, "As many as mentioned in the Nivid of the Visvadevas, namely three hundred and three, three thousand and three."

"Agreed," he said, "how many gods are there really, Yajnavalkya?"

"Thirty-three."

"Agreed," he said, "how many gods are there, Yajnavalkya?"

"Six."

"Agreed," he said, "how many gods are there, Yajnavalkya?"

"Three."

"Agreed," he said, "how many gods are there, Yajnavalkya?"

"Two"

"Agreed," he said, "how many gods are there, Yajnavalkya?"

"One and a half."

"Agreed," he said, "how many gods are there, Yajnavalkya?"

"One."

"Agreed," he said, "which are those three hundred and three and three thousand and three?"

Notes: Nivid refers to a group of very ancient, and possibly the earliest, adulatory mantras found in the Rigveda and Yajurveda, many of which are said to have been lost. The Hotri priests used to address them to a single deity or a group of deities (Visvadevas) during the midday and evening libations associated with the Soma rituals, in which their numbers, titles, and qualities were mentioned. Yajnavalkya gave their number as 303 and 3003.

2. sa hovaca, mahimana evaisam ete, trayas trimsat tv eva deva iti. katame te trayas trimsad iti. astau vasavah ekadasa rudrah, dvadasadityah, te ekatrimsat indras caiva prajapatis ca trayastrimsav iti.

2. He said, "They are but their manifestations. There are only thirty-three gods." "Which are these thirty-three? "The eight Vasus, the eleven Rudras, and the twelve Adityas, these are thirty-one. With Indra and Prajapati, it is thirty-three.

Notes: The 33 gods mentioned here are found not only in God's creation but also in the human body as organs.

3. katame vasava iti. agnis ca prthivi ca vayus cantariksam cadityas ca dyaus ca candramas ca naksatrani ca, ete vasavah, etesu hidam sarvam hitam iti, tasmad vasava iti.

3. "Which are the Vasus?" "Fire, earth, air, the mid-region, the sun, heaven, the moon and stars, these are the Vasus, for in this well-placed all this is. Therefore, they are called the residents (Vasus)."

4. katame rudra iti. daseme puruse pranah atmaikadasah; te yadasmat sariran martyad utkramanti, atha rodayanti, tad yad rodayanti, tasmad rudra iti.

4· "Which are the Rudras?" "The ten breaths in the person, with the mind as the eleventh. When they rise up and depart from the mortal body, others weep. They make them weep. Therefore, they are called the Rudras.

Notes: The ten Rudras mentioned here are actually the ten sense organs, not breaths (prana).

5. katama aditya iti. dvadasa vai masah samvatsarasya, eta adityah, ete hidam sarvam adadana yanti; te yad idam sarvam adadana yanti, tasmad aditya iti.

5· "Which are the Adityas?" "Truly, the twelve months in the year, they are the Adityas. They move, taking away all this with them. Hence, they are called the Adityas.

Notes: Adityas are solar deities, 12 in number, each corresponding to a month in a solar year. Since each takes away a month from the life of a living being, they are known as Adityas, the takers (Āda).

6. katama indrah, katamah prajapatir iti, stanayitnur evendrah, yajnah prajapatir iti. katamah stanayitnur iti. asanir iti. katamo yajna iti, pasava iti.

6. "Which is Indra, and which is Prajapati?" "Indra is the thundercloud, Prajapati is the sacrifice." "Which is the thundercloud?" "The flashes of lightning." "Which is the sacrifice." "The animals."

Notes: Stanayithnur means thundercloud, which is often equated with death. Indra, the thundercloud, is the cause of death. He sacrifices the animals through flashes of lightning.

7. katame saḍ iti. agnis ca prthivi ca vayus cantariksam cadityas ca dyaus ca, ete sat; ete hidam sarvaṃ sad iti.

7. "Which are the six?" "Fire, earth, air, the mid-region, the sun, and heaven, these are the six, and all this exists in these six."

Notes: These are the six of the Vasus mentioned in verse 3. The 33, 303, and 3003 gods inhabit these six spheres.

8. katame te trayo deva iti. ima eva trayo lokah, esu hime sarve deva iti. katamau tau dvau devav iti, annam caiva pranas ceti. katamo'dhyardha iti, yo yam pavata iti.

8. "Which are the three gods?" "These are the three worlds. In them exist all the deities." "Which are the two gods." "Food and breath." "Which is one and a half?" "This one who blows."

Notes: The six spheres are reduced to three worlds: earth and fire, air and mid-region, and the sun and heaven. The two gods are the gross (annam) body and the subtle (pranam) body. All the deities in the body or the cosmos exist in these two.

9. tad ahuh, yad ayam eka ivaiva pavate, atha katham adhyardha iti. yad asminn idam sarvam adhyardhnot, tenadhyardha iti, katama eko deva iti. prana iti, sa brahma, tyad ity acaksate.

9. "Of that, some say, 'He blows as one.' Now, how can he be one and a half?? In him, all this becomes one and a half by expanding." "Which is the one deity?" "He is Brahman. They call him Tyat (That).

Notes: The one deity is Brahman. The one-and-a-half deities are the breath and its extension. They are one and a half because breath is not confined to the body only. It goes beyond the gross body and connects to the breath outside. It extends infinitely since, apart from Brahman (pure consciousness), all this is filled with prana only.

10. prthivy eva yasyayatanam, agnir lokah, mano jyotih, yo vai tam purusam vidyat sarvasyatmanah parayanam, sa vai vedita syat, yajnavalkya. veda va aham tam purusam sarvasyatmanah parayanam, yam attha; ya evayam sarirah purusah, sa esah. vadaiva sakalya, tasya ka devata iti. amrtam iti hovaca.

10. "Indeed He who knows that being whose body is the earth, whose world is fire, whose light is the mind, who is the ultimate support from within all, he is the true knower, O Yajnavalkya." "I do know that person, who is the ultimate support from within all, of whom you speak. This one who is in the body is that person. Tell me, Sakalya, who is his deity?" "Amrit," he said.

Notes: Amrit, in this context, may mean life-giving food or the fruit or the remains of a sacrifice. It is the deity (cause) of the person in the body.

11. kama eva yasyayatanam, hrdayam lokah, mano jyotih, yo vai tam purusam vidyat sarvasyatmanah parayanam, sa vai vedita syat, yajnavalkya. veda va aham tam purusam sarvasya atmanah parayanam, yam attha; ya evayam kamamayah purusah sa esah. vadaiva, sakalya, tasya ka devata iti. striyah, iti hovaca.

11. "Indeed, he who knows that being whose body is desire, whose world is the heart, whose light is the mind, who is the ultimate support from within all, he is the true knower, Yajnavalkya." "I do know that person, who is the ultimate support from within all, of whom you speak. This one who desires is that person. Tell me Sakalya, who is his deity?" "Women," he said.

Notes: Women induce desires in men, which results in their union and the birth of a newborn, the person in the body.

12. rupany eva yasyayatanam, caksur lokah, mano jyotih, yo vai tam purusam vidyat sarvasyatmanah parayanam, sa vai vedita syat, yajnavalkya. veda va aham tam purusam sarvasyatmanah parayanam, yam attha; ya evasav aditye purusah, sa esah. vadaiva, sakalya. tasya ka devata iti. satyam iti hovaca.

12. "Indeed, He who knows that being whose body is the form, whose world is the eye, whose light is the mind, who is the ultimate support from within all, he is the true knower, Yajnavalkya." "I do know that person, who is the ultimate support from within all, of whom you speak. This one who is in the sun is that person. Tell me Sakalya, who is his deity?" "Truth," he said.

Notes: The eye sees truth. Hence, it is equated with truth.

13. akasa eva yasyayatanam, srotram lokah, mano jyotih, yo vai tam purusam vidyat sarvasyatmanah parayanam, sa vai vedita syat, yajnavalkya. veda va aham tam purusam sarvasyatmanah parayanam, yam attha; ya evayam srautrah pratisrutkah purusah sa esah. vadaiva, sakalya. tasya ka devata iti. disah iti hovaca.

Chapter 3

13. "Indeed, He who knows that being whose body is space, whose world is the ear, whose light is the mind, who is the ultimate support from within all, he is the true knower, Yajnavalkya." "I do know that person, who is the ultimate support from within all, of whom you speak. This one who hears is that person. Tell me, Sakalya, who is his deity?" "The quarters," he said.

14. tama eva yasyayatanam, hrdayam lokah, mano jyotih, yo vai tam purusam vidyat sarvasyatmanah parayanam, sa vai vedita syat, yajnavalkya. veda va aham tam purusam sarvasyatmanah parayanam, yam attha; ya evayam chayamayah purusah sa esah. vadaiva, sakalya. tasya ka devata iti, mrtyur iti hovaca.

14. "Indeed He who knows that being whose body is darkness, whose world is the heart, whose light is the mind, who is the ultimate support from within all, he is the true knower, Yajnavalkya." "I do know that person, who is the ultimate support from within all, of whom you speak. This one who is enveloped by shadow is that person. Tell me Sakalya, who is his deity?" "Death," he said.

15. rupany eva yasyayatanam, caksur lokah, mano jyotih, yo vai tam purusam vidyat sarvasyatmanah parayanam, sa vai vedita syat, yajnavalkya. veda va aham tam purusam sarvasyatmanah parayanam, yam attha; ya evayam adarse purusah, sa esah. vadaiva, sakalya. tasya ka devata iti, asur iti hovaca.

15. "Indeed He who knows that being whose body is forms, whose world is the eye, whose light is the eye, who is the ultimate support from within all, he is the true knower, Yajnavalkya." "I do know that person, who is the ultimate support from within all, of whom you speak. This one who is in the reflection is that person. Tell me Sakalya, who is his deity?" "Breath," he said.

16. apa eva yasyayatanam, hrdayam lokah, mano jyotih, yo vai tam purusam vidyat sarvasyatmanah parayanam, sa vai vedita syat, yajnavalkya. veda va aham tam purusam sarvasyatmanah parayanam, yam attha. ya evayam apsu purusah sa esah. vadaiva, sakalya, tasya ka devata iti. varuna iti hovaca.

16. "Indeed He who knows that being whose body is water, whose world is the heart, whose light is the mind, who is the ultimate support from within all, he is the true knower, Yajnavalkya." "I do know that person, who is the ultimate support from within all, of whom you speak. This one who is in the water is that person. Tell me Sakalya, who is his deity?" "Varuna," he said.

17. reta eva yasyayatanam hrdayam lokah, mano jyotih, yo vai tam purusam vidyat sarvasyatmanah parayanam, sa vai vedita syat, yajnavalkya. veda va aham tam purusam sarvasyatmanah parayanam, yam attha. ya evayam apsu putramayah purusah, sa esah. vadaiva, sakalya, tasya ka devata iti. prajapatih iti hovaca.

17. *"Indeed, He who knows that being whose body is semen, whose world is the heart, whose light is the mind, who is the ultimate support from within all, he is the true knower, Yajnavalkya." "I do know that person, who is the ultimate support from within all, of whom you speak. This one who is filled with sons is that person. Tell me Sakalya, who is his deity?" "Prajapati," he said.*

18. sakalya, iti hovaca yajnavalkyah, tvam svid ime brahmana angaravaksayanam akrata u iti.

18. *"Sakalya," said Yajnavalkya, "have these Brahmanas tricked you into gathering the burning coals?"*

Notes: Yajnavalkya tauntingly asked Sakalya whether the rest of the Brahmanas left him behind to face the humiliating defeat in the fierce debate they were engaged in. His situation was comparable to the ordeal of waiting until the end of the sacrifice to collect the burning embers from the sacrificial pit and carry them to another place.

19. yajnavalkya, iti hovaca sakalyah, yad idam kuru-pancalanam brahmanan atyavadih, kim brahma vidvan iti, diso veda sadevah sapratistha iti. yad diso vettha sa devah sapratisthah.

19. *"Yajnavalkya," said Sakalya, "Tell me who is that Brahman you know by which you have outwitted all these Brahmanas of Kuru and Panchala?" "I know the quarters with their deities and supports." "If you know the quarters with their deities and supports..."*

20. kim-devato'syam pracyam disy asiti. aditya-devata iti. sa adityah kasmin pratisthita iti. caksusiti. kasmin nu caksuh pratisthitam iti. rupesv iti. caksusa hi rupani pasyati. kasmin nu rupani pratisthitaniti. hrdaye iti hovaca, hrdayena hi rupani janati, hrdaye hy eva rupani pratisthitani bhavantiti. evam evaitat, yajnavalkya.

20. *"Which deity you say exists in the eastern quarters?"*

"The deity Aditya (the sun)."

"That sun upon what does it rest?"

"Upon the eye."

"Upon what does the eye rest?"

"Upon the forms. By eyes only, the forms are seen."

"Upon what do the forms rest?"

"Upon the heart," he said. In the heart, one discerns forms. In the heart only do the forms rest."

"Yes, it does indeed, Yajnavalkya."

21. kim-devato'syam daksinayam disy asiti. yama-devata iti sa yamah kasmin pratisthita iti. yajna iti. kasmin nu yajnah pratisthita iti. daksinayam iti. kasmin nu daksina pratisthita iti. sraddhayam iti. yada hy eva sraddhatte atha daksinam dadati; sraddhayam hy eva daksina pratisthita iti. kasmin nu sraddha pratisthita iti. hrdaye iti. hovaca hrdayena hi sraddham janati, hrdaye hy eva sraddha pratisthita bhavatiti. evam evaitat, yajnavalkya.

21. *"Which deity do you say exists in the southern quarters?"*

"The deity Yama (Death)."

"That Yama upon what does he rest?"

"Upon the sacrifice."

"Upon what does the sacrifice rest?"

"Upon the gifts made to the Brahmanas."

"Upon what do the gifts made to the Brahmanas rest?"

"Upon faith, for when one has faith, one gives gifts. Therefore, it is upon faith do the gifts made to the Brahmanas are supported."

"By what is faith supported?"

"By the heart," he said. It is in the heart that one becomes aware of faith. In the heart only, faith is established."

"Yes, it does indeed, Yajnavalkya."

22. kim-devato'syam praticyam disy asiti. varuna-devata iti, sa varunah kasmin pratisthita iti. apsv iti. kasmin nv apah pratisthita iti. retasiti, kasmin nv retah pratisthitam iti. hrdaye iti, hovaca; tasmad api pratirupam jatam ahuh, hrdayad iva srptah, hrdayad iva nirmita iti, hrdaye hy eva retah pratisthitam bhavatiti. evam evaitat, yajnavalkya.

22. *Which deity you say exists in the western quarters?"*

"The deity Varuna."

"That Varuna, upon what does he rest?"

"Upon water."

"Upon what does water rest?"

"Upon the semen."

"Upon what does the semen rest?"

"Upon the heart," he said.

"Therefore, they say of a newly born who resembles his father, who appears as if he has sprung out of his heart, that he is made out of his heart. It is in the heart the semen becomes established."

"Yes, it does indeed, Yajnavalkya."

23. kim-devato'syam udicyam disy asiti. soma-devata iti. sa somah kasmin pratisthita iti. diksayam iti. kasmin nu diksa pratisthita iti. satya iti. tasmad api diksitam ahuh, satyam vada iti: satye hy eva diksa pratisthita iti. kasmin nu satyam pratisthitam iti. hrdaye iti hovaca, hrdayena hi satyam janati, hrdaye hy eva satyam pratisthitam bhavatiti. evam evaitat, yajnavalkya.

23. Which deity do you say exists in the northern quarters?"

"The deity Soma."

"That Soma, upon what does he rest?"

"Upon initiation."

"Upon what does initiation rest?"

"Upon truth. Therefore, they say to the initiated, 'Speak truth,' for initiation is supported only by truth."

"On what does truth rest?"

"Upon the heart," he said. "In the heart does one discern the truth. In the heart only, truth finds its support"

"Yes, it does indeed, Yajnavalkya."

24. kim-devato'syam dhruvayam disy asiti. agni-devata iti. so'gnih kasmin pratisthita iti. vaci iti. kasmin nu vak pratisthita iti. hrdaye iti. kasmin nu hrdayam pratisthitam iti.

24. "Which deity you say exists in the fixed quarter?"

"The deity Fire."

"That deity Agni, upon what does he rest?

"Upon speech."

"Upon what does speech rest?"

"Upon the heart."

"Upon what does the heart rest?"

25. ahallika iti hovaca yajnavalkyah, yatraitad anyatrasman manyasai, yaddhy etad anyatrasmat syat, svano vainad adyuh vayamsi vainad vimathnirann iti.

25. *" You ghost," said Yajnavalkya. "If you think the heart is elsewhere than within us, and if it is elsewhere than in us, either the dogs would eat it, or the birds would tear it to pieces."*

Notes: In this, the heart symbolizes the Self. By addressing Sakalya as a ghost, Yajnavalkya implied that if the heart was elsewhere than in the body, the person would be a ghost without a body.

26. kasmin nu tvam catma ca pratisthitau stha iti. prana iti. kasmin nu pranah pratisthita iti. apana iti. kasmin nv apanah pratisthita iti. vyana iti. kasmin nu vyanah pratisthita iti. udana iti. kasminn udanah pratisthita iti. samana iti. sa esa, na iti. na ity atma, agrhyah na hi grhyate, asiryah, na hi siryate, asangah na hi sajyate, asito na vyathate, na risyati. etany astav ayatanani, astau lokah, astau devah, astau purusah. sa yas tan purusan niruhya pratyuhyatyakramat, tam tva aupanisadam purusam prcchami. tam cen me na vivaksyasi murdha te vipatisatiti. tam ha na mene sakalyah, tasya ha murdha vipapata, api hasya parimosino'sthiny apajahruh, anyan manyamanah.

26. *"By what do you and your Self are supported?"*

"By breath."

"Upon what is breath supported?"

"Upon the downward breath, Apana."

"Upon what is Apana supported?"

"Upon the diffused breath, Vyana."

"Upon what is Vyana supported?"

"Upon the upward breath, Udana."

"Upon what Udana is supported?"

"Upon the equalizing breath, Samana. That Self is not this, not this. It is imperceptible, for it cannot be perceived; it is imperishable because it

does not decay; it is unattached, for it is not attached; and it is unfettered, it does not feel pain, and it is not injured. These are the eight worlds, the eight gods, and the eight beings. He who separates and unites these beings and goes beyond them, I ask you about that person who is taught in the Upanishad. If you do not explain him to me clearly, your head shall fall off."

Sakalya did not know Him; his head fell off, and, indeed, robbers carried away his bones, mistaking them for something else.

27. atha hovaca, brahmana bhagavanto, yo vah kamayate sa ma prcchatu, sarve va ma prcchata, yo vah kamayate, tam vah prchami, sarvan va vah prcchamiti. te ha brahmana na dadhrsuh.

27. Then he said. "Godly Brahmanas, whoever among you wishes to ask me questions, you may do so, or you may all ask me; Or I will ask him, or I will ask all of you. Those Brahmanas, indeed, did not dare.

28. tan haitaih slokaih papraccha:

1. yatha vrkso vanaspatih, tathaiva puruso'mrsa tasya lomani parnani, tvag asyotpatika bahih.

2. tvaca evasya rudhiram prasyandi, tvaca utpatah; tasmat, tad atrnnat praiti, raso vrksad ivahatat.

3. mamsany asya sakarani, kinatam snava, tat sthiram; asthiny antarato daruni, majja majjopama krta.

4. yad vrkso vrkno rohati mulan navatarah punah, martyah svin mrtyuna vrknah kasman mulat prarohati.

5. retasa iti ma vocata; jivatas tat prajayate; dhanaruha iva vai vrksah anjasa pretyasambhavah.

6. yat samulam avrheyuh vrksam, na punar abhavet, martyah svin mrtyuna vrknah kasman mulat prarohati.

7. jata eva na jayate, konvenam janayet punah; vijnanam anandam brahma, ratir datuh parayanam, tisthamanasya tadvidah.

28. He asked them using these verses:

1. As a large tree in a forest, so indeed is the person. His hairs are its leaves; his skin is its outer bark.

2. Blood flows out of his skin, and sap flows out of the bark. Therefore, when a man is wounded, blood flows out, like sap from a tree that is struck.

3. His flesh is its inner bark, and his nerves are tough like the innermost layer of the bark. His bones are the wood within, and his marrow is made like its pith.

4. When a tree is felled, it springs forth again from its root as if it is newly born; but then from what root does a man spring forth after he is cut off by death?

5. Do not say, "From the seed." It is produced in those who are alive. A tree also springs from the seed. It certainly springs again (from the seed) after it is dead also.

6. If a tree is pulled out along with its roots, it will not become alive again. From what root does a mortal spring forth again when he is cut off by death?

7. Once he is born, he is not born again. Who should create him again? Brahman, who is knowledge and bliss, is the supreme goal of him who is the distributor of wealth as well as of him who knows Brahman and whose mind is fixed upon Him.

Chapter 4

First Brahmana

Yajnavalkya on Partial Definitions of Brahman

1. aum, janako ha vaideha asam cakre. atha ha yajnavalkya avavraja. tam hovaca: yajnavalkya, kim artham acarih, pasun icchan, anvantan-iti. ubhayam eva, samraḍ iti hovaca.

1. *Janaka (king) of Videha was sitting on a chair when Yajnavalkya arrived. He said, "Yajnavalkya, what is the purpose of your visit? Is it for cattle or to ask some subtle questions?" "For both indeed, O Emperor," he said*

2. yat te kas cid abravit tat srnavameti. abravin me jitva sailinih, vag vai brahmeti. yatha matrman pitrman acaryavan bruyat, tatha. tat sailinir abravit: vag vai brahmeti, avadato hi kim syad iti. abravit tu te tasyayatanam pratistham. na me' bravid iti. eka-pad va etat, samrat, iti. sa vai no bruhi, yajnavalkya. vag evayatanam, akasah pratistha, prajnety enad upasita. ka prajnata, yajnavalkya. vag eva, samrat, iti hovaca. vaca vai, samrat, bandhuh prajnayate; rg-vedo yajur-vedah, sama-vedo' tharvangirasa, itihasah, puranam, vidya upanisadah, slokah, sutrany anuvyakhyanani, vyakhyananistam hutam asitam payitam, ayam ca lokah, paras ca lokah, sarvani ca bhutani vacaiva, samrat, prajnayante; vag vai, samrat, paramam brahma; nainam vag jahati, sarvany enam bhutany abhiksaranti, devo bhutva devan apyeti, ya evam vidvan etad upaste. hasty-rsabham sahasram dadami, iti hovaca janako vaidehah. sa hovaca yajnavalkyah, pita me" manyata nananusisya hareteti.

2. *"Whatever anyone may have told you recently, let me hear about it."*

"Jitvan Sailni said this to me: Speech, indeed, is Brahman."

"Just as his mother, father, and teacher spoke, so did Sailini might have said that speech was Brahman. What can one have who cannot speak? But did he tell you the abode and support of it?"

"He did not tell me."

"This one, O Emperor, is only one-footed."

"Then, Yajnavalkya, you should only tell us."

"Speech is its abode, space is its support. It should be worshipped as intelligence."

"What kind of intelligence, Yajnavalkya?"

"Speech only, O Emperor," he said, "A friend or a relation is discerned by speech only. By speech only, O Emperor, are known the Rigveda, Yajurveda, Samaveda, Atharvangirasa, (Vedic) history, Puranas, Brahma vidyas, the Upanishads, slokas, sutras, elaborations, commentaries, the knowledge of making offerings, oblations and the offering of food and drinks, knowledge of this world and the next world, and all beings. O Emperor! Speech verily is the supreme Brahman. Speech does not desert him, who, knowing thus, worships speech. All beings come to him. He even becomes a god and goes to the gods."

Janaka of Videha said, "I shall give you a thousand cows and a large elephant-sized bull."

Yajnavalkya said, "It is my father's opinion that one should not accept gifts from a student without teaching him fully."

Notes: Now, if something is incomplete and depends upon another, it is not Brahman who is independent and without support. Hence, Yajnavalkya refuted the argument that speech was Brahman, saying it was only one-footed Brahman, meaning it was an aspect of Brahman or Brahman in a limited sense. He further said that speech should be worshipped as intelligence but not as Brahman. Liberation is attained only by knowing Brahman, and speech would not lead one to him. Therefore, those who excel in speech and the scriptural knowledge acquired through it gain riches and attain the heaven of gods but not liberation. The same argument is repeated in the subsequent verses about the other parts of the body.

3. yad eva te kas cid abravit tat srnavameti. abravin ma udankah saulbayanah, prano vai brahmeti: yatha matrman pitrman acaryavan bruyat, tatha tat saulbayano'bravit, prano vai brahmeti, apranato hi kim syad iti. abravit tu te tasyayatanam pratistham. na me'bravid iti. eka-pad va etat, samrad, iti. sa vai no bruhi, yajnavalkya, prana evayatanam, akasah pratistha, priyam ity enad upasita, ka priyata, yajnavalkya, prana eva, samrad, iti hovaca: pranasya vai, samrat, kamayayajyam yajayati, apratigrhyasya pratigrhnati, api tatra vadhasankam bhavati, yam disam eti, pranasyaivya, samrat, kamaya, prano vai, samrat, paramam brahma, nainam prano jahati, sarvany enam bhutany abhiksaranti, devo bhutva devan apyeti, ya evam vidvan etad upaste. hasty-rsabham sahasram dadami, iti hovaca, janako vaidehah. sa hovaca yajnavalkyah, pita me"manyata nananusisya hareteti.

3. *"Whatever else anyone may have told you recently, let me hear about it."*

"Udanka Saulbayana told me that breath, indeed, is Brahman."

"Just as his mother, father, and teacher spoke, so did Saulbayana say that breath was Brahman. What can one have who cannot breathe? But did he tell you the abode and support of it?"

"He did not tell me."

"This one, O Emperor, is also one-footed."

"Then, Yajnavalkya, you should only tell us."

"Breath is its abode; space is its support. It should be worshipped as the beloved."

"What kind of beloved one, Yajnavalkya?"

"As breath only, O Emperor," he said, *"For the sake of breath only, O Emperor, one pours oblations into the sacrifice, out of desires, grasps things that should not be grasped. Because of breath only, O Emperor, in whatever direction one goes there, the fear of losing life arises. Breath verily, O Emperor, is the supreme Brahman. Breath does not desert him, who, knowing thus, worships breath. All beings come to him. He even becomes a god and goes to the gods."*

Janaka of Videha said, *"I shall give you a thousand cows and a large elephant-sized bull."*

Yajnavalkya said, *"It is my father's opinion that one should not accept gifts from a student without teaching him fully."*

4. yad eva te kas cid abravit tat srnavameti. abravin me barkur varsnah caksur vai brahmeti: yatha matrman pitrman acarya-van bruyat, tatha tad varsno'bravit. caksur vai brahmeti, apasyato hi kim syad iti. abravit tu te tasyayatanam pratistham. na me'bravid iti. eka-pad va etat, samraḍ, iti. sa vai no bruhi, yajnavalkya. caksur evayatanam, akasah pratistha; satyam iti etad upasita. ka satyata, yajnavalkya. caksur eva, samraḍ, iti hovaca, caksusa vai, samrat, pasyantam ahuh; adraksir iti, sa aha; adraksam iti tat satyam bhavati. caksur vai, samrat, paramam brahma. nainam caksur jahati, sarvany enam bhutany abhiksaranti, devo bhutva devan apyeti, ya evam vidvan etad upaste. hasty-rsabham sahasram dadami, iti hovaca janako vaidehah. sa hovaca yajnavalkyah. pita me"manyata, nananusisya hareteti.

4. *"Whatever else anyone may have told you recently, let me hear about it."*

"Barku Varsna told me that the eye, indeed, is Brahman."

"Just as his mother, father and teacher spoke, so did Varsna say that eye was Brahman. What can one have, who cannot see? But did he tell you the abode and support of it?"

"He did not tell me."

"This one, O Emperor, is also one-footed."

"Then, Yajnavalkya, you should only tell us."

"The eye is its abode; space is its support. It should be worshipped as truth."

"What kind of truth, Yajnavalkya?"

"The eye itself, O Emperor," said Yajnavalkya. *"Truly, if they say to a person who has seen with his eyes, 'Have you seen?' he says, 'I have seen.' That is the truth. The eye verily, O Emperor, is the supreme Brahman. Vision does not desert him, who, knowing thus, worships speech. All beings come to him. He even becomes a god and goes to the gods.*

Janaka of Videha said, "I shall give you a thousand cows and a large elephant-sized bull."

Yajnavalkya said, "It is my father's opinion that one should not accept gifts from a student without teaching him fully."

5. yad eva te kas cid abravit, tat srnavameti. abravin me gardhabhivipito bharadvajah: srotram vai brahmeti. yatha matrman pitrman acaryavan bruyat, tatha tad bharadvajo' bravit. srotram vai brahmeti, asrnvato hi kim syad iti. abravit tu te tasyayatanam pratistham. na me'bravid iti. eka-pad va etat, samraḍ, iti. sa vai no bruhi, yajnavalkya. srotram evayatanam, akasah pratistha, ananta ity enad upasita. ka anantata, yajnavalkya. disa eva, samraḍ, iti hovaca. tasmad vai, samraḍ, api yam kam ca disam gacchati, naivasya antam gacchati, ananta hi disah diso vai, samrat, srotram. srotram vai, samrat, paramam brahma nainam srotram jahati, sarvany enam bhutany abhiksaranti, devo bhutva devan apyeti, ya evam vidvan etad upaste. hasty- rsabham sahasram dadami iti. hovaca janako vaidehah, sa hovaca yajnavalkyah, pita me'manyata, nananusisya hareteti.

5. *"Whatever else anyone may have told you recently, let me hear about it."*

"Gardabhivipita Bharadvaja told me that the ear, indeed, is Brahman."

"Just as his mother, father, and teacher spoke, so did Bharadvaja say that the ear was Brahman. What can one have who cannot hear? But did he tell you the abode and support of it?"

"He did not tell me."

"This one, O Emperor, is also one-footed."

"Then, Yajnavalkya, you should only tell us."

"The ear is its abode; space is its support. It should be worshipped as the endless."

"What kind of endlessness, Yajnavalkya?"

"That of quarters only, O Emperor," said Yajnavalkya. *"Truly, in whatever direction one goes, one keeps on going endlessly, for the directions are endless. The quarters verily, O Emperor, are the ears of the ears. O Emperor, they are the supreme Brahman. Hearing does not desert him, who, knowing thus, worships the quarters. All beings come to him. He even becomes a god and goes to the gods.*

Janaka of Videha said, *"I shall give you a thousand cows and a large elephant-sized bull."*

Yajnavalkya said, *"It is my father's opinion that one should not accept gifts from a student without teaching him fully."*

6. yad eva kas cid abravit tat srnavameti. abravin satyakamo jabalah, mano vai brahmeti: yatha matrman pitrman acaryavan bruyat, tatha taj jabalo'bravit, mano vai brahmeti, amanaso hi kim syad iti. abravit tu te tasyayatanam pratistham. na me'bravid iti. eka-pad va etat samraḍ iti. sa vai no bruhi, yajnavalkya. mana evayatanam, akasah pratistha, ananda ity enad upasita, ka anandata, yajnavalkya. mana eva, samraḍ, iti hovaca, manasa vai, samrat. striyam abhiharyate, tasyam pratirupah putro samrat, paraman brahma. nainam mano jahati, sarvany enam bhutany abhiksaranti, devo bhutva devan apyeti, ya evam vidvan etad upaste. hasty-rsabham sahasram dadami, iti hovaca janako vaidehah. sa hovaca yajnavalkyah, pita me"manyata nananusisya hareteti.

6. *"Whatever else anyone may have told you recently, let me hear about it."*

"Satyakama Jabala told me that the mind, indeed, is Brahman."

Brihadaranyaka Upanishad

Chapter 4

"Just as his mother, father, and teacher spoke, so did Jabala say that the mind was Brahman. What can one have who is mindless? But did he tell you the abode and support of it?"

"He did not tell me."

"This one, O Emperor, is only one-footed."

"Then, Yajnavalkya, you should only tell us."

"The mind is its abode; space is its support. It should be worshipped as the blissful."

"What kind of blissfulness, Yajnavalkya?"

"Of the mind only, O Emperor," said Yajnavalkya. *"Truly, by the mind only, O Emperor, one enjoys a woman, whereby a son with his resemblance is born to her. O Emperor, it is the supreme Brahman. His mind does not desert him, who, knowing thus, worships it. All beings come to him. He even becomes a god and goes to the gods.*

Janaka of Videha said, *"I shall give you a thousand cows and a large elephant-sized bull."*

Yajnavalkya said, *"It is my father's opinion that one should not accept gifts from a student without teaching him fully."*

Notes: The moon is the presiding deity of the mind. It is in the mind one enjoys the bliss of conjugal pleasures and obtains progeny. However, it is not Brahman because it goes as far as the moon but not beyond it.

7. yad eva kas cid abravit, tat srnavameti. abravin me vidagdhah sakalyah, hrdayam vai brahmeti, yatha matrman pitrman acaryavan bruyat, tatha tat sakalyo'bravit, hrdayam vai brahmeti, ahrdayasya hi kim syad iti. abravit tu te tasya-yatanam pratistham. na me"bravid iti. eka-pad va, etat, samrad, iti. sa vai no bruhi, yajnavalkya. hrdayam evayatanam, akasah pratistha, sthitir ity enad upasita. ka sthitita, yajnavalkya. hrdayam eva samrad, iti hovaca, hrdayam vai, samrat, sarvesam bhutanam ayatanam, hrdayam vai, samrat, sarvesam bhutanam pratistha, hrdaye hy eva, samrat, sarvani bhutani pratisthitani bhavanti. hrdayam vai, samrat, paramam brahma. nainam hrdayam jahati, sarvany enam bhutany abhiksaranti, devo bhutva devan apyeti, ya evam vidvan etad upaste. hasty rsabham sahasram dadami, iti hovaca janako vaidehah. sa hovaca yajnavalkyah, pita me"manyata nananusisya hareteti. Iti prathamam brahmanam.

7. *"Whatever else anyone may have told you recently, let me hear about it."*

"Vidagdha Sakala told me that the heart, indeed, is Brahman."

"Just as his mother, father, and teacher spoke, so did Sakala say that the heart was Brahman. What can one have who is without a heart? But did he tell you the abode and support of it?"

"He did not tell me."

"This one, O Emperor, is only one-footed."

"Then, Yajnavalkya, you should only tell us."

"The heart is its abode; space is its support. It should be worshipped as the stable."

"What kind of stability, Yajnavalkya?"

"Of the heart only, O Emperor," said Yajnavalkya. *"The heart, O Emperor, is the abode of all things, and the heart, O Emperor, is the support of all beings. On the heart, O Emperor, all beings rest. The heart truly, O Emperor, is the supreme Brahman. His heart does not desert him, who, knowing thus, worships it. All beings come to him. He even becomes a god and goes to the gods.*

Janaka of Videha said, *"I shall give you a thousand cows and a large elephant-sized bull."*

Yajnavalkya said, *"It is my father's opinion that one should not accept gifts from a student without teaching him fully."*

Notes: In this section, Yajnavalkya described Brahman as intelligent, adorable, truthful, infinite (endless), and the stable (fixed) foundation or support of all. They are aspects of Brahman and may be considered Brahman, but only in a limited sense. The ultimate support of all these, the ultimate source of their functioning and the ultimate object of their functioning, that alone should be considered Brahman. This is the essence of this teaching.

Second Brahmana

Yajnavalkya on the Person in the Body

1. janako ha vaidehah kurcad upavasarpann uvaca: namas te'stu yajnavalkya, anu ma sadhiti. sa hovaca: yatha vai, samrat, mahantam adhvanam esyan ratham va navam va samadadita, evam evaitabhir upanisadbhih samahitatmasi, evam brndaraka adhyah sann adhita-veda ukta-upanisatkah ito vimucyamanah kva gamisyasiti. naham tad, bhagavan, ve-

da, yatra, gamisyamiti; atha vai te'ham tad vaksyami, yatra gamisyasiti, bravitu, bhagavan, iti.

1. *Janaka of Videha got down from his couch and said, coming nearer, "Salutations to you, Yajnavalkya; please instruct me."*

He said, "O Emperor, as one who wishes to travel a long distance, assembles a chariot or a boat, so have you fully equipped your mind with the teachings of the Upanishads. You are likewise respected and wealthy. You have studied the Vedas and heard the Upanishads. Where will you go when you are freed?"

"I do not know Godman, where I may go."

"Then I will tell you where you will go."

"Certainly, Godman."

2. indho ha vai namaisa yo'yam daksine'ksan purusah: tam va etam indham santam indra ity acaksate paroksenaiva, paroksa-priya iva hi devah, pratyaksa-dvisah.

2. Indha, indeed, is the name of this person who is in the right eye. He who is called that Indha by all is regarded indirectly as Indra. The gods are indeed fond of the indirect, as such, since they are averse to the direct.

Notes: The person in the right eye refers to the Self, the enjoyer. Indra, the lord of the senses, is the enjoyer. He is compared here to the Self. Indha also means the sustainer or the nourisher, a reference to the fuel or fire in the body whose source is Brahman or the Sun. Gods do not want to be known by their direct name. Therefore, they call Indra as Indha.

3. athaitad vame'ksani purusa-rupam, esasya patni virat, tayor esa samstavo ya eso'ntar-hrdaya akasah, athainayor etad annam ya eso'ntar-hrdaye lohita-pindah, athainayor etat pravaranam yad etad antar-hrdaye jalakam iva; athainayor esa srtih samcarani yaisa hrdayad urdhva nady uccarati. yatha kesah sahasradha bhinnah evam asyaita hita nama nadyo'ntar-hrdaye pratisthita bhavanti; etabhir va etad asravad asravati; tasmad esa praviviktaharatara ivaiva bhavaty asmac carirad atmanah.

3· Now, that which is in the form of a person in the left eye is his wife, Virat. Their place of union is the space within the heart. Now, their food is the red-colored ball of rice in the heart. Now, their outer sheath is the net of arteries within the heart. Their flowing movement is along the channel that goes upward. Just as hair is a thousandfold, so become the arteries called Hita that are established in the heart. Through them flows that which flows. Therefore, that, as such, is an eater of finer food than the (gross) body.

Notes: The subtle body, consisting of Indra and Virat, has access to the subtle food distributed by the diffused breath (vyana). It is finer than the normal food (annam) with which we nourish our gross bodies. Hita refers to the bundle of 72,000 subtle energy channels that extend from the heart to the entire body.

4. tasya praci dik prancah pranah, daksina dig daksine pranah, pratici dik pratyancah pranah, udici dig udancah pranah, urdhva dig urdhvah pranah, avaci dig avancah pranah: sarva disah, sarve pranah, sa esa neti nety atma agrhyah na hi grhyate; asiryah, na hi siryate; asangah na hi sajyate; asito na vyathate; na risyati abhayam vai, janaka, prapto'si, iti hovaca yajnavalkyah. sa hovaca janako vaidehah, abhayam tva gacchatat, yajnavalkya, yo nah, bhagavan, abhayam vedayase; namas te'stu; ime videhah ayam aham asmiti.

4. Of him, the eastern direction is the eastern breath, the southern direction is the southern breath, the western direction is the western breath, the northern direction is the northern breath, the upward direction is the upward breath, the downward direction is the downward breath, and all the quarters are all the breaths. This one is the Self, which is (understood as) 'not this, not this.' He is not perceptible because he cannot be perceived with the senses. He is indestructible, for he cannot be destroyed. He is without attachments, for he does not hold on to anything. He is unfettered, free from suffering, and free from injury. Indeed, Janaka, you have attained that which is fearless," said Yajnavalkya. Said Janaka of Videha, "May you too come to that which is fearless, O Yajnavalkya, Godman, who makes us know about the fearless. Salutations to you. Here is all of Videha and ourselves (at your feet).

Notes: By entering these different breath channels through concentration and meditation, one enters That which is their support. He who attains that immortal Self transcends death and becomes fearless.

Third Brahmana

Yajnavalkya on the Light Within

1. janakam ha vaideham yajnavalkyo jagama: sa mene: na vadisya iti. atha ha yaj janakas ca vaideho yajnavalkyas cagnihotre samudate, tasmai ha yajnavalkyo varam dadau: sa ha kama-prasnam eva vavre, tam hasmai dadau. tam ha samraḍ eva purvah papraccha.

Chapter 4

1. Yajnavalkya went to Janaka of Videha. He thought within himself, "I will not speak. "Now, in the past, Janaka of Videha and Yajnavalkya happened to speak about the Agnihotra sacrifice, during which Yajnavalkya gave him a boon. (Referring to that) he now expressed his desire to pursue an inquiry, and Yajnavalkya granted him his wish. Therefore, the emperor now proceeds with the previous discussion.

Notes: It seems Yajnavalkya was obliged to speak because, as the host and patron of the Agnihotra Sacrifice, King Janaka must have rewarded him richly and obtained a promise from him to answer his metaphysical questions about the Self.

2. yajnavalkya, kim-jyotir ayam purusa iti. aditya-jyotih, samrat, iti hovaca, adityenaivayam jyotisaste, palyayate, karma kurute, vipalyetiti. evam evaitat, yajnavalkya.

2. "Yajnavalkya, what light is within the person here?" "The light of the sun, O Emperor," he said. It is with the light of the sun that the person sits, goes out, performs actions, and returns." "Yes, it is so, Yajnavalkya."

Notes: The light within the person is the light within the eye. It is the external light that comes from the sun. Because of this light only, one is able to see, move and perform actions or return to home after going out to some place.

3. astam ita aditye, yajnavalkya, kim-jyotir evayam purusa iti. candrama evasya jyotir bhavati, candramasaivayam jyotisaste, palyayate, karma kurute, vipalyetiti. evam evaitat, yajnavalkya.

3. "When this sun sets, Yajnavalkya, what light is within this person?" " The moon becomes the light of this person. It is through the light of the moon that the person sits, goes out, performs actions, and returns." "Yes, it is so, Yajnavalkya."

Notes: In the night, when the sun is absent, what helps the people to see is the moon light. Nowadays, we have electricity. But it was not so in the past. The verse also means that when the eyes are closed, what light guides the person? It is the light of the dreams or the light of the mind from which dreams arise. As we have seen before, the mind represents the moon only.

4. astam ita aditye, yajnavalkya, candramasy astam ite, kim-jyotir evayam purusa iti. agnir evasya jyotir bhavati, agninaivayam jyotisaste, palyayate, karma kurute, vipalyetiti. evam evaitat, yajnavalkya.

4. "When the sun sets, Yajnavalkya, and the moon sets, what light is within this person?" "The fire, indeed, becomes his light. It is through

the fire that this person sits, goes out, performs actions, and returns."
"Yes, it is so, Yajnavalkya."

Notes: When there is no sun and no moon in the sky, what guides a person? It is indeed fire because, in total darkness, a lamp, torch, or fire guides the person. This also means that when a person is lost in the darkness of ignorance and delusion, the fire of knowledge guides him.

5. astam ita aditye, yajnavalkya, candramasi astam ite, sante agnau, kim-jyotir evayam purusa iti. vag evasya jyotir bhavati, vacaivayam jyotisaste, palyayate, karma karute, vipalyeti, tasmad vai, samraḍ, api yatra panir na vinirjnayate, atha yatra vag uccarati, upaiva tatra nyetiti. evam evaitat, yajnavalkya.

5. *"When the sun sets, Yajnavalkya, the moon sets, and the fires subside, what is the light within this person? "Speech becomes his light. It is through the light of speech that one sits, goes out, performs actions, and returns. Therefore, O Emperor, even if one's own hand is not clearly discernible, wherever speech is uttered, there one goes." "Yes, it is so, Yajnavalkya."*

Notes: When there is no light whatsoever, what will you do in total darkness? You will indeed shout or speak loudly to let others know where you are or where they may find you. Therefore, in complete darkness, speech is your support and guide.

6. astam ita aditye, yajnavalkya, candramasy astam ite, sante agnau, santayam vaci, kim-jyotir evayam purusa iti. atmaivasya jyotir bhavati, atmanaivayam jyotisaste, palyayate, karma karute, vipalyeti.

6. *"When the sun sets, Yajnavalkya, the moon sets, the fire subsides, and speech is tranquil; what is the light for this person (that guides him)?" "The Self becomes his light. It is through the light of the Self one sits, goes out, performs actions, and returns."*

Notes: When there is no light whatsoever, and no one is speaking, or the senses are inactive, what guides a person? He depends upon himself and guides himself using his mind, intelligence, intuition, or memory. Since they are not self-luminous, they are illuminated by the Self. In other words, that light is not of the mind and body but of the Self, which illuminates all the organs, tattvas, and gunas in the body.

7. katama atmeti. yo'yam vijnanamayah pranesu, hrdy antarjyotih purusah sa samanah sann ubhau lokav anusancarati, dhyayativa lelayativa, sa hi svapno bhutva, imam lokam atikramati, mrtyo rupani.

7. "Who is the Self?" "He who is full of intelligence among the senses, the light within the heart, that person, remaining equal, wanders about in both the worlds as if thinking (and) as if moving. When he enters dreams, he goes above this world and the forms of death."

Notes: The Self is not the mind and body or any of its parts. However, the Self illuminates them all, creating the illusion in the mind of the person that he, with his name and form, is indeed the Self. The same Self moves effortlessly from one state of consciousness to another, illuminating the mind, the senses, and intelligence and creating the illusion of activity and movement. In dreams, he transcends the limitation of the mind and body since the Self leaves the body and wanders in the astral worlds. He temporarily goes beyond death and all its associated forms. The mortal world is the world of death. The forms of death are the divisions of time, impermanence, partial or complete destruction, and modifications of the mind and body. In the dream world, a person is no more subject to the limitations or conditions of this world. Whatever reality he creates in the dreams becomes his reality. He may become young or old or do whatever he wishes to do or what his desires prompt him to do.

8. sa va ayam puruso jayamanah, sariram abhisampadyamanah papmabhih samsrjyate, sa utkraman, mriyamanah papmano vijahati.

8. "Truly, when this person is born, he obtains a body and becomes afflicted with evils. When he gives up (the body) or dies, he casts off the evils."

Notes: When a person is born, he becomes associated with the tattvas, gunas, and organs of his body and subject to the impurities of egoism, delusion, and desires that arise from them, in addition to the good and bad karma he accumulates through his actions. When he dies, he discards his body, breaths, and all the evils associated with it and departs from there. In dreams also, he temporarily rises from the body, departs from here, casting off all the impurities associated with his body, and shines in his own light.

9. tasya va etasya purusasya dve eva sthane bhavatah: idam ca para-loka-sthanam ca; sandhyam trtiyam svapna-sthanam; tasmin sandhye sthane tisthann, ubhe sthane pasyati, idam ca para-loka-sthanam ca atha yathakramo'yam para-lokasthane bhavati, tam akramam akramya, ubhayan papmana anandams ca pasyati. sa yatra prasvapiti, asya lokasya sarvavato matram apadaya, svayam vihatya, svayam nirmaya, svena bhasa, svena jyotisa prasvapiti; atrayam purusah svayam-jyotir bhavati.

9. "For this person, there are only two places of existence, this and a place of existence in the higher world. Joining the two is the third, the dream state. Standing in that third state, he sees both the states, this

existence, and other existence in the higher world. Now, by whatever steps one has to ascend, by that only he goes to the abode in the higher world and sees both the evils (of this world) and the joys (of the higher world). When he goes into dreams, he takes all the objects of this world along with him. He breaks himself apart (in his dreams) and rebuilds himself again. He shines in his own light and radiates his own light. In that state, that person becomes self-luminous."

Notes: In dreams, he leaves the body behind, rebuilds a new body, and becomes self-luminous. In other words, unlike in the wakeful state, he is not illuminated by any external light but by his own light.

10. na tatra rathah, na ratha-yogah, na panthano bhavanti; atha rathan, ratha-yogan, pathah srjate; na tatranandah, mudah pramudo bhavanti, athanandan, mudah, pramudah srjate; na tatra vesantah puskarinyah sravantyo bhavanti; atha vesantan, puskarinih sravantih srjate. sa hi karta.

10. "There are neither chariots nor animals to yoke to the chariots, nor roads. Therefore, he creates chariots, animals to fasten to the chariots, and roads. There are no joys, no pleasures, and no delights. Therefore, he creates joys, pleasures, and delights. There are no water tanks, no sacred ponds, and no running streams. Therefore, he creates water tanks, sacred ponds, and running streams."

Notes: In dreams, he becomes a creator and creates everything out of himself.

11. tad ete sloka bhavanti: svapnena sariram abhiprahatya-suptah suptan abhicakasiti; sukram adaya punar aiti sthanam, hiranmayah purusa eka-hamsah.

11. "Regarding this, there are the following verses: 'Leaving his body which is asleep, taking the shining functions of his senses with him, and taking the light into himself, the golden person, the lonely swan, watches those that are asleep and returns to his (original) place.'"

Notes: In sleep, the luminous Self becomes free from the shackles of the body, assumes the light of the deities (sense organs) that are tired and asleep, and flies away into the dream world. The light of the dream world is the light from within, not the light from outside. A dream is illuminated by oneself and one's own light. He return to his place means he wakes up or returns to his wakeful state.

12. pranena raksann avaram kulayam bahis kulayad amrtas caritva, sa iyate amrto yatra kamam, hiran-mayah purusa eka-hamsah.

Chapter 4

12. "Guarding his lower nest with breath, the immortal one moves out of the nest and roams around. The immortal one, the golden person, the lonely swan, goes wherever he wishes to."

Notes: His lower nest is the body. He leaves that behind and wanders into the dream world or the astral world. Since it is his own creation, there are no limits to what he can or cannot do in dreams.

13. svapnanta uccavacam iyamano rupani devah kurute bahuni uteva stribhih saha modamanah jaksat, utevapi bhayani pasyan.

13. "In his dream world, moving up and down, this deity of the mind creates numerous forms for himself, as if he were enjoying the company of women, or laughing or even seeing fearful things."

14. aramam asya pasyanti, na tam pasyati kas cana: iti. tam nayatam bodhayed ity ahuh; durbhisajyam hasmai bhavati, yam esa na pratipadyate. atho khalv ahuh, jagarita-desa evasyaisah; yani hi eva jagrat pasyati, tani sputa iti. atrayam purusah svayam-jyotir bhavati. so'ham bhagavate sahasram dadami; ata urdhvam vimoksaya bruhiti.

14. "Everyone sees his resting place, but no one sees him. They say not to wake him up suddenly, for if he does not return to his body, it will be difficult to revive him. Others, however, say it (the dream state) is a wakeful state only because whatever he perceives when awake he perceives in his sleep. However, in the dream state he himself becomes the light." "Godman, I give you a thousand cows; please speak to me further about liberation."

Notes: The dream state and the wakeful state are not the same, although one may perceive the same objects or experience similar things in both.

15. sa va esa etasmin samprasade ratva caritva drstvaiva punyam ca papam ca, punah pratinyayam pratiyony adravati svapnayaiva; sa yat tatra kim cit pasyati ananvagatas tena bhavati; asango hy ayam purusa iti. evam evaitat, yajnavalkya. so'ham bhagavate sahasram dadami, ata urdhvam vimoksayaiva bruhiti.

15. "Having enjoyed the deep sleep and seen both good and evil while roaming, he returns again inversely to the place from where he started, the dream state. Whatever he has seen in that state does not follow him, for this person is not attached to anything." "I am that. Godman, I give you a thousand cows. Please speak to me further about liberation."

Notes: A dreamer does not return with his dream. He does not bring anything back from his dream except memories. Yajnavalkya says this is because the dreamer is unattached (asanga) to his dreams. Therefore, even if he has seen both good and evil, he is not tainted by them. It is good that we do not bring our dreams with us into our wakeful world. Imagine you are going through a nightmare. You suddenly wake up and find yourself really in the middle of that!

16. sa va esa etasmin svapne ratva caritva drstvaiva punyam ca papam ca, punah, pratinyayam pratiyony adravati buddhantayaiva sa yat tatra kim cit pasyati, ananvagatas tena bhavati: asango hy ayam, purusa iti. evam evaitat, yajnavalkya. so'ham bhagavate sahasram dadami, ata urdhvam vimoksayaiva bruh-iti.

16. "Having enjoyed the dream state and seen both good and evil while roaming, he returns again inversely to the place from where he started, the wakeful state. Whatever he has seen in that state does not follow him, for this person is not attached to anything." "I am that. Godman, I give you a thousand cows. Please speak to me further about liberation."

17. sa va esa etasmin buddhante ratva caritva drstvaiva punyam ca papam ca, punah pratinyayam pratiyony adravati svapnantayaiva.

17. "Having enjoyed the wakeful state and seen both good and evil while roaming, he returns again inversely to the place from where he started, the dream state."

18. tad yatha mahamatsya ubhe kule anusamcarati, purvam caparam ca, evam evayam purusa etav ubhav antav anusamcarati, svapnantam ca buddhantam ca.

18. Just as the great fish traverses between the two banks, this side and that side, so does this infinite person move between the two ends, the dream state and the wakeful state.

19. tad yathasminn akase syena va suparno va viparipatya srantah samhatya paksau samlayayaiva dhriyate, evam evayam purusa etasma antaya dhavati yatra na kam cana kamam kamayate, na kam cana svapnam pasyati.

19. "Just as a falcon or any bird flying in the sky becomes tired and folding its wings flies down to its nest, so does this infinite being return to that state where he desires no desires and sees no dreams."

Notes: He falls into a deep sleep where he desires no desires and sees no dreams.

20. ta va asyaita hita nama naḍyah, yatha kesah sahasradha bhinnah, tavatanimna tisthanti, suklasya, nilasya, pingalasya,

haritasya, lohitasya purnah; atha yatrainam ghnativa, jinantiva, hastiva vicchayayati, gartam iva patati, yad eva jagrad bhayam pasyati, tad atravidyaya manyate, atha yatra deva iva rajeva; aham evedam, sarvo'smiti manyate; so'sya paramo lokah.

20. *"In him are those nerves called Hita, fine as a hair, divided into a thousand times and filled with white, blue, yellow, green, and red. Now, whenever he feels as if he were killed, overpowered, pursued by an elephant, or thrown into a well, he imagines whatever fears he experienced in his waking state. But when he thinks he were a god, he were a king, that I am all this, that is his supreme world."*

Notes: The fluids that flow in the body have different colors. The same is the case with the subtle energies that flow inside the body or through the nerve channels. They have different colors and serve different purposes. In dreams, as in life, one may experience different states and emotions, both high and low and both positive and negative. The material for his dreams arises from the impressions stored in his subtle body. The quality and nature of his dreams depend upon the purity or impurity of his mind and body. He will have bad dreams if he has excessive negative energy and positive and uplifting dreams if he has a divine nature.

21. tad va asyaitad aticchando'pahatapapmabhyam rupam. tad yatha priyaya striya samparisvakto na bahyam kim cana veda nantaram, evam evayam purusah prajnenatmana samparisvakto na bahyam kim cana veda nantaram. tad va asyaitad aptakamam, atmakamam, akamam rupam sokantaram.

21. *"That, verily, is his form, which is without desires, free from sins, and without fear. Just like a man who is embraced by his wife does not know at all what is (going on) outside or inside, so does this person in the embrace of his intelligent Self do not know at all what is (happening) outside or inside. That, verily, is his form in which all desires are fulfilled, desire is only for the Self, desires are absent, and there is freedom from sorrow."*

Notes: In the deeper states of consciousness, individuality becomes hazy. Consciousness extends beyond the boundaries of name and form and into all, into whatever is conceived. In dreams, a person becomes the God of the worlds he creates, extending his consciousness and personality into everything he creates. His dreams are made up of himself and his essential nature. They are the projections of his consciousness, just as this world is the projection of Isvara. In deep sleep, all that activity, imagination, and dreaming come to an end. Everything disappears, and the Self alone remains without a second or any emotion, feeling, desire, or awareness.

22. atra pita'pita bhavati, mata'mata, lokah alokah, deva adevah, veda avedah; atra steno'steno bhavati bhrunahabhrunaha, candalo'candalah paulkaso' paulkasah, sramano'sramanah, tapaso'tapasah, ananvagatam punyena, ananvagatatam ananvagatam papena, tirno hi tada sarvan sokan hrdayasya bhavati.

22. *"There, a father is not a father, a mother is not a mother, the worlds are not the worlds, the gods not the gods, and the Vedas are not the Vedas. There, a thief is not a thief, the killing of a fetus is not killing of a fetus, a Chandala is not a Chandala, a half-caste is not a half-caste, a mendicant is not a mendicant, an ascetic is not an ascetic. He is not accompanied by good works; he is not accompanied by bad works, for he has moved beyond all the sorrows of his heart."*

Notes: The state described here is the state of nonduality (Advaita) in which neither knowledge nor ignorance, relationships nor social values, and neither good nor evil exit. Bhruna-hatya means killing or aborting a fetus or killing a Brahmana. Paulaska is the one born to a Shudra father and a Kshatriya mother. Chandala literally means an impure or irreligious person. In ancient India, people who belonged to the lowest order of society were called Chandalas. In the Self, these distinctions disappear.

23. yad vai tan na pasyati, pasyan vai tan na pasyati; na hi drastur drster viparilopo vidyate, avinasitvat; na tu tad dvitiy-am asti, tato'nyad vibhaktam yat pasyet.

23. *"In that state, indeed, he does not see. Yet, he does verily see even while not seeing because the seeing of the seer, who is imperishable, is never interrupted. There is no second (or the other) that is different and distinct from him, which he can see."*

Notes: The unified state of seeing in which the duality of the subject and the object or the seer and the seen is absent is different from ordinary seeing, in which perceptions are supported by relationships, duality, and objectivity. This seeing is not continuous.

24. yad vai tan na jighrati, jighran vai tan na jighrati: na hi ghratur ghrater viparilopo vidyate, avinasitvat; na tu tad dvitiyam asti, tato'nyad vibhaktam yaj jighret.

24. *"In that state, indeed, he does not smell. Yet, he does verily smell even while not smelling because the smelling of the smelling person, who is imperishable, is never interrupted. There is no second that is different and distinct from him, which he can smell."*

25. yad vai tan na rasayati, rasayan vai tan na rasayati na hi rasayitu rasayater viparilopo vidyate, avinasitvat; na tu tad dvitiyam asti, tato'nyad vibhaktam yad rasayet.

25. "In that state, indeed, he does not taste. Yet, he does verily taste even while not tasting because the tasting of the taster, who is imperishable, is never interrupted. There is no second that is different and distinct from him, which he can taste."

26. yad vai tan na vadati, vadan vai tan na vadati, na hi vaktur vakter viparilopo vidyate, avinasitvat; na tu tad dvitiyam asti, tato'nyad vibhaktam yad vadet.

26. "In that state, indeed, he does not speak. Yet he does verily speak even while not speaking because the speaking of the speaker, who is imperishable, is never interrupted. There is no second that is different and distinct from him, which he can speak."

27. yad vai tan na srnoti, srnvan vai tan na srnoti; na hi srotuh sruter viparilopo vidyate, avinasitvat; na tu tad dvitiyam asti, tato'nyad vibhaktam yat srnuyat.

27. "In that state, indeed, he does not hear. Yet he does verily hear even while not hearing because the hearing of the listener, who is imperishable, is never interrupted. There is no second, which is different and distinct from him, which he can hear."

28. yad vai tan na manute, manvano vai tan na manute, na hi mantur mater viparilopo vidyate, avinasitvat; na tu tad dvitiyam asti, tato'nyad vibhaktam yan manvita.

28. "In that state, indeed, he does not think. Yet he does verily think even while not thinking because the thinking of the thinker, who is imperishable, is never interrupted. There is no second that is different and distinct from him, which he can think."

29. yad vai tan na sprsati, sprsan vai tan na sprsati, na hi sprastuh sprster viparilopo vidyate, avinasitvat, na tu tad dvitiyam asti, tato'nyad vibhaktam yat sprset.

29. "In that state, indeed, he does not touch. Yet he does verily touch even while not touching because the touching of the touching person, who is imperishable, is never interrupted. There is no second that is different and distinct from him, which he can touch."

30. yad vai tan na vijanati, vijanan vai tan na vijanati, na hi vijnatur vijnater viparilopo vidyate, avinasitvat; na tu tad dvitiyam asti, tato'nyad vibhaktam yad vijaniyat.

30. "In that state, indeed, he does not know. Yet he does verily know even while not knowing because the knowing of the knower, who is imperishable, is never interrupted. There is no second that is different and distinct from him, which he can know."

31. yatra vanyad iva syat, tatranyo'nyat pasyet, anyo'nyaj jighret, anyo'nyad rasayet, anyo'nyad vadet, anyo'nyat srnuyat, anyo'nyan manvita, anyo'nyat sprset, anyo'nyad vijaniyat.

31. *"When there, verily, is the other, as it were, then only one does see the other, one does smell the other, one does taste the other, one does speak to the other, one does listen to the other, one does think of the other, one does touch the other, and one does know the other."*

Notes: Perception and knowing happen in a state of duality only. If the perceived and the perceiver are the same, there is perception but no perception of the perception. It means the Self is self-aware and cognizes without any external agency. In other words, he is not ignorant and is self-knowing continuously and uninterruptedly.

32. salila eko drastadvaito bhavati, esa brahma-lokah, samraḍ iti. hainam anusasasa yajnavalkyah; esasya parama gatih, esasya parama sampat, eso'sya paramo lokah, eso'sya parama anandah; estasyaivanandasyanyani bhutani matram upajivanti.

32. *"One like water becomes the seer in the state of non-duality. This is the world of Brahman, O Emperor," thus did instruct Yajnavalkya. "This is the highest goal; this is the highest wealth; this is his highest world, and this is his highest bliss. On a particle of this very bliss only, all beings live."*

33. sa yo manusyanam raddhah samrddho bhavati, anyesam adhipatih, sarvair manusyakair bhogaih sampannatamah, sa manusyanam parama anandah; atha ye satam manusyanam anandah, sa ekah pitrnam jitalokanam anandah; atha ye satam pitrnam jita-lokanam anandah; sa eko gandharvaloka anandah; atha ye satam gandharva-loka anandah, sa eka karma devanam anandah, ye karmana devatvam abhisampadyante; atha ye satam karma-devanam anandah, sa eka ajana-devanam anandah, yas ca strotriyo'vrjino'kama-hatah; atha ye satam ajana-devanam anandah, sa ekah prajapati-loka anandah, yas ca srotriyo'vrjino'kama-hatah; atha ye satam Prajapati loka anandah, sa eko brahma loka anandah, yas ca srotriyo'vrjino'kama hatah; athaisa eva parama anandah, yas ca strotriyo'vrjino'kama-hatah; athaisa eva parama anandah, esa brahma-lokah samraḍ, iti hovaca yajnavalkyah. so'ham bhagavate sahasram dadami; ata urdhvam vimoksayaiva bruhiti. atra ha yajnavalkyo bibhayam cakara; medhavi raja, sarvebhyo mantebhya udarautsid iti.

33. *That human being who has a perfect body, who is abundantly wealthy, who is the lord of others, who is richly endowed with all the*

joys of human beings, that is the highest bliss of human beings. Now, a hundred time this bliss of human beings is equal to one measure of the bliss of the ancestors who have won the ancestral world. Now, a hundred times this bliss of ancestors who won the ancestral world is equal to one measure of the bliss of the world of Gandharvas. Now, a hundred times this bliss of the world of the Gandharva, is equal to one measure of the bliss of the Karma-devas, those who become gods by their actions. Now, a hundred times this bliss of Karma-devas is equal to one measure of the bliss of the Ajana Devas (gods by birth) as well as the one who is well versed in the Vedas, who is without sin and who has ended all his desires. Now, a hundred times this bliss of the Ajana Devas is equal to one measure of the bliss of the world of Prajapati as well as the one who is well versed in the Vedas, who is without sin and who has ended all his desires. Now, a hundred times this bliss of the world of Prajapati is equal to the bliss of the world Brahma as well as the one who is well versed in the Vedas, who is without sin and who has ended all his desires. This, indeed, is the highest bliss, this is the world of Brahma, O Emperor," said Yajnavalkya. "I will give you a thousand cows, godman. Please speak to me further about liberation." At this, Yajnavalkya was afraid that the intelligent king was driving to him to the very end of his thinking.

34. sa va esa, etasmin svapnante ratva caritva drstvaiva punyam ca papam ca, punah pratinyayam pratiyony adravati buddhantayaiva.

34. "Having enjoyed his dreams until the end and wandered about seeing both good and evil, he returns inversely by the same order to his former condition, the waking state."

35. tad yatha'nah su-samahitam utsarjad yayat, evam evayam sarira atma prajnenatmananvarudha utsarjam yati, yatraitad urdhva ucchvasi bhavati.

35. "Just as a cart, heavily loaded, goes on making creaking sounds, so does the Self in this body, loaded with self-sustaining supreme intelligence, goes on making creaking sounds when the upward breathing becomes difficult."

Notes: That is when a person is about to die, his breathing becomes difficult and noisy.

36. sa yatrayam animanam nyeti, jaraya vopatapata vanimanam nigacchati, tad yathamram va udumbaram va pippalam va bandhanat pramucyate, evam evayam purusa ebhyo'ngebhyah sampramucya punah pratinyayam pratiyony adravati pranayaiva.

36. *"When this body becomes emaciated, whether that emaciation arises from old age or disease, then just as a mango or a fig or a fruit of the pipal tree breaks its attachment, so does this person break free from the organs of his body and returns again by the same way to the source from where he began breathing."*

Notes: He begins his journey into the world from a womb, and after death, he returns to another womb and begins his new life again.

37. tad yatha rajanam ayantam ugrah, pratyenasah, suta-gramanyo'nnaih panair avasathaih pratikalpante: ayam ayati, ayam agacchatiti, evam haivam-vidam sarvani bhutani pratikalpante, idam brahmayati, idam agacchatiti.

37. *"Just as when a king arrives (in a village), the Ugras who sit in judgment to deliver punishments for specific offenses, and the Sutas of the village wait for him readily with food, drink and a resting place, saying, 'He is coming, he is coming,' so do all beings wait for him who knows this, saying, 'Here comes Brahman, here he comes.'"*

Notes: The Ugras are the fierce-looking lords or administrators appointed by the King to deliver punishments for specific offenses. The Sutas are the half-castes born to a Kshatriya father and a Brahmana woman. They used to serve the King as local landlords, revenue collectors, charioteers, and warriors who protected the village in peace times.

38. tad yatha rajanam prayiyasantam, ugrah pratyenasah, suta-gramanyo'bhisamayanti, evam evaimam atmanam, antak-ale sarve prana prana abhisamayanti, yatraitad urdhvocchvasi bhavati.

38. *Just as when a King departs, the Ugras who sit in judgment to deliver punishments for specific offenses, and the Sutas of the village gather around him (to give him farewell), so do all the organs of the body gather around the Self in the end when his upward breathing becomes difficult."*

Fourth Brahmana

The Fate of the Departing Souls

1. sa yatrayam atma-abalyam nyetya sammoham iva nyeti, athainam ete prana abhisamayanti; sa etas tejomatrah samabhyadadano hrdayam evanvavakramati, sa yatraisa caksusah purusah paran paryavartate, atharupajno bhavati.

1. *"When that Self becomes weak and benumbed, as it were, then the breaths gather around him. Taking with him these effulgent ones, he*

descends into the heart. When that person in the eye withdraws from all sides, then he becomes unconscious of forms."

Notes: The effulgent ones are the deities located in the sense-organs. He gathers them up and takes them with him into the heart. What becomes weak is the physical Self, the body, not the inner Self, for it is eternal and inexhaustible.

2. eki-bhavati, na pasyati, ity ahuh; eki-bhavati, na jighrati ity ahuh; eki-bhavati na rasayati, ity ahuh; eki-bhavati, na vadati, ity ahuh; eki-bhavati na srnoti, ity ahuh; eki-bhavati, na manute, ity ahuh; eki-bhavati na sprsati, ity ahuh; ekibhavati, na vijanati, ity ahuh. tasya haitasya hrdayasyagram pradyotate, tena pradyotenaisa atma niskramati, caksuso va murdhno va anyebhyo va sarira desebhyah; tam utkramantam prano anutkramati, pranam anutkramantam sarve prana anutkramanti; sa vijnano bhavati, sa vijnanam evanvavakramati; tam vidya-karmani samanvarabhete purva-prajna ca.

2. "Having become one, he cannot see; they say it. Having become one, he cannot smell; they say it. Having become one, he cannot taste; they say it. Having become one, he cannot speak; they say it. Having become one, he cannot hear; they say it. Having become one, he cannot think; they say it. Having become one, he cannot touch; they say it. Having become one, he does not know; they say it. The foremost part of his heart lightens up. By that light, the Self departs either through the eye, through the head, or through some other part of the body. When he rises up, breath follows, and when breath follows, all the breaths (organs) in the body follow it. Then he becomes (one with) intelligence. That intelligence rises up. Then his knowledge, karmas, and past experience follow."

Notes: When the deities in the organs are withdrawn and joined with the subtle body, the organs do not function. Hence, a dying person loses all his senses as he is about to depart. Purva-prajna refers to latent or dominant memories and impressions of the mind that become a part of the seed for one's next birth.

3. tad yatha trnajalayuka, trnasyantam gatva, anyam akramam akramya, atmanam upasamharati, evam evayam atma, idam sariram nihatya, avidam gamayitva, anyam akramam akramya, atmanam upasamharati.

3. Just as a leach, having reached the end of a blade of grass, takes hold of another support and pulls itself towards it, so does the Self, having discarded this body and made it incapable of knowing, take hold of another support (body) and gather itself into it.

Chapter 4

4. tad yatha pesaskari pesaso matram upadaya, anyan navataram kalyanataram rupam tanute, evam evayam atma, idam sariram nihatya, avidyam gamayitva, anyan navataram kalyanataram rupam kurute, pitryam va, gandharvam va, daivam va, prajapatyam va, brahmam va anyesam va bhutanam.

4. *"Just as a goldsmith taking a fragment of gold and carves it into another, newer and more pleasing form, even so, this Self, having discarded this body and made it incapable of knowing, makes for itself another, newer and more auspicious form, fit for the ancestors, the celestial Gandharvas, gods, Prajapati, Brahma or other beings."*

Notes: He makes himself a new body that is fit for the sacrifice and enjoyment of gods, manes, etc.

5. sa va ayam atma brahma, vijnanamayo manomayah pranamayas caksurmayah, srotramayah, prthivimaya apomayo vayumaya akasamayas tejomayo'tejomayah, kamamayo 'kamamayah, krodhamayo'krodhamayo, dharmamayo 'dharmamayah sarvamayah tad yad etat; idam-mayah adomaya iti. yathakari yathacari tatha bhavati, sadhukari sadhur bhavati, papakari papo bhavati; punyah punyena karmana bhavati, papah papena; athau khalv ahuh; kamamaya evayam purusa iti, sa yathakamo bhavati, tat kratur bhavati, yat kratur bhavati, tat karma kurute, yat karma kurute, tat abhisampadyate.

5. *"That Self, indeed, is Brahman who is made of intelligence, mind, breath, eyes, ears, the earth, the water, the air, the space, the light, no light, desires, no desire, anger, no anger, duty, non-duty, and all things. Regarding this, there is this, 'He consists of this, and he consists of that. As he acts and as he behaves, so does he become. The doer of good becomes good. The doer of sinful actions becomes sinful. By virtuous actions, he becomes virtuous; and by evil actions evil.' Others, however, say, 'This person consists of desires only. As he desires, so is his will. As is his will, so does he act. Whatever actions he performs, that he attains.'"*

Notes: Brahman contains everything. He is made of desires, anger, duty, etc., and their opposites also. The second part of the verse mentions the two beliefs about how a person becomes what he is. According to the first, a person becomes so by his actions. The other is that a person becomes so by his desires. Both are, in fact, interrelated. When actions are performed with desires, they produce consequences, which bind the person to death and rebirth. Each jiva is shaped by its karma and its consequences. The record of karma is imprinted in the subtle energy that flows in the body. It, too, becomes pure or tainted according to karma only.

6. tad esa sloko bhavati: tad eva saktah saha karmanaiti lingam mano yatra nisaktam asya; prapyantam karmanas tasya yat kim ceha karoty ayam. tasmal lokat punar aiti asmai lokaya karmane iti nu kamayamanah; athakamayamanah, yo'kamo niskama apta-kama atmakamah, na tasya prana utkramanti, brahmaiva san brahmapyeti.

6. *"Of this, there is this verse, 'That one who performs actions with desires in his mind, his subtle body goes together with the deed, being attached to it alone. After exhausting the fruit of whatever actions he performed in this life, he returns from that world to this world for doing (more) actions.' This is with regard to a man whose mind is filled with desires. Now, regarding the one who is free from desires. He who is without desires, who is freed from desires, whose desire is satisfied, who desires only the Self, his breaths do not depart. Being Brahman only, he goes to Brahman."*

Notes: This is a direct and clear reference to the doctrine of Karma. Yajnavalkya was conversant with it and spoke about it in the previous section. All the subsequent beliefs and philosophies about karma, rebirth, and liberation of jiva are found in this teaching of Yajnavalkya. He was not the first one to propound them since they existed from the early Vedic period. The state of desires is the state of ignorance and delusion. Freedom from that ignorant state of pursuing desires for selfish enjoyment is liberation.

7. tad esa sloko bhavati: yada sarve pramucyante kama ye'sya hrdi sritah, atha martyo'mrto bhavati, atra brahma samasnute iti tad yathahinirvlayani valmike mrta pratyasta sayita, evam evedam sariram sete. athayam asariro'amrtah prano brahmaiva, teja eva; so'ham bhagavate sahasram dadami, iti hovaca janako vaidehah.

7. *"Of this, there is this verse, 'When all the desires that dwell in the heart are gone, then the mortal becomes an immortal and attains Brahman here (in this body).' Just as the dead slough of a snake is cast off and lies on an anthill, so does the body lie. Now, this incorporeal and immortal life is Brahman only and light only." "I give you a thousand (cows), Godman," said Janaka of Videha.*

Notes: When one gives up desires, one gives up the body. When one subdues and silences all his desires fully, he permanently detaches himself from his body and becomes liberated even while still embodied. For him, his body becomes detached like the skin shed by a snake.

8. tad eta sloka bhavanti: anuh pantha vitatah puranah; mam sprsto'nuvitto mayaiva, tena dhira api yanti brahmavidah svargam lokam ita urdhvam vimuktah.

8. "Of this, there is this verse, 'The subtle path which is extensive and ancient has touched me. No, I have known it by myself. By that, the wise, the knowers of Brahman, go to the heavenly world after they ascend (leaving the body behind), being free."

Notes: The path to Brahman is subtle because it is not easily discernable or knowable. It is broad or extensive, meaning it can accommodate many seekers from diverse backgrounds. It is ancient because it must have been in existence through several cycles of creation. It cannot be known otherwise than by oneself.

9. tasmin suklam uta nilam ahuh, pingalam, haritam, lohitam ca esa pantha brahmana hanuvittah tenaiti brahmavit punyakrt taijasas ca.

9. "That path they say is white, is blue, is yellow, is green, and is red. That path is realized by a Brahmana (a knower of Brahman) and on it goes the knower of Brahman who has done good deeds and who is filled with the brilliance (of sattva)."

Notes: The colors of the path represent the different subtle energies that flow in the nerve channels (nadis) by which the knowers of Brahman attain liberation. However, they all must be virtuous and pure.

10. andham tamah pravisanti ye vidyam upasate tato bhuya iva te tamah ya u vidyayam ratah.

10. "Into blinding darkness enter those who worship the (mantra) vidyas. Into greater darkness enter those who take delight in the (brahma) vidyas."

Notes: A similar verse is also found in the Isa Upanishad. This can be interpreted differently. Vidya means any branch of Vedic study. Many types of vidyas exist, the lower ones and the higher ones. They lead to different ends. The central idea is that those who pursue any vidya out of ignorance, be it the knowledge of the rituals, the study of the shastras, or even the study of the Upanishads to fulfill desires or for personal gain, will remain in blinding ignorance bound to samsara. To escape from ignorance and delusion, one must use the knowledge for righteous purposes. Those who pursue liberation must perform sacrifices as an offering to the Lord without desiring their fruit. They must study the Vedas and other scriptures for the knowledge of Brahman and practice it sincerely until they attain liberation. The knowledge that does not lead to liberation is ignorance only.

11. ananda nama te lokah, andhena tamasavrtah tams te pretyabhigacchanti avidvamso'budho janah.

11. "Joyless are the worlds that are covered with blinding darkness. To them go after death those who are ignorant and unwise."

Notes: The ignorant and unwise who lack discernment and the right knowledge remain in the blinding darkness of Samsara and, upon death, fall into the lower worlds.

12. atmanam ced vijaniyad ayam asmiti purusah kim icchan, kasya kamaya sariram anusamjvaret.

12. "When one knows the Self as 'I am this person,' desiring what and for which desires will he suffer in the body?"

Notes: All desires and cravings cease when one sees oneself in all and as all-pervading

13. yasyanuvittah pratibuddha atmasmin samdehye gahane pravistah, sa visva-krt, sa hi sarvasya karta, tasya lokah sa u loka eva.

13. "Whoever has known and understood this Self that has entered into this place of impenetrable suffering and darkness, he is the creator of the universe, doer of all actions. The world is his, and he is the world itself."

Notes: The body is described as gahana, a thicket, labyrinth, or an impenetrable place of darkness and suffering. By knowing Brahman as himself, he overcomes it.

14. ihaiva santo'tha vidmas tad vayam, na cet avedir mahati vinastih. ye tad viduh, amrtas te bhavanti, athetare duhkham evapiyanti.

14. "Being in the body, we somehow know it. If not, it is ignorance and great destruction. Those who know it become immortal. The others go to only sorrow."

15. yadaitam anupasyati atmanam devam anjasa, isanam bhuta bhavyasya, na tato vijugupsate.

15. "When one sees this effulgent Self as the deity and as the lord of the past and present, does not turn away from him."

Notes: Vijugupsate means hiding, shrinking away, or avoiding. When the Seer sees the Self within himself, he no longer wishes to hide behind a veil of delusion and duality. He sees the Self in all and everywhere and does not wish to avoid or hide from anyone.

16. yasmad arvak samvatsarah ahobhih parivartate, tad deva jyotisam jyotih ayur hopasate'mrtam.

16. That under whom the year with its days revolves, that the gods worship as the light of the lights, and whose life is immortal.

Notes: The year represents mortality and limited time with its division of past, present, future, months, days, hours, seconds, etc., to which all beings are subject. Brahman represents immortality and unlimited time that is without such divisions. These divisions are for the earth not for the world of Brahman.

17. yasmin panca panca-janah akasas ca pratisthitah, tam eva manya atmanam, vidvan brahma'mrto'mrtam.

17. "That in which the five groups of five and the space are established, that alone I regard as my Self. Knowing that immortal Brahman, I become immortal."

Notes: The body is that in which the five groups of five (the senses, elements, etc.) are established.

18. pranasya pranam uta caksusas uta srotrasya srotram, manaso ye mano viduh, te nicikyur brahma puranam agryam.

18. It is the breath of the breaths (organs), the seeing of the eye, the hearing of the ears, and the thinking of the mind; those who know it as such have realized the ancient and the primordial Brahman.

19. manasaivanudrastavyam, naiha nanasti kim cana: mrtyoh sa mrtyum apnoti ya iha naneva pasyati.

19. "By the mind alone, it is perceived. There is no diversity in it whatsoever. From death to death goes here he who perceives as if it were many."

20. ekadhaivanudrastavyam etad aprameyam dhruvam, virajah para akasad aja atma mahan dhruvah.

20. "It is perceived as One only. It is unknowable and fixed. The Self is taintless, above the space, unborn, great, and fixed."

Notes: The Self is perceived as One only without a second and without duality and distinctions. It is unknowable because to know something, you need a second. It is one and indestructible; therefore, it is also fixed.

21. tam eva dhiro vijnaya prajnam kurvita bramanah nanudhyayad bahun sabdan, vaco viglapanam hi tat iti.

21. "Let him, the stable-minded one, attain the supreme knowledge of Brahman after knowing this only. He should not reflect upon many words, for they tire the speech."

Notes: Brahman is truly known only by knowing the Self. He cannot be known through study, debate, or discussions. Those efforts make one weary but do not lead to true knowledge.

22. sa va esa mahan aja atma yo'yam vijnanamayah pranesu; ya eso'ntar-hrdaya akasah tasmin sete, sarvasya vasi, sarvasyesanah, sarvasyadhipatih; sa na sadhuna karmana bhuyan no evasadhuna kaniyan. esa sarvesvarah, esa bhutadhipatih, esa

bhutapalah. esa setur vidharana esam lokanam asambhedaya. tam etam vedanuvacanena brahmana vividisanti, yajnena, danena, tapasanasakena; etam eva viditva munir bhavati, etam eva pravrajino lokam icchantah pravrajanti. etadd ha sma vai tat purve vidvamsah prajam na kamayante: kim prajaya karisyamah; yesam no'yam atmayam loka iti. te ha sma putraisanayas ca vittaisanayas ca lokaisanayas ca vyutthaya, atha bhiksacaryam caranti; ya hy eva putraisana sa vittaisana, ya vittaisana sa lokaisana; ubhe hy ete esane eva bhavatah sa esa neti nety atma; agrhyah, na hi grhyate; asiryah, na hi siryate; asangah, na hi sajyate; asito na vyathate, na risyati; etam u haivaite na tarata iti, atah papam akaravam iti, atah kalyanam akaravam iti; ubhe u haivaisa ete tarati, nainam krtakrte tapatah.

22. "He, verily, is the great unborn Self who is filled with intelligence among the breaths (organs). He is the Lord who lies in the space within the heart. He is the indweller of all, the lord of all, and the ruler of all. He does not become pious by pious actions or not-pious through evil actions. He is the lord of all, the ruler of all beings, and the protector of all beings. He is the bridge that upholds and keeps apart these different worlds. The Brahmanas endeavor to know Him by the study and recitation of the Vedas, by sacrifices, by charity, by austerity, and by cultivating dispassion. By knowing Him only, one becomes the silent ascetic (muni). Desiring Him only as their world, the traveling ascetics (Parivrajakas) wander around. Indeed, by knowing this only, in the past, the ancient sages did not desire children. 'What shall we do with children, we who have attained this Self, this world?' (they thought). It is said that having renounced their desire for sons, having renounced their wealth, and having renounced their attachment to the worlds (the earth and heaven), they led the life of a mendicant, begging for alms. Indeed, that which is the desire for sons is the desire for wealth, and that which is the desire for wealth is the desire for worlds. Both these, verily, are desires only. This one is the Self, which is 'not this, not this.' He is not perceptible because he cannot be perceived with the senses. He is indestructible, for he cannot be destroyed. He is without attachments, for he does not hold on to anything. He is without fetters, without suffering, without injury. Him (who knows the Self) these two thoughts do not trouble, 'Now for some reason I have done this evil act,' and 'Now for some reason I have done this good act.' He overcomes both. He is not troubled by what he has done or what he has not done."

Notes: It is the highest and the most exalted state in which one does not have any desires. A person without desires is a person without fetters. He is not concerned by the consequences of his actions, since he is not subject to karma. The Self is 'not this, not this' (neti neti) because it is known only by knowing what it is not.

23. tad esa rcabhyuktam: esa nityo mahima brahmanasya na vardhate karmana no kaniyan tasyaiva syat pada-vit, tam viditva na lipyate karmana papakena, iti tasmad evam-vit, santo danta uparatas titiksuh samahito bhutva, atmany evatmanam pasyati, sarvam atmanam pasyati; nainam papma tarati, sarvam papmanam tarati; nainam papma tapati, sarvam papmanam tapati; vipapo virajo'vicikitso brahmano bhavati; esa brahma-lokah, samrat; enam prapito'si iti hovaca yajnavalkyah; so'ham bhagavate videhan dadami, mam capi saha dasyayeti.

23. "This has been expressed in a hymn of the Rigveda, 'This eternal greatness of a knower of Brahman neither increases through actions nor decreases.' One should know its essential meaning. Knowing it, one is not tainted by the evil arising from actions. Therefore, who knows this thus becomes peaceful, self-controlled, withdrawn, patient, and collected. He sees the Self in himself and sees all in himself. Evil does not overtake him. He transcends all evil. Evil does not burn him. He burns away all evil. Without evil, free from the quality of rajas, free from doubt, he becomes a knower of Brahman. This is the world of Brahman, O Emperor. You have attained it, "thus said Yajnavalkya. Janaka of Videha said, "I am that, God man. I offer you the empire of Videha and myself also, along with it, to be in your service."

Notes: 'So ham,' I am That,' is a powerful mantra used in chants and meditation to absorb the mind into the Self and dissolve it.

24. sa va esa mahan aja atma'nnado vasudanah; vindate vasu ya evam veda.

24. This, indeed, is the great unborn Self, the eater of food and the giver of hidden wealth. He who knows this attains hidden wealth.

25. sa va esa mahan ajatma, ajaro amaro'mrto'bhayo brahma; abhayam vai brahma, abhayam hi vai brahma bhavati ya evam veda.

25. This, indeed, is the great unborn Self, imperishable, undying, immortal, and fearless Brahman. Brahman, indeed, is fearless. Fearless as Brahman he becomes who knows thus.

Fifth Brahmana

Yajnavalkya and Maitreyi

1. atha ha yajnavalkyasya dve bharye babhuvatuh, maitreyi ca katyayani ca tayor ha maitreyi brahma-vadini babhuva, stri-

Chapter 4

prajnaiva tarhi katyayani, atha yajnavalkyo'nyad-vrttam upakarisyan

1. *Now, Yajnavalkya was blessed with two wives: Maitreyi and Katyayani. Of them, Maitreyi was blessed to be a debater of Brahman, while Katyani was more into feminine matters. Then, Yajnavalkya, having decided to go on another journey...*

Notes: Thus far, Yajnavalkya has been a householder. He had two wives, Maitreyi and Katyayani; one was spiritual and drawn to Brahman, and the other, an ordinary housewife, was into feminine ways. Yajnavalkya decided to renounce worldly life, take up sannyasa, and go on a journey of adventure as a renunciant. This and the fourth Brahmana of the Second Chapter are almost identical.

2. maitreyi, iti hovaca yajnavalkyah, ud yasyan va are "ham asmat sthanad asmi; hanta hanta, te" naya katyayanyantam karavaniti.

2. *"Maitreyi, my dear, said Yajnavalkya, "I am ready to leave this place. Let me make a settlement between you and Katyayani."*

3. sa hovaca maitreyi, yan nu ma iyam, bhagoh, sarva prthivi vittena purna syat, katham tenamrta syam iti. na, iti hovaca yajnavalkyah; yathaivopakaranavatam jivitam, tathaiva te jivitam syad amrtatvasya tu nasasti vitteneti.

3. *Then Maitreyi said, "Indeed, my lord, if this whole earth filled with wealth is mine, shall I become immortal through that?" "No," said Yajnavalkya. "Your life will be just like that of wealthy people, but there is no hope of immortality through wealth."*

4. sa hovaca maitreyi, yenaham namrta syam, kim aham tena kuryam, yad eva bhagavan veda tad eva me bruhiti.

4. *Then Maitreyi said, "What shall I do with that by which I will not become immortal? Please tell me that only Godman, which you know (about immortality).*

5. sa hovaca yajnavalkyah, priya bata are nah sati priyam bhasase; ehi, assva, vyakhyasyami te; vyacaksanasya tu me nididhyasasva iti.

5. *Yajnavalkya said, "My dear, you have been dearer to me, and you spoke words that are even dearer. Come, sit here. I will explain it to you. As I speak, listen with utmost attention, restraining your mind and reflecting upon it."*

6. sa hovaca: na va are patyuh kamaya patih priyo bhavati, atmanas tu kamaya patih priyo bhavati: na va are jayayai kamaya jaya priya bhavati, atmanas tu kamaya jaya priya bha-

vati; na va are putranam kamaya putrah priya bhavanti, atmanas tu kamaya putrah priya bhavanti; na va are vittasya kamaya vittam priyam bhavati, atmanas tu kamaya vittam priyam bhavati; na va are brahmanah kamaya brahma priyam bhavati, atmanas tu kamaya brahma priyam bhavati; na va are ksatrasya kamaya ksatram priyam bhavati atmanas tu kamaya ksatram priyam bhavati; na va are lokanam kamaya lokah priya bhavanti, atmanas tu kamaya lokah priya bhavanti; na va are devanam kamaya devah priya bhavanti, atmanas tu kamaya devah priya bhavanti; na va are bhutanam kamaya bhutani priyani bhavanti, atmanas tu kamaya bhutani priyani bhavanti; na va are sarvasya kamaya sarvam priyam bhavati, atmanas tu kamaya sarvam priyam bhavati; atma va are drastavyah srotavyo mantavyo nididhyasitavyah: maitreyi atmano va are darsanena sravanena matya vijnanenedam sarvam viditam.

6. He said, "Truly, it is not because the husband is desirable that the husband becomes dearer, but because the Self is desirable, the husband becomes dearer. It is not because the wife is desirable that the wife becomes dearer, but because the Self is desirable, the wife becomes dearer. It is not because the sons are desirable that the sons become dearer, but because the Self is desirable, the sons become dearer. It is not because wealth is desirable that wealth becomes dearer, but because the Self is desirable, wealth becomes dearer. It is not because a Brahmana is desirable that the Brahmana becomes dearer, but because the Self is desirable, the Brahmana becomes dearer. It is not because a Kshatriya is desirable that the Kshatriya becomes dearer, but because the Self is desirable, the Kshatriya becomes dearer. It is not because the worlds are desirable that the worlds become dearer, but because the Self is desirable, the worlds become dearer. It is not because gods are desirable that the gods become dearer, but because the Self is desirable, the gods become dearer. It is not because the beings are desirable that the beings become dearer, but because the Self is desirable, the being becomes dearer. It is not because all this is desirable that all this becomes dearer, but because the Self is desirable, all this becomes dearer. Indeed, the Self should be seen, heard, meditated upon, and concentrated upon. Truly, Maitreyi, by seeing, hearing, thinking, and discerning the Self within, all this is known.

7. brahma tam paradad yo'nyatratmano brahma veda. ksatram tam paradad yo'nyatratmanah ksatram veda. lokas tam paradur yo'nyatratmano lokan veda. devas tam paradur yo'nyatratmano devan veda. bhutani tam paradur yo'nyatratmano bhutani veda. sarvam tam paradad yo'nyatratmano sarvam veda. idam

brahma, idam ksatram, ime lokah, ime devah, imami bhutani, idam sarvam, yad ayam atma.

7. A brahmana regards him as distant (or adverse) who thinks he (the brahmana) is different from himself. A Kshatriya regards him as distant who thinks he is different from himself. The worlds regard him as distant who thinks the worlds are different from himself. The gods regard him as distant who thinks the gods are different from himself. Beings regard him as distant who think the beings are different from himself. All this regards him as distant who thinks all this is different from himself. The Brahmana, the Kshatriya, the worlds, the gods, the beings, and all this are this Self only.

8. sa yatha dundubher hanyamanasya na bahyan sabdan saknuyad grahanaya, dundubhes tu grahanena dundubhyaghatasya va sabdo grhitah.

8. Just as when a drum is beaten, one cannot distinguish its particular sound, but by seeing the drum or the bearer of the drum the sound is grasped...

9. sa yatha sankhasya dhmayamanasya na bahyan sabdan saknuyad grahanaya, sankhasya tu grahaenan sankhadhmasya va sabdo grhitah.

9. Just as when a conch is blown, one cannot distinguish its particular sound, but by seeing the conch or the blower of the conch, the sound is grasped...

10. sa yatha vinayai vadyamanayai na bahyan sabdan saknuyad grahanaya, vinayai tu grahanena vina-vadasya va sabdo grhitah.

10. Just as when a Vina (a musical instrument) is played, one cannot distinguish its particular sound, but by seeing the Vina or the player of the Vina the sound is grasped...

11. sa yathardra-edhagner abhyahitat prthag dhūma viniscaranti, evam va are'sya mahato bhūtasya nihsvasitam, etad yad rgvedo yajurvedah samavedo'tharvangirasa itihasah puranam vidya upanisadah slokah sūtrany anuvyakhyanani vyakhyanani: asyaivaitani sarvani nihsvasitani.

11. Just as different kinds of smoke arise from a fire kindled with wet wood, even so, my dear, the Rigveda, Yajurveda, Samaveda, Atharvangirasah, history, Puranas, various branches of supreme knowledge, Upanishads, verses, aphorisms, explanations, and commentaries. From this, indeed, all these are breathed out.

12. sa yatha sarvasam apam samudra ekayanam, evam sarvesam sparsanam tvag ekayanam, evam sarvesam sarvesam gandhanam nasike ekayanam, evam sarvesam rasanam jihva ekayanam, evam sarvesam rupanam caksur ekayanam, evam sarvesam sarvesam sabdanam srotram ekayanam, evam sarvesam samkalpanam mana ekayanam, evam sarvasam vidyanam hrdayam ekayanam, evam sarvasam karmanam hastav ekayanam, evam sarvasam anandanam upastha ekayanam, evam sarvesam sarvesam visarganam payur ekayanam, evam sarvesam adhvanam padav ekayanam, evam sarvesam vedanam vag ekayanam.

12. *Just as all the waters become one with the ocean, just as all forms of touch become one with the skin, just as all odors become one with the nose, just as all tastes become one with the tongue, just as all forms become one with the eyes, just as all sounds become one with the ears, just all intentions become one with the mind, just all types of supreme knowledge (brahma-vidyas) become one with the heart, just as all actions become one with the hands, just as all forms of enjoyment become one with the reproductive organs, just as all forms of excretion become one in the anus, just as all movements become one in the feet, just as all the Vedas become one in the speech...*

13. sa yatha saindhavakhilya udake prasta udakam evanuviliyeta, na hasya udgrahanayeva syat, yato yatas tv adadita lavanam eva, evam va ara idam mahad bhutam anantam apa-ram vijnana-ghana eva; etebhyo bhutebhyah samutthaya, tany evanuvinasyati; na pretya samjnasti, iti are bravimi, iti hovaca yajnavalkyah.

13. *Just as a lump of salt dropped into water is dissolved and no one can grasp it thereafter, but whenever one sips it tastes salty, so does, my dear, this great being, who is infinite, limitless, and filled with intelligence joins with these beings and vanishes into them. When he departs, there is no more intelligence. This is what I say, my dear," said Yajnavalkya.*

14. sa hovaca maitreyi, atraiva ma bhagavan amumuhat, na pretya samjnastiti. sa hovaca, na va are"ham moham bravimi, alam va are idam vijnanaya.

14. *Then Maitreyi said, "Godman, indeed you have now put me in confusion, saying that, 'when he departs, there is no more intelligence,'" Yajnavalkya said, "Certainly, I have not said anything confusing. This should be intelligent enough."*

15. yatra hi dvaitam iva bhavati, tad itara itaram pasyati, tad itara itaram jighrati, tad itara itaram rasayate, tad itara itaram abhivadati, tad itara itaram srnoti, tad itara itaram vijanati, yatra tv asya sarvam atmaivabhut, tat kena kam pasyet, tat kena kam jighret, tat kena kam rasayet, tat kena kam abhivadet, tat kena kam srnuyat, tat kena kam manvita, tat kena kam sprset, tat kena kam vijaniyat, sa esa neti nety atma; agrhyah, na hi grhyate, asiryah na hi siryate; asangah, na hi sajyate asit, na vyathate, asiryah na hi siryate; asangah, na hi sajyate, asito, na vathate, na risyati, vijnataram are kena vijaniyat, iti utkanusasanasi, maitreyi; etavad are khalv amrtatvam, it hoktva, yajnavakyo vijahara.

15. When there is duality, then only one sees another, one smells another, one tastes another, one speaks to another, one hears another, and one knows another. Truly, when everything becomes the Self, then by what and whom one sees, by what and whom one smells, by what and whom one tastes, by what and to whom one speaks, by what and whom one hears, by what and about whom one thinks, by what and whom one touches, and by what and whom one should know? He is that 'Not this, not this' Self. He is imperceptible, for he cannot be perceived. He is indestructible, for he cannot be destroyed. He is unattached, for he does not hold on to anything. He is unfettered, he does not suffer, and he cannot be injured. By what means, indeed, the knower can be known? This much is the instruction, Maitreyi. This is about the immortality." Having said that, Yajnavalkya went away.

Sixth Brahmana

The Line of Teachers and Students

Editor's Note: This section contains the uninterrupted succession of teachers who transmitted this knowledge and preserved it for future generations. Once again, to avoid redundancy we have not included the Sanskrit verses for this section.

1. Now, as to the lineage of teachers: Pautimasya (received it) from Gaupavana. Gaupavana from Pautimasya. Pautimasya from Gaupavana. Gaupavana from Kausika. Kausika from Kaundinya. Kaundinya from Sandilya. Sandilya from Kausika and Gautama. Gautama -

2. From Agnivesya. Agnivesya from Gargya. Gargya from Gargya. Gargya from Gautama. Gautama from Saitava. Saitava from Parasaryayana. Parasaryayana from Gargyayana. Gargyayana from Uddalakayana. Uddalakayana from Jabalayana. Jabalayana from Madhyandinayana. Madhyandinayana from Saukarayana. Saukaraya-

na from Kasayana. Kasayana from Sayakayana. Sayakayana from Kausikayani. Kausikayani-

3· *From Ghrtakausika. Ghrtakausika from Parasaryayana. Parasaryayana from Parasarya. Parasarya from Jatiikarnya. Jatiikarnya from Asurayana and Yaska. Asurayana from Traivani. Traivani from Aupajandhani. Aupajandhani from Asuri. Asuri from Bharadvaja. Bharadvaja from Atreya. Atreya from Manp. Manti from Gautama. Gautama from another Gautama. This Gautama from Vatsya. Vatsya from Sandlilya. Sandilya from Kaisorya Kapya. Kaisorya Kapya from Kumaraharita. Kumaraharita from Galava. Galava from Vidarbhikaundinya. Vidarbhikaundinya from Vatsanapat Babhrava. Vatsanapat Babhrava from Pathin Saubhara. Pathin Saubhara from Ayasya Angirasa. Ayasya Angirasa from Abhuti Tvastra. Abhuti Tvastra from Visvariipa Tvastra. Visvariipa Tvastra from the two Asvins. The two Asvins from Dadhyac Atharvana. Dadhyac Atharvana from Atharvan Daiva. Atharvan Daiva from Mrtyu Pradhvamsana. Mrtyu Pradhvamsana from Pradhvarilsana. Pradhvamsana from Ekarsi. Ekarsi from Viprachitti. Viprachitti from Vyasti. Vyasti from Sanaru. Sanaru from Sanatana. Sanatana from Sanaga. Sanaga from Paramesthin (Viraj). Paramesthin from Brahma. Brahma is self-born. Salutation to Brahma.*

Chapter 5

First Brahmana

Invocation to Brahman, the Full

1. aum, puranam adah, purnam idam, purnat purnam udacyate purnasya purnam adaya purnam evavasisyate. aum khambrahma, kham puranam, vayuram kham, iti ha smahakauravyayani-putrah, vedo'yam brahmana viduh; vedainenayad veditavyam. iti prathamam brahmanam

I. Aum! That is full. This is full. From the full arises the full. Taking the full from the full, the full still remains full. "Aum is spatial Brahman, space that is ancient, space that is filled with air," thus verily the sons of Kauravyayani used to say. This is the knowledge which the knower of Brahman knows. Through it, one knows what is to be known.

Notes: Brahman is infinite. Now, whatever you take out of Brahman does not diminish him. Still, he remains the same because you are not taking anything out of Him or separate from Him. All duality and diversity exist within Brahman. Therefore, despite the changes and the transience, the sum of existence always remains the same. To understand the concept of purna or fullness, consider the number zero. Zero among the numbers symbolizes infinity. Zero among the numbers symbolizes infinity. From zero, you can produce another zero without diminishing the former, and even if you deduct a zero from a zero, it remains a zero even then. This is a simple and direct example of Brahman's infinity and indestructibility. Everything emanates from Brahman. Yet Brahman remains the same. Space also remains the same, even though a myriad of objects appear and disappear in it during creation. He is like Aum, which is described as the spatial Brahman (Aum, Kham Brahma). Aum is the primordial subtle sound hidden in space. When joined with the breath in speech, it manifests as a sacred syllable, just as Brahman manifests by joining with the subtle energy called prana that is hidden in the universe. Hence, Aum is considered the connecting link. Traditionally, pursuers of Brahman are advised to meditate on him as Aum only. So is with the sun, the shining zero in the sky, whose brightness remains undiminished even when he sheds light.

Second Brahmana

Prajapati's Advice to Gods, Humans and Demons

1. trayah prajapatyah prajapatau pitari brahma-caryam usuh, deva manusya asurah, usitva brahmacaryam deva uchu; bravitu no bhavan iti; tebhyo haitad aksaram uvaca; da iti,

Chapter 5

vyajnasista iti; vyajnasisma iti hocuh, damyata, iti na attheti, aum iti hovaca, vyajnasisteti.

1. *The three kinds of Prajapati's offspring, the gods, humans, and the demons, lived with their father Prajapati as students practicing celibacy. Having practiced celibacy and completed their studies, the gods said, "Please tell us (something)." To them, then he spoke this syllable, "Da," and said, "Have you understood?" They said, "Yes, we understood; you spoke to us about 'damyata, self-control.'" "Yes," he said, "you have understood."*

Notes: Damyata means self-control or restraint of the senses. The gods, by nature, pursue enjoyment and seek sensuous pleasures. They preside over the sense organs in our bodies. Hence, they are always busy and outgoing, looking for sense objects to experience various types of pleasures. Hence, Brahma suggested that the gods should practice self-restraint while performing their duties and stay free from evil.

2. atha hainam manusya ucuh: bravitu no bhavan iti; tebhyo haitad evaksaram uvaca; da iti; vyajnasista iti, vyajnasisma iti hocuh, datta iti na attheti; aum iti hovaca vyajnasisteti.

2. *Then the humans said to him, "Please tell us (something)." To them, then he spoke the same syllable, "Da," and said, "Have you understood?" They said, "Yes, we understood, you spoke to us about 'datta, to give.'" "Yes," he said, "you have understood."*

Notes: Humans are, by nature, selfish and do not easily give charity, whereas they are supposed to overcome the evil of selfishness by performing sacrifices, helping the needy, and giving gifts as a part of their obligatory duties. Hence, he advised them to practice giving.

3. atha hainam asura ucuh, bravitu no bhavan iti; tebhyo haitad evaksaram uvaca; da iti, vyajnasista iti, vyajnasisma iti hocuh, dayadhvam iti na attheti, aum iti hovaca vyajnasisteti. tad etad evaisa daivi vag anuvadati stanayitnuhda—da, da, iti, damyata, datta, dayadhvam iti. tad etat trayam sikset, damam, danam, dayam iti.

3. *Then the humans said to him, "Please tell us (something)." To them then he spoke the same syllable, "Da," and said, "Have you understood?" They said, "Yes, we understood, you spoke to us about 'dayadhvam, compassion.'" "Yes," he said, "you have understood." This very thing is also repeated by the heavenly voice, the thunder, "Da, Da, Da, meaning, control yourselves, give charity and show compassion."*

Notes: The Asuras are, by nature, cruel and deluded. They take pleasure in harassing and inflicting pain and suffering upon others.

Brahma taught them to show compassion so they could learn to restrain their evil nature. This section is about cultivating divine qualities, balance, and restraint. Both gods and demons live inside the human body as organs, thoughts, desires, and tendencies. When they are used for selfless and sacrificial actions, they uplift humans. When they are used for selfish and violent purposes, it leads to their downfall. Therefore, human beings who possess both the divine and demonic nature must cultivate all three qualities.

Third Brahmana

Brahman as Hrdayam - The Heart

1. esa prajapatir yad hrdayam, etad brahma, etad sarvam. tad etat try-aksaram; hr-da-yam iti. hr ity ekam aksaram; abhiharanty asmai svas canye ca, ya evam veda; da ity ekam aksaram, dadatyasmai svas canye ca ya evam veda; yam, ity ekam aksaram; eti svargam lokam ya evam veda.

1. This is Prajapati, this heart. This is Brahman, this is all. This has triple syllables. They are: 'Hr,' 'Da,' and 'Yam.' Hr is one syllable. To him, who knows this, his own people and others make offerings. Da is one syllable. To him who knows that, his own people give. Ya is one syllable. He who knows this goes to the heavenly world.

Notes: 'Hr' literally means to make offerings to a deity or to perform a sacrifice. 'Da' means to give, as in dana or charity. 'Yam' means going. These three syllables make up the word Hridayam, which is symbolized here as Brahman. The heart is described as the sustainer and nourisher of the body since the bundle of Hita nadis (subtle channels) spread out into the whole body from the heart only like the branches of the inverted Asvattha tree. They carry prana (the subtle energy) filled with the nourishment extracted from the food to all the organs and keep them nourished. Hence, whoever acts like the heart, knowing the meaning of 'Hr,' and makes offerings to gods with devotion, his own people treat him like a god in human form and make offerings of respect, love, etc. Whoever knows the meaning of 'Da' and gives charity like the heart, his own people reciprocate his benevolence and give gifts of love and support in return. Whoever knows the meaning of 'Ya' and meditates on the heart as the seat of Brahman will eventually go to the immortal world.

Fourth Brahmana

Brahman as That and Sat

1. tad vai tat, etad tad asa, satyam eva. sa yo haitan mahad yaksam prathamajam veda; satyam brahmeti, jayatimaml lokan. jita in nv asav asat, ya evam etan mahad yaksam prathamajam veda; satyam brahmetip; satyam hy eva brahma.

I. This, verily, is That. This, indeed, was That verily what is Sat (True). He who knows this great Yaksha as the firstborn, he conquers these worlds and attains Brahman, who is Sat. Likewise, would be conquered (the enemy of) his and (they) become non-existent (for him), who knows thus this great Yaksha, the firstborn as Brahman, who is Sat. Indeed, Brahman is Sat only.

Notes: The Way (yam) to realizing Brahman is by knowing and meditating on Tad or That (the Supreme Brahman or the Supreme Self) as indeed Sat, the True (the Self). Only Brahman or Atman (the Self) represents Sat. The rest is Asat (untrue), temporary illusion, projection, or manifestation. Hence, we have the famous mantra, Aum Tat Sat, which is used in rituals and meditative practices to realize Brahman or remind oneself of one's divine nature and, except that, all this is an illusion and, hence, we should not be too particular about our beliefs, attachments, and endeavors. The Yakshas are a class of celestial beings or fairies with beauty, wealth, and supernatural powers. Yaskha also means a celestial spirit. In Vedic imagery, Brahman is often depicted as Yaksha because He once appeared to the gods in that form. Please refer to the Kena Upanishad in the Selected Upanishads.

Fifth Brahmana

Brahman as Satyam - the Truth

1. apa evadam agra asuh, ta apah satyam asrjanta, satyam brahma, brahma prajapatim, prajapatir devan. te devah satyam evopasate, tad etat try-aksaram: sa ity ekam aksaram; ti ity ekam aksaram, yam it ekam aksaram: prathama uttame aksare satyam, madhyato'nrtam; tad etad anrtam ubhayatah satyena parigrhitam satyabhuyam eva bhavati. naivam vidvamsam amrtam hinasti.

I. Water only was all this in the beginning. That water created the Satyam, the truth. The truth was Brahman. Brahman (created) Prajapati. Prajapati created the gods. The gods worshipped Satyam, the truth. That(truth) has these three syllables: Sa is one syllable, Ti is one syllable, and Yam is one syllable. The first and the third syllables are true. The middle one is untrue. This untruth is enclosed from both sides by the truth. Hence, Truth predominates. The knower of this is never hurt by the untrue.

Notes: The water mentioned here is not the physical water but the subtle pure energy (the plasma of the universe) that flows endlessly in the whole existence. From that ocean of pure energy manifested the First Being, Sat Brahman. He then produced Prajapati, gods, and all other manifestations. They all worship Him because He is their source. The three syllables, 'Sa,' 'Ta,' and 'Yam,' represent the three realities: the Supreme Self (Sat), the mortal body or the projection (tan), and the embodiedSelf that keeps wandering (Yam) in Samsara. The first and the last are true and everlasting. The middle one is Asat because it is impermanent and subject to death and destruction. Shankara interpreted 'Ti' as death since the words mrtyu (death) and anrita (death) contained the common syllable 'T.'

2. tad yat tat satyam asau sa adityah. ya esa etasmin mandale puruso yas cayam daksine'ksan purusah. tav etav anyo'nyasmin pratisthitau; rasmibhir eso'smin pratisthitah pranair ayam amusmin, sa yadotkramisyan bhavati. suddham evaitan mandalam pasyati. nainam ete rasmayah pratyayanti.

2. That which is True is the sun up above. He is the Person who is in the disc of the sun and the Person who is here in the right eye. The two are established in each other. Through the shining rays, that one is established in this one. Through the breaths (pranas) this one in That. When one becomes ready to depart, he sees the orb of the sun as pure, and those rays no longer reach him.

Notes: The same analogy is used here. Sa is the Supreme Self or the Cosmic Being (Aditya or Purusha) in the Sun. Yam is the individual Self seen in the right eye. The rays of the sun connect them through that eye. When the eye ceases to function due to death, that connection is lost, and he cannot go to the immortal world but remains stuck in the lower worlds.

3. ya esa etasmin mandale purusah, tasya bhur iti sirah; ekam sirah, ekam etad aksaram; bhuva iti bahu; dvau ete aksare; svar iti pratistha; dve pratisthe dve ete aksare. tasyopanisad ahar iti; hanti papmanam jahati ca, ya evam veda.

3. Of the person who is in the disc of the sun, the syllable Bhuh is the head. One is the head, and one is this syllable. His arms are Bhuvah. Two are the arms, and two are the syllables. His feet are Svah. He stands on two feet, and two are the syllables. His secret name is Ahar. He who knows this destroys evil and turns away from it.

Notes: Ahar means he who dispels darkness. It is, therefore, another name for the day. The evil that the knower of Brahman destroys with this knowledge is death or mortality.

Yo'yam daksine;ksan pursah, tasya bhur iti sirah, ekam sirah, ekam etad aksaram; bhuva it bahu; dvau bahu, dve ete aksare; svar iti pratistha; dev pratisthe, dve ete akasare, tasyo'panisad aham iti; hanta papmanam jahati ca ya evam veda.

4. Of the person who is in the right eye, the syllable Bhuh is the head. One is the head, and one is this syllable. His arms are Bhuvah. Two are the arms, and two are the syllables. His feet are Svah. He stands on two feet, and two are the syllables. His secret name is Aham. He who knows this destroys evil and turns away from it.

Notes: Aham means ego or the self-sense. The sun is described here in inverse form, with his feet up in heaven and his head down in the mortal body or world (bhuh). He is like the Asvattha tree, with roots (feet) in heaven and branches (rest of the body) below.

Sixth Brahmana

Brahman as the Person in the Mind

1. manomayo'yam purusah, bhah satyah tasminn antarhrdaye yatha vrihir va yavo va. sa esa sarvasyesanah, sarvasya-dhipatih, sarvam idam prasasti yad idam kim ca

I. The person who consists of the mind is (seen as or is meditated as) the light within the heart, like a grain of rice or barley. He is the lord of all and governs whatever there is.

Notes: The Purusha, or the Self in the body, should be meditated as a small point of light the size of a rice or barley grain. By doing so, one attains oneness with the Self.

Seventh Brahmana

Brahman as the Lightning

1. vidyud brahma ity ahuh; vidanad vidyut, vidyaty enam papmanah, ya evam veda, vidyud brahmeti, vidyud hy eva brahma.

I. Lightning is Brahman, they say. It scatters (dark clouds); hence it is lightning. He who knows that lightning, in fact, is Brahman, he does indeed scatter all sins, for lightning, verily, is Brahman.

Notes: This is the meditation on the Sat Purusha as lightning.

Eight Brahmana

Speech Symbolized as the Cow

1. vacam dhenum upasita tasyas catvarah stanah; svaha-karo vasat-karo hanta-karah svadha-karah; tasyai dvau stanau deva upajivanti, svaha-karam ca, vasat-karam ca; hantakaram manusyah, svadha-karam pitarah. tasyah prana rsabhah, mano vatsah.

I. One should meditate upon speech as a cow. She has four teats: the sound Svaha, the sound Vasat, the sound Hanta, and the sound Svadha. The gods live on two of her teats: the sound Svaha and the sound Vasat. The human upon the sound Hanta; and the ancestors on the sound Svadha. Her breath is her bull, and her mind her calf.

Notes: This is a meditation on speech or the Vedas since they personify speech. These four sounds are uttered while offering oblations to gods. Two, Svaha and Vasat, are made to the gods, and one, Svadha, is made to the ancestors. Hanta is uttered while offering food to the guests who are invited to the sacrifice.

Nineth Brahmana

The Digestive Fire Within the Body

1. ayam agnir vaisvanaro yo'yam antah puruse, yenedam annam pacyate yad idam adyate; tasyaisa ghoso bhavati yam etat karnav apidhaya srnoti, sa yadotkramisyan bhavati, nainam ghosam srnoti.

I. The fire that is within this person is the Vaisvanarah fire, which cooks (digests) the food that is eaten. Because of that, arises the sound one hears when the ears are closed thus. When this one is about to depart from here, he no longer hears the sound.

Notes: This is the meditation on fire as the subtle energy in the body, which is responsible for the bodily heat (tapas). The sound that one hears when both the ears are closed by the hands is the sound of the flow of prana or the subtle energy in the body, which is responsible for that heat. This heat or subtle energy comes from the food when it is digested and transformed into energy by the Vaisvanara fire. When a person dies, his body loses heat. Hence, he no longer hears the sound.

Tenth Brahmana

The Journey of Souls After Death

1. yada vai puruso'smal lokat praiti, sa vayum agacchati; tasmai sa tatra vijihite yatha ratha-cakrasya kham; tena sa urdhva akramate, sa adityam agacchati; tasmai sa tatra vijihite yatha lambarasya kham; tena sa urdhva akramate, sa candramasam agacchati, tasmai sa tatra vijihite yatha dundubheh kham; tena sa urdhva akramate, sa lokam agacchaty asokam ahimam; tasmin vasati sasvatih samah.

I. When a person does depart from this world, he reaches the air, which creates an opening for him, like the opening in a chariot wheel. Through that, he goes upwards and reaches the sun, who makes an opening for him like the opening in Lambara. Through that, he goes up and reaches the moon, who makes an opening for him like the opening in a Dundubhi. Through that, he goes up and reaches the world, which is without sorrow and without cold. There, he lives forever.

Notes: Lambara and Dundubhi are the names of ancient drums. Of the two, Dundubhi makes a much bigger noise and is usually used on important occasions such as a war or a large public ceremony. This verse describes the journey of a pious one who has realized Brahman through these meditations. When he departs from the words, the sun and the moon, which usually do not open up for everyone, open up and let the sage pass through them to the immortal world of Brahman, which is beyond them and which is free from sorrow and cold (death).

Eleventh Brahmana

Death and Illness as Austerities

1. etad vai paramam tapo yad vyahitas tapyate; paramam haiva lokam jayati, ya evam veda; etad vai paramam tapo yam pretam aranyam haranti; paramam haiva lokam jayati, ya evam veda; etad vai paramam tapo yam pretam agnav abhyadadhati. paramam haiva lokam jayati, ya evam veda.

I. This, indeed, is the highest austerity when a man is heated by illness. He who knows thus wins the highest world. This, indeed, is supreme austerity when they carry a dead person to the forest. He who knows thus wins the highest world. This, indeed, is the highest austerity a dead person is cremated in the fire. He who knows thus wins the highest world.

Notes: Sickness should be considered a form of austerity since through the suffering caused by the illness, the sick person pays for his past karma and cleanses himself. He should, therefore, stay positive during that suffering rather than feeling dejected or fearful. Similarly, a dying person should not be worried about death. He should consider death as his Vanaprastha (journey to the forest before renunciation). He who knows and acts likewise will attain better worlds like a yogi who performs penances and austerities.

Twelfth Brahmana

The Interconnection Between Food and Breath

1. annam brahma ity eka ahuh, tan na tatha, puyati va annam rte pranat; prano brahma ity eka ahuh, tan na tatha, susyati vai prana rte'nnat, ete ha tv eva devate, ekadhabhuyam bhutva, paramatam gacchatah tadd ha smaha pratrdah pitaram, kim svid evaivam viduse sadhu kuryam, kim evasma asadhu kuryam iti. sa ha smaha panina: ma pratrda, kas tv enayor ekadha bhuyam bhutva paramatam gacchatiti. tasma u haitad uvaca;

vi, iti; annam vai vi; anne himani sarvani bhutani vistani; ram iti prano vai ram, prane himani sarvani bhutani ramante; sarvani ha va asmin bhutani visanti, sarvani bhutani ramante, ya evam veda. iti dvadasam brahmanam

I. Food is Brahman; this is one opinion. It is not so because food decomposes without breath. Therefore, breath is Brahman; this is another opinion. It is not so because breath dries up without food. Indeed, when these two deities are united into one, they attain the highest. Therefore, Patrada said to his father, "What good, indeed, may I do to him who knows this, and what evil may I do to him?" " With the gesture of his hand, his father said to him, "Oh no, Patrada, who can indeed attain the highest state by being united with these two?" Then he said to him, "This is Vi. Food, indeed, is Vi, for all these beings depend upon food only. This is Ram. Breath, indeed, is Ram, for all beings delight in breath." All beings rest in him, and all beings take delight in him who knows this."

Notes: Meditation on food and breath may lead to the realization that they are not Brahman because both are perishable. However, they should not be ignored or slighted since they do serve an important purpose in creation. They both support and sustain life. People depend upon food for nourishment. They enjoy life as long as they breathe. They sleep and rest well because of the food they eat and the air they breathe. Thus, existence and enjoyment, and even liberation, are not possible without them. Therefore, even if they are not Brahman, they are still important and deserve respect because beings depend upon them and are sustained by them until they attain the highest and leave the world.

Thirteenth Brahmana

Breath as Ukta, the Hymn of Praise

1. uktham; prano va uktham, prano hidam sarvam utthapayati. uddhasmad uktha-vid viras tisthati, ukthasya sayujyam salokatam jayati, ya evam veda.

I. Regarding (the meditation on) the hymn of praise, breath, indeed, is the hymn of praise, for it is the breath which uplifts all this. From him who knows this arises a son who knows the hymn of praise. By means of the hymn praise, he who knows, thus, achieves union with (the presiding deities of) Ukta and an abode in the same world.

Notes: Uktha means speech or utterance. Uktham means uttering eulogy or praise, usually a reference to chanting the hymns of the Rigveda during Soma rituals. The chanting requires a lot of breathing power. The verse says that whoever knows the subtle energy that flows in the chanting of the Ukta and excels in the chanting will obtain a son who will also be well-versed in it. That son, he so begets with the help of the presiding deities of the Soma rituals (Indra, Soma, Varuna, etc.), will help his father unite the subtle breath energy flowing in his body with the auspicious energy flowing in the Ukta, enjoy the bliss of the intoxicating Soma juice, and reside in the same world as the deities. Sayujyam means union, and Salokyam means living in the same world.

2. yajuh. prano vai yajuh, prane himani sarvani bhutani yujyante; yujyante hasmai sarvani bhutani sraisthyaya. yajusah sayujyam salokatam jayati, ya evam veda.

2. Regarding (meditation on) the hymns of Yajurveda, breath, indeed, is Yaju (the hymn of Yajurveda), for all beings are united by it. Indeed, all beings become united for the eminent or superior person who knows this, and he achieves union with (the deities of) Yajus and an abode in the same world.

Notes: Whoever knows that the mystic power hidden in the Yajus, the mystic formulas of the Yajurveda, is the same subtle energy that flows in breath, achieves preeminence in chanting them, unites his subtle breath energy with the energy flowing in them, and attains the same world as their presiding deities. It is because the same energy flows in them.

3. sama: prano vai sama, prane himani sarvani bhutani samyanci; samyanci hasmai sarvani bhutani sraisthyaya kalpante. samnah sayujyam salokatam jayati, ya evam veda.

3. Regarding the hymns of Samaveda, breath is, indeed, the song of the Samaveda. In breath, all beings are united. United, indeed, all beings become for his eminence who knows thus and by means of Samans, he achieves union with (the presiding deities of) Samans and wins the same world.

Notes: Whoever knows that the subtle breath energy that flows in his body is the same as the energy that flows from the Samans when they are sung achieves preeminence in singing Samans, unites his energy with the energy flowing in the Samans and attains the same world as their presiding deities who also possess the same energy.

4. ksatram: prano vai ksatram, prano hi vai ksatram: trayate hainam pranah ksanitoh. pra ksatram atram apnoti, ksatrasya sayujyam salokatam jayati, ya evam veda.

4. Regarding the (meditation on the) body, breath, indeed, is the body. This body is sustained by breath alone. Breath protects the body from injury and decay. He who knows thus attains a body that needs no protection; and by means of the body, he achieves liberation and wins its associated world.

Notes: By knowing the connection between the body and the auspicious, healing, and cleansing power of the breath energy, one attains a strong body that will help him withstand the ordeals of renunciation and austerities and achieve liberation. He achieves the same world as the breath, which is the immortal world of Brahman. Thus, meditating on the prana that flows in the body is more powerful and liberating than meditating and uniting with the power hidden in the Uktas, Yajus, and Samans. Perhaps, if they meditate on them without duality as the all-pervading power of Brahman, they may achieve the same results.

Fourteenth Brahmana

The Four Feet of Gayatri

1. bhumir antariksam dyauh ity astav aksarani; astaksaram ha va ekam gayatryai padam. etad u haivasya etat, sa yavad esu trisu lokesu, tavaddha jayati, yo'sya etad evam padam veda.

1. The earth, the mid-region, and the heaven - these represent the eight syllables. Eight syllables, indeed, make up one foot of the Gayatri meter. So, this (foot of eight syllables) makes up that (three worlds). He who knows the foot of the Gayatri as such wins up to the end of the three worlds.

Notes: Gayatri is the most auspicious of the Vedic mantras. It protects the reciters from physical and mental harm by creating a shield of Savitur's light around their bodies. Whoever chants this mantra becomes a Brahman by virtue of its cleansing and elevating power. According to Shankara, those who chant it will attain the birth of a Brahmana in the next life. By chanting it, a person born as a Brahmana becomes a Dvija, the twice-born. This verse suggests that by chanting this mantra, one will attain the three worlds that it represents: Bhur, Bhuva, and Suva.

2. rco yajumsi samani, ity astav aksarani; astaksaram ha va ekam gayatrai padam. etad u haivasya etat. sa yavadiyam trayi vidya, tavad ha jayati. yo'sya etad evam padam veda.

2. Rcha, Yajumsi, and Samani are eight syllables. Eight syllables, indeed, make up the one foot of the Gayatri meter. So, this (foot of eight syllables) makes up that (three Vedas). He who knows the foot of the Gayatri as such wins the knowledge of the three Vedas up to the end.

3. prano'pano vyanah, ity astav aksarani; astaksaram ha va ekam gayatrai padam: etad u haivasya etat. sa yavad idam prani, tavad ha jayati yo'sya etad evam padam veda. athasya etad eva turiyam darsatam padam paroraja ya esa tapati; yad vai caturtham tat turiyam; darsatam padam iti, dadrsa iva. hy esah; paroraja iti, sarvam u hy evaisa raja upari upari tapati. evam haiva sriya, yasasa tapati, yo'sya etad evam padam veda.

3. *Prana, Apana, and Vyana are the eight syllables. Eight syllables, indeed, make up the one foot of the Gayatri meter. So, this (foot of eight syllables) makes up that (the three breaths). He who knows the foot of the Gayatri as such wins up to the end of the three breaths. The visible foot beyond the dark skies that glows with intense heat is indeed the fourth foot of this (Gayatri). That which is the fourth (feet) is that Turiya. It is the visible foot because it is visible indeed. He is called above the dark skies because he glows with intense heat up and above every darkness. He who knows that foot of it as such, he shines in fame and fortune with the same glow.*

Notes: The visible foot of Gayatri is Aditya, the solar deity, who shines in the sky. He is called Paroraja (above the dark skies) because he is the same as the transcendental overlord who shines in our consciousness beyond the dark cloud of the impurities of the mind and body. Therefore, whoever knows him shines like him.

4. saisa gayatry etasmims turiye darsate pade parorajasi pratisthita, tad vai tat satye pratisthitam; caksur vai satyam, caksur hi vai satyam; tasmad yad idanim dvau vivadamanav eyatam aham adarsam, aham asurausam iti. ya evam bruyat; aham adarsam iti, tasma eva sraddadhyama. tad vai tat satyam bale pratisthitam; prano vai balam; tat prane pratisthitam; tasmad ahuh: balam satyad ogiya iti. evam vesa gayatry adhyatmam. pratisthita sa haisa gayams tatre; prana vai gahah; tat pranams tatre; tad yad gayams tatre, tasmad gayatri nama. sa yam evamum savitrim anvaha, esaiva sa. sa yasma anvaha, tasya pranams trayate.

4. *That Gayatri rests on the fourth visible foot, which rests high above the dark skies. That, again, rests on truth (Sat). The eye, indeed, is truth, for by the eyes only, truth (is perceived). Therefore, even today, if two persons are engaged in a dispute saying "I have seen" and "I have heard," we should keep faith in the one who says, "I have seen." Truth also rests on strength. Breath, verily, is strength. It rests upon breath. Therefore, they say, strength is stronger than truth. Thus does Gayatri rest within oneself. That Gayatri protects the Gayas. The Gayas are the breaths. It protects the breaths. Since it protects the Gayas, hence it is named Gayatri. That Savitr verse, which is taught, it is just this. To whomsoever it is taught, it protects his breaths.*

Notes: Truth (Sat) rests upon the eyes means eyes do not lie. They show you the truth or what is. Strength is more powerful than truth means with strength, a person who wields power and authority can force others to accept his words even if they are untrue. People do not like to cross him and incur his displeasure. Therefore, he prevails even if he is dishonest and evil. Gayas are the breaths. Gayatri is prana, the subtle energy. Therefore, the chanting of the Gayatri protects the breath channels and ensures the free circulation of prana through them.

5. tam haitam eke savritrim anustubham anvahuh: vag anustup; etad vacam anubruma iti. na tatha kuryat. gayatrim eva savitrim anubruyat. yadi ha va apy evam-vid bahv iva pratigrhnati, na haivatad gayatrya ekam cana padam prati.

5. Some teach the Savitri verse as Anustubh, "Speech is Anustubh. We impart that speech." However, one should not do it. Gayatri alone should be imparted as Savitri. If a person who knows this receives (gifts or food) even excessively, it does not amount to even one foot of the Gayatri.

Notes: Gayatri should not be sung in the Anustubh meter, equated with speech, or attributed to Saraswati, the goddess of speech. It should be sung in the Gayatri meter, equated with breath (prana), and attributed to goddess Savitri only since they are the source of prana that supports speech. He who knows thus, even if you give him many gifts, it does not equal to what he deserves.

6. sa ya imams trin lokan purnan pratigrhniyat, so'sya etat prathamam padam apnuyat; atha yavatiyam trayi vidya, yas tavat pratigrhniyat, so'sya etad dvitiyam padam apnuyat; atha yavad idam prani, yas tavat pratigrhniyat, so'sya etat trtiyam padam apnuyat, athasya etad eva turiyam darsatam padam, poroja ya esa tapati, naiva kenacanapyam; kuta u etavat pratigrhniyat.

6. He who receives as much as the entire wealth of the three worlds as a gift, that would be like receiving for the first foot only. Now, he who receives as much as the knowledge of the triple Vedas, that would be like receiving for the second foot. Now, he who receives as much as all the living beings, that would be like receiving for the third foot. Now, the fourth foot, which is visible and which glows with intense heat high above the dark skies is not attainable by anyone whatsoever. Then, who can receive anything for that?

Notes: All the wealth in the three worlds will not be equal to the wealth one gains by knowing the four feet of Gayatri. Even if we assume that all the wealth in the three worlds is equal to the triple feet of Gayatri, nothing can match the wealth of the fourth foot represented by Brahman, the resplendent sun, who shines beyond the dark clouds. Why? Because he is limitless.

7. tasya upasthanam: gayatri, asy eka-padi dvi-padi tri-padi catus-pady a-pad asi, na hi padyase. namas te turiyaya darsa-taya padaya parorajase; asav ado ma prapad iti; yam dvisyat, asav asmai kamo ma samrddhiti va; na haivasmai sa kamah

samrddhyate yasma evam upatisthate; aham adah prapam iti va.

7. Of that, this is the adoration, "O Gayatri, you are one-footed, two-footed, three-footed, and four-footed. You are without feet, for indeed you are indivisible. Salutations to you, the fourth foot, which is visible and which is high above the dark sky. May the enemy never attain his desired wish. He who bears hatred towards anyone may (sing Gayatri and) say, "May such and such person's desire never flourish," indeed, that desire of him will never flourish against whom he renders the service of Gayatri with those remarks. Or he may say, "May I attain that (wish of his)."

Notes: According to this verse, any positive or negative wish expressed after uttering the Gayatri chant during the prayers to the sun comes to fruition. Such is the power of Gayatri. Upastanam means adoration, salutation, or method of attendance, service, remembrance, worship, meditation, or reverence associated with the Sandhya Vandanam, evening adoration of the sun.

8. etadd ha vai taj janako vaideho buḍilam asvatarasvim uvaca: yan nu ho tad gayatri-vid abruthah, atha katham hasti bhuto vahasiti. mukham hy asyah, samrat, na vidam cakara, iti hovaca; tasya agnir eva mukham: yadi ha va api bahu ivagnau abhyadadhati, sarvam eva tat samdahati; evam haivaivam-vid yady api bahv iva papam kurute, sarvam eva tat sampsaya suddhah puto'jaro'mrtah sambhavati. iti caturdasam brahmanam

8. Regarding this, Janaka of Videha, said to Budila Asvatarasvi, "Well, you declared yourself as a knower of the Gayatri. Then, how come you are carrying me like an elephant?" "Because I do not know its mouth, O Emperor," he said. "Fire, indeed, is its mouth. Truly, indeed, even when they pour large quantities of fuel into the fire, it burns it all. Similarly, he who knows this, even if he commits a great many sins, (he) burns them all and becomes pure, clean, imperishable, and immortal.

Notes: Budila knew some aspects of Gayatri but lacked complete knowledge. When King Janaka pointed this out, he replied that he did not know its mouth. The King then explained to him the fire was its mouth. The symbolism is that chanting Gayatri with full knowledge of its four feet and mouth has the same beneficent merit as performing a fire sacrifice. In this section, Gayatri, with the description of its four feet, is equated with Brahman, who is also described as four-footed and compared to a horse in the opening verse of this Upanishad.

Chapter 5
Fifteenth Brahmana

Prayer to Pusan and Agni by a Dying Person

1. hiranmayena patrena satyasyapihitam muktam: tat tvam, pusan, apavrnu, satya-dharmaya drstaye.

1. The face of Truth is concealed by a golden vessel. That you, Pusan, please remove so that I, who love truth and duty, may see it.

Notes: This is the prayer of a dying person to Sat Brahman, the fourth foot of Gayatri, who shines above and beyond the dark clouds. Whoever knows him attains the highest world. On the death bed, he is now praying to Brahman, addressing him as Pusan and Agni, and reminding him that all his life, he lived truthfully and discharged his duties. Therefore, he is now requesting him to remove the obstacles and absolve him of his past sins so that he may reach him and join him. A similar prayer is found in the Isa Upanishad also. The golden vessel is the sun's shining orb or disc in the sky. Brahman, the Cosmic Person, is hidden behind it. The dying person is requesting him to remove it so that he can see him clearly.

2. pusann, ekarse, yama, surya, praja-patya, vyuha rasmin samuha, tejah yat te rupam kalyanatamam, tat te pasyami yo sav asau purusas, so'ham asmi.

2. O Pusan, O one traveler, O controller, O Sun, O son of Prajapati, remove your rays, withdraw your vigorous heat, so that I may see your most benign and auspicious form. The person who is there in the Sun, that I am also.

Notes: He wants the sun to reduce his intensity so that he may see him without difficulty during his heavenward journey and the Person (the Self) in him can reach him and join him.

3. vayur anilam amrtam athedam bhasmantam sariram: aum krato smara, krtam smara, krato smara, krtam smara.

3. May this breath reach the immortal breath! Now, let this body end in ashes. Aum! O Mind! Remember, remember, what has been done. O Mind! Remember, remember, what has been done.

Notes: The dying person wants to dissolve his energy (prana) in its source, Brahman's indestructible and inexhaustible energy. As the body begins to burn, he wishes the presiding deity of his mind to remember all the good deeds he performed in this life so that they stand testimony to his truthfulness and help him reach Sat Brahman.

4. agne naya supatha, raye asman; visvani, deva, vayunani vidvan; yuyodhy asmaj juharanam eno: bhuyistham te nama-uktim vidhema.

4. *O Agni, O god, knower of all our thoughts and deeds, may you lead us along the auspicious path by virtue of the fruit of our good karma. Remove from us all crooked and deceitful sins. We offer you many words of obeisance.*

Notes: Fire is a purifier. During cremation, the last sacrifice in a human being's life, the body is consumed and cleansed by fire. The departing soul is now praying to Agni and requesting him to cleanse him of his past sins and lead him along the auspicious Path of liberation towards Sat Brahman, who shines beyond the dark clouds.

Chapter 6

First Brahmana

Breath is Superior to the Organs of the Body

1. aum. yo ha vai jyestham ca srestham ca veda, jyesthas ca srestha ca svanam bhavati, prano vai jyesthas ca, sresthas ca, jyesthas ca sresthas ca svanam bhavati; api ca yesam bubhusati, ya evam veda.

I. Aum. Truly, he who knows the oldest and the best becomes the oldest and the best among his own relations. Breath, indeed, is the oldest and the best. He who knows this as such becomes the oldest and the best among his own relations as well as those among whom he wishes to be such.

Notes: The vital force (prana) existed even before creation and even before the Cosmic Purusha manifested. It exists in the fetus even before the organs are formed, and it exists even in the reproductive material before they are united. Hence, prana, the life force, the subtle energy that pervades the whole universe, is the oldest and the best.

2. yo ha vai vasistham veda, vasisthah svanam bhavati vag vai vasistha, vasisthah svanam bhavati. api ca yesam bhubhusati ya evam veda.

2. He who knows the most excellent becomes the most excellent among his own relations. Speech, indeed, is the oldest. He who knows this as such becomes the most excellent among his own relations as well as among those whom he wishes to be as such.

Notes: Through speech and erudition, or the knowledge of the Vedas, for the Vedas are but the personification of speech only, one becomes excellent (Vasishta) and famous in his family and community.

3. yo ha vai pratistham veda, pratitisthati same, pratitisthati durge; caskur vai pratistha; caksusa hi same ca durge ca pratitisthati. pratitisthati same, pratitisthati durge, ya evam veda.

3. He who knows the stable remains stable in even conditions and remains stable in uneven conditions. The eye, indeed, is the stable, for with the eye only, one is able to remain stable on even and uneven grounds. He who knows this as such remains stable in even conditions, and stable in uneven conditions.

Notes: Pratishta means firmly established. However, it also means a higher position or status among people. The eye represents direct knowledge (Pratyaksha). He who excels in seeing things as they are excels in discernment, truthfulness, and sameness. He will be respected by people for his knowledge and wisdom.

4. yo ha vai sampadam veda, sam hasmai padyate, yam kamam kamayate; srotram vai sampat; srotre hime sarve veda abhisampannah. sam hasmai padyate, yam kamam kamayate, ya evam veda.

4. He who knows the source of wealth attains whatever desire he desires. The ear, indeed, is the source of wealth, for one becomes endowed with the wealth of the Vedas through the ear only. He who knows this as such attains whatever desire he desires.

Notes: In the past, the Vedas were learned by listening only. Hence, for a Brahmana, the ear was the source of wealth. Even now, if you listen to others, you will understand others well and improve your effectiveness.

5. yo ha va ayatanam veda, ayatanam svanam bhavati, ayatanam jananam mano va ayatanam, ayatanam svanam bhavati ayatanam jananam, ya evam veda.

5. He who knows the abode becomes an abode for his own relations as well as an abode for other people. The mind, indeed, is the abode. He who knows this as such becomes an abode for his own relations and for other people.

6. yo ha vai prajatim veda, prajayate ha prajaya pasubhih reto vai prajatih, prajayate ha prajaya pasubhih, ya evam veda.

6. He who knows the source of procreation procreates offspring and creates more cattle (by knowing their method of impregnation). Semen, verily, is the source of procreation. He who knows this as such procreates offspring and creates more cattle.

7. te heme pranah, aham sreyase vivadamanah brahma jagmuh; tadd hocuh; ko no vasistha iti. tadd hovaca, yasmin va utkranta idam sariram papiyo manyate, sa vo vasistha iti.

7. The breaths (organs), disputing among themselves, "I am the best," went to Brahma. They said, "Who is the most excellent (Vasishta) among us?" He said, "Upon anyone among you departing if the body is considered impure, he is the most excellent."

8. vag ghoccakrama: sa samvatsaram prosya, agatya, uvaca. katham asakata mad rte jivitum iti; te hocuh; yatha kalah avadanto vaca, pranantah pranena, pasyantas caksusa, srnvantah srotrena, vidvamso manasa, prajayamana retasa, evam ajivismeti, pravivesa ha vak.

8. *Speech went away. After staying away for a year, it returned and asked, "How was life without me?" They said, "Just like the dumb, without using speech, but breathing with the breath, seeing with the eye, hearing with the ear, knowing with the mind, and procreating with the semen. Thus, we have lived." Speech entered back.*

9. caksur hoccakrama, tat samavatsaram prosya, agatya, uvaca katham asakata mad rte jivitum iti, te hocuh yathandhah, apasyantas caksusa, prahantah pranena, vadanto vaca, srnvantah srotrena, vidvamso manasa, prajayamana retasa, evam ajivismeti, pravivesa ha caksuh.

9. *The eye went away. After staying away for a year, it returned and asked, "How was life without me?" They said, "Just like the blind, without using sight, but breathing with the breath, speaking with the speech, hearing with the ear, knowing with the mind, and procreating with the semen. Thus, we have lived." The eye entered back.*

10. srotram hoccakrama. tat samvatsaram porsya, agatya uvaca, katham asakata mad rte jivitium iti, te hocuh; yatha badhirah asrnvantah srotrena, pranantah pranena, vadanto vaca, pasyantas caksusa, vidvamso manasa, prajayamana retasa, evam ajivismeti. pravivesa ha srotram.

10. *The ear went away. After staying away for a year, it returned and asked, "How was life without me?" They said, "Just like the deaf, without using hearing, but breathing with the breath, speaking with the speech, seeing with the eye, knowing with the mind, and procreating with the semen. Thus, we have lived." The ear entered back.*

11. mano hoccakaram. tat samvatsaram prosya, agatya, uvaca, katham asakata mad rte jivitum iti, te hocuh. yatha mugdha avidvamso manasa, pranantah pranena, vadanto vaca, pasyantah caksusa, srnvantah srotrena, prajayamana retasa, evam ajivismeti, pravivesa ha manah.

11. *The mind went away. After staying away for a year, it returned and asked, "How was life without me?" They said, "Just like the deluded, without knowing with the mind, but breathing with the breath, speaking with the speech, seeing with the eye, hearing with the ear, and procreating with the semen. Thus, we have lived." The mind entered back.*

12. reto hoccakrama, tat samvatsaram prosya, agatya, uvaca: katham asakata mad rte jivitum iti. te hocuh, yatha klibah, aprajayamana retasa, pranantah pranena, vadanto vaca, pasyantah caksusa, srvnvantah srotrena, vidvamso manasa, evam ajivismeti pravivesa ha retah.

12. Semen went away. After staying away for a year, it returned and asked, "How was life without me?" They said, "Just like the childless, unable to procreate with the semen, but breathing with the breath, speaking with the speech, seeing with the eye, hearing with the ear, and knowing with the mind. Thus, we have lived." Then semen entered back.

13. atha ha prana utkramisyan, yatha maha-su-hayah saidhavah, padvisa-sankhun samvrhet, evam haiveman pranan samvarha. te hocuh: ma bhagavah utkramih, ha vai saksyamas tvad rte jivitum it tasyo me balim kuruteti tatheti.

13. Now, as the breath tried to go away, just as a great and well-bred horse from the land of Sindhu might pull out the pegs to which his feet are tied, it pulled out all the breaths (organs). They said, "Godman, please do not depart. Without you, we cannot live." "Then give me my share of the offering." "Yes, we do."

Notes: Bali means sacrificial offering. In the case of the body, it is the share of the food and its resultant energy shared by the organs. This story should not be interpreted literally. It is meant to convey the importance of breath and the fact that the body remains alive as long as breath circulates in it. The importance of anything or any person is known only by its absence.

14. sa ha vag uvaca: yad va aham vasisthasmi, tvam tad vasistho siti. yad va aham pratisthasmi, tvam tat pratistho'si ti caksuh. yad va aham sampad asmi tvam tat sampad asi iti srotram. yad va aham ayatanam asmi, tvam tad ayatanam asi, iti manah; yad va aham prajatir asmi, tvam tat prajatir asi, iti retah, tasyo me kim annam, kim vasa iti, tat te annam; apo vasa iti. na ha va asyan annam jagdham bhavati, nanannam pratigrahitam, ya evam etad anasyannam veda, tad vidvamsah srotriya asisyanta acamanti, asitvacamanti, etam eva tad anam anagnam kurvanto manyante.

14. Speech said, "In which I am the most excellent, in that you are the most excellent.

The eye said, "In which I am stable, in that you are stable."

The ear said, "In which I am wealthy, in that you are wealthy."

The mind said, "In which I am the abode, in that you are the abode,"

The reproductive organ said, "In which I am the source of procreation, in that, you are the source of procreation."

"If that is so, then what is my food? What is my abode?"

"Whatever food is here (in this body) is your food. Whatever water is here (in this body) is your abode."

Whoever knows this as the food of breath never eats anything that is not food and never receives it as an offering that is not food. Therefore, wise men who recite the Vedas regularly take a sip of water before eating and take a sip after eating. By doing it, they think they remove the nakedness of breath.

Notes: The organs made peace with breath and offered their tributes, acknowledging it as the lord in the body; food should not be eaten without sipping water. It is well known that water is as important as food to keep one's breath going. Water is also important for digestion. According to the Vedas, the food consumed by the body and digested in the stomach by the Vaisvanara digestive fire is taken up by breath (prana) first and circulated among the various organs in the body according to their due share. The process is more or less similar to the manner in which the sacrificial offerings are distributed among the various deities by Fire (Agni) according to their due share.

Second Brahmana

The Path of Gods and the Path of Ancestors

1. svetaketur ha va aruneyah pancalanam parisadam ajagama. sa ajagama jaivalim pravahanam paricarayamanam. tam udiksya, abhyuvada, kumara iti. sa, bhoh, iti partisusrava anusisto nv asi pitreti, aum iti hovaca.

I. Svetaketu Aruneya went to the assembly of the Panchalas. He went to Pravahana Jaivali, who was being attended by his servants. Seeing him, he said, "Yes, young man?"

He replied, "Yes, sir."

"Have you been taught by your father?"

"Yes, sir," he said.

2. vettah yathcmah pajah prayatyo vipratipadyante , iti. na iti hovaca. vetho yatemam lokam punar apadyante, iti. na it haivovaca. vetho yathasau loka evam bahubhih punah punah prayabhir na sampuryate iti. na iti haivovaca. vetho yatihyam ahutyam hutayam apah purusa-vaco bhutva samutthaya vadanti, iti. na iti haivovaca. vetho deva-yanasya va pathah pratipadam pitr-yanasya va, yat krtva deva-yanam va panthanam pratipadyante pitr-yanam va. api hi rscr vacah srutam. dve srti asrnavam pitrnam aham devanam uta martyanam;

Chapter 6

tabhyam idam visvam ejat sameti yad antara pitaram mataram ca. iti naham ata ekam cana veda, iti hovaca.

2. "Do you know in what manner people go in different directions after they depart from here?"

"No, sir, "he said.

"Do you know how they return to this world?"

"No, sir," he said.

"Do you know why the other world is not filled even after many people go there again and again.?"

"No, sir, "he said.

"Do you know after how many offerings of oblations water rises up to become the voice of the (offering) person?

"No, sir," he said.

"Do you know the way to the path of gods and the way to the path of ancestors? And by doing what one obtains the path of gods or the path of the ancestors? We have, indeed, heard the words of the seers, 'I have heard of two paths, that which goes to the ancestors and that which goes to the gods. By these two, all that lives moves on, whatever that arises between a father and a mother.'"

He said, "I do not know any of that."

Notes: After being tutored by his father, Svetaketu went to the court of Pravahana Jaivali, proud of his learning and confident that he would prove his erudition and earn some gifts from the King. The King, in his wisdom, raised a few questions about the paths by which the souls departed to the other worlds, challenging the young student's knowledge, asking him five questions. The student had no answer. This story is also found in the Chandogya Upanishad (5.3). What his father, Uddalaka Aruni, taught him is described in the sixth chapter of the same Upanishad.

3. athainam vasatyopamantrayam cakre anadrtya vasatim kumarah pradudrava, sa ajagama pitaram, tam hovaca. Iti vava kila no bhavan puranusistan avocado iti; katham sumedha, iti. panca ma prasnan rajanya-bandhur apraksit; tato naikam cana vedeti: katame ta iti. ima iti ha pratikany udajahara.

3. Then he invited him to stay. Disregarding the invitation, the boy left in a hurry. He went to his father. He said to him, "You did, indeed, tell me before that I was fully instructed."

"Why you say so, wise one?"

"Five questions that royal acquaintance of ours asked me, and I did not know even one."

"Which are they?"

"These," he repeated the main points.

4. sa hovaca: tatha nas tvam, tata, janitha, yatha yad aham kim ca veda sarvam aham tat tubhyam avocam. prehi tu tara pratiya, brahmacaryam vatsyava iti. bavan eva gacchatu iti. sa ajagama gautamo yatra pravahansasya jaivaler asa. tasma asanam ahrtya udakam aharayam cakara; atha hasma arghyam cakara; tam hovaca, varam bhagavate gautamaya dadma iti.

4. He said, "This you should know, my son. As much as I know, all that I have spoken to you. But let us go and live there as students practicing celibacy." "You may go alone, sir." Thereupon, Gautama went to where Pravahana Jaivali lived. He offered him a seat, arranged for him water, and gave him a respectful welcome due to a venerable person. Then he said, "A boon, Godman Gautama, we offer you."

Notes: Svetaketu's responses here and in the previous verse show that he was angry and uninterested in pursuing knowledge. Unlike him, his father went to the King with humility to learn from him the answers to his questions.

5. sa hovaca: pratijnato ma esa varah; yam tu kumarasyante vacam abhasathah, tam me brhuiti.

5. He said, "You have made up your mind to give me a boon. Please tell me about the statements you made in the presence of my son

6. sa hovaca: daivesu vai, gautama, tad varesu; manusanam bruhiti.

6. He said, "That boon, indeed, is for gods only. Please ask for a boon that is suitable for humans."

7. sa hovaca: vijnayate ha asti hiranyasyapattam, go-asvanam dasinum pravaranam paridhanasya; ma no bhavan bahor anantasyaparyantasyabhyavadanyo bhud iti. sa vai, Gautama, tirthenechasa iti. upaimy aham bhavantam. Iti vaca ha smaiva purva upayanti. sa hopayana-kirtyovasa.

7. He said, "You know that I have plenty of gold, cattle, horses, maidservants, attendants, and dresses. Please do not be ungenerous towards me about that which is plentiful, infinite, and unlimited."

"Then, Gautama, you must seek it in the right manner."

"I come to you." Indeed, the ancients used to approach a teacher with this declaration. So, he lived with that announcement to earn the recognition of having served his master.

Notes: Gautama was a Brahmana. Pravahana Jaivali was a Kshatriya. In the Vedic period, if a Brahmana wanted to learn from a Kshatriya teacher, all he had to do was approach the teacher with this declaration, "I come to you as a pupil." The teacher had to accept him as his student without further scrutiny. The student also had no obligation to touch his feet, serve in his household, or personally attend to him.

8. sa hovaca: tatha nas tvam, Gautama, maparadhas tava ca pitamaha yatha, iyam vidyetah purvam na kasmims can brahmana uvasa; tam tv aham tubhyam vaksyami. ko hi tvaivam bruvantam arhati prayakhyatum iti.

8. The King said, "Please do not take offense, Gautama, just as your forefathers never did. In the past, this knowledge never rested with a Brahmana. But I shall teach it to you, for who can refuse you when you speak like this?

Notes: The teacher tradition associated with this teaching remained with the Kshatriyas for several generations. Hence, Pravahana Jaivali was reluctant to admit a Brahmana as a student and break that tradition.

9. asau vai loko agnih gautama. tasyaditya eva samit, rasmayo dhumah, ahar arcih, diso'ngarah, avantaradiso visphulingah; tasminn etasminn agnau devah sraddham juhvati; tasya ahutyai somo raja sambhavati.

9. That world, O Gautama, is fire. The sun itself is its fuel. The rays are its smoke, the day its flame, the quarters its coal, and the intermediate quarters its sparks. In this fire, the gods pour faith as the oblation. Out of that offering manifests Soma, the king.

Notes: The sacrifice from which the ancient gods manifested Soma, the Lord of the Moon, is compared to the Agnihotra (fire) sacrifice and the moon (ancestral world) to Ahavaiya fire. In that sacrifice, gods poured faith as oblation, which resulted in the creation of the ancestral world with Soma (moon) as its lord. This world is obtained by humans through sacrifices only.

10. Prajanyo va agnih Gautama. Tasya samvatsara eva samit, abhrani dhumah, vidyud arcih, asanir angarah, hradunayo visphulingah, tasminn etasminn agnau devah somani rajanam juhvati; tasya ahutyai vrstih sambhavati.

10. Prajanya, O Gautama, is fire. The year itself is its fuel. The cloud, its smoke, the lightning, its flame, the thunder, its coal, and the rum-

bling, its sparks. In this second fire, the gods sacrificed King Soma (produced from the first sacrifice) as the oblation. Out of that sacrifice, rain manifested.

Notes: Prajanya is the god of rain. In this second fire sacrifice, gods poured Soma oblation to produce rain and nourish the earth.

11. ayam vai loko'gnih, gautam. Tasya prthivy eva samit, agnir dhumah, ratrir arcih, candrama angarah, nakstrani visphulingah; tasminn etasminn agnau deva vrstim juhvati; tasya ahutya annam sambhavti.

11. This world, O Gautama, is fire. The earth itself is its fuel. The (earthly) fire, its smoke, the night, its flame, the moon, its coal, and the stars, its sparks. In this fire, the gods pour rain as the oblation. Out of that offering, food manifests.

Notes: In this third sacrifice, gods sacrificed Parjanya, produced from the second sacrifice, as oblation to produce food.

12. puruso va agnih, Gautama. Tasya vyattam eva samit, prano dhumah, vag arcih, caksur angarah, srotram visphlingah, tasminn etasminn agnau deva annam juhvati, tasya ahutyai retah sambhavati.

12. The person, O Gautama, is fire. The open mouth itself is its fuel. Breath is its smoke, speech, its flame, the eye, its coal, and the ears, its sparks. In this fire, the gods pour food as the oblation. Out of that offering, semen manifests.

Notes: In this fourth sacrifice, gods poured food that was produced from the third sacrifice as the oblation. From that, semen manifested. Food is the source of all the energy in the body. It is also the source of reproductive materials.

13. yosa va agnih, gautama. tasya upastha eva samit, lomani dhumah, yonir arcih, yad antah karoti te'ngarah, abhianda vishphulingah; tasmin etasminn agnau deva reto juhavati, tasya ahutyai pursah sambhavati, sa jivati yavaj jivati. atha yada mriyate.

13. The woman, O Gautama, is fire. Her sexual organ itself is the fuel. The hairs are its smoke, the womb its flame, what is placed inside the coals, and the sensations of pleasure its sparks. In this fire, the gods pour semen as the oblation. Out of that offering manifests a person. He lives for the span of his life. When he dies.

Notes: All the jivas are born from sacrifices only, just as rain, food, this world, the world of ancestors, and the heaven of Indra. Who are the gods? In the body, they are the organs. In the macrocosm, they are the ancient gods of the unknown past who served as priests in the sacrifice performed by Brahma Prajapati, the First Cosmic Purusha to manifest creation. This verse describes the birth of a human being from the union between a man and a woman. The woman is fire. Into that fire, the gods (organs) pour semen.

14. athainam agnaye haranti. tasyagnir evagnir bhavati, samit samit dhumo dhumah, arcir arcih, angara angarah, visphulinga visphulingah, tasminn etasminn agnau evah purusam juvahati; tasya ahutyai puruso bhasvara-varnah sambhavati.

14. They carry him as an offering to fire. That fire becomes his fire, the fuel his fuel, the smoke his smoke, the flame his flame, the coals his coals, and the sparks his sparks. In this fire, the gods pour the person as the oblation. Out of that offering manifests a person of radiant color.

Notes: When a person dies, he is offered to fire as the last sacrifice of his life. In this sacrifice, the person, or the jiva, becomes the offering. From that offering emerges the embodied Self, ready to depart to another world.

15. te ya evam etad viduh, ye cami aranye sraddam satyam upasate, te'rcir abhisambhavanti, arciso'hah, ahna apurya manapaksam, apuryamana-paksad yan san masan udann aditya eti masebhyo deva-lokam, deva-lokad adityam, adityad vaidyutam, tan vaidyutan puruso manasa etya brahma-lokan gamayati, tesu brahma-lokesu parah paravato vasanti. Tesam na punar avrttih.

15. Those who know this and those who meditate upon this truth in the forests with faith - they pass into the region of light rays. From the region of light rays into the day, from the day into the fortnight of the waxing moon, from the fortnight of the waxing moon into the six months during which the sun flies northward, from these months into the world of gods, from the world of gods into the sun, and from the sun into the lightning. Then, a mind-born (son of Brahma) goes to that world of lightning and leads them to the world of Brahman. In those worlds of Brahman, they live for very long periods. Of them, none returns.

Notes: The day, the fortnight, and the first six months of the year refer to the time during which the souls ascend to the immortal world of Brahman. By this path, known as the path of the gods (Devayana), they ascend higher and higher into brighter regions until they reach the world of Brahman. The journey takes a year. The year symbolizes immortality.

16. atha ye yajnena danena tapasa lokan jayanti te dhimam abhisambhavanti, dhumad ratrim, ratrer apaksiyamana-paksam, paksiyamana-paksad yan san masan daksinaditya eti, masebhyah pitr-lokam, pitr-lokac candram, te candram prapya-

nnam bhavanti; tams tatra deva yatha somam rajanam apyayasva, apaksiyasveti, evam enams tatra bhaksanti; tesam yadd tat paryavaiti athemam evakasam abhinispadyante, akasad vayum, vayor vrstim, vrsteh prathvim; te prathivim prapyannam bhavanti; te punah purusagnau huyante, tato yosagnau jayante. lokan prayutthayinas ta evam evan uparivartante. atha ya etau panthanau na viduh, te kitah, patangah, yad idam dadasukam.

16. Now, those who win the worlds by sacrifices, charity, and austerity they pass into the smoke, from the smoke into the night, from the night into the fortnight of the waning moon, from the fortnight of the waning moon into the six months during which the sun files southwards, from these months into the world of ancestors, from the world of ancestors into the moon. Upon reaching the moon, they become food. There, the gods enjoy them, just as the priests enjoy the drink of Soma, watching the moon wax and wane. When that ends (due to the exhaustion of karmas), they enter into space, from space into air, from air into rain, from rain into the earth. Having reached the earth, they become food. Then they are again offered in the fire of man and from there into the fire of a woman so that they can go again to the other worlds. Thus, they keep rotating. Now, those who do not know these two paths become insects, moths, and whatever is here that bites.

Notes: This verse describes the path that leads to the ancestral world to which the performers of sacrifices and pious deeds go and the world below to which those who commit mortal sins go. There is no dispenser of justice in these rewards and punishments. Humans attain these words according to their deeds. With this, Pravahana Jaivali answered all the questions he asked Svetaketu.

Third Brahmana

A Sacrifice for Greatness and Prosperity

1. sa yah, kamayeta: mahat prapnuyam iti, udagayana apuryamana-paksasya punyahe dvadasaham upasad-vrati bhutva, audumbare kamse camase va sarvausadham phalanti sambhrtya, parisamukhya, parilipya, agnim upasamadhaya, paristirya, avrtajyam samskrtya, pumas maksatrena, mantham samniya, juhoti. yavanto devas tvayi, jata-vedah, tiryanco ghnanti purusasya kaman, tebho'ham bhaga-dheyam jukomi: te ma trptah sarvaih kamais tarpayantu: svaha ya tirasci nipa-dyate aham vidharaniti tam tva ghrtasya dharaya yaje samra-dhanim aham: svaha.

1. He who desires, "I should attain greatness," when the sun is moving northwards, on an auspicious day in the fortnight during which the moon wanes, having observed the vow of twelve days and subsisted on milk, having collected all herbs and fruits in a cup or a dish made of fig wood, after sweeping and plastering the floor, after purifying the offering of clarified butter in the prescribed manner, having mixed the offerings into a paste in a mortar called Mantha on a day when a male star presides over, should pour the oblation into the fire saying, "O fire, to all those gods you know, who vehemently obstruct the desires of a person, I offer them their share. May they, becoming satisfied, satisfy me with all my desires! Svaha. To that deity who has turned spiteful under your protection, thinking she is the support of all, I offer this pouring of clarified butter. Svaha."

Notes: Svaha is uttered with each pouring of an oblation into the sacrificial fire to convey that the oblation has been poured so that the deity may take note and enjoy it. There is no equivalent of it in English. Hence, it is used as it is in the translation. This verse refers to a special rite called Mantha meant to attain greatness and wealth.

2. jyesthaya svaha, sresthaya svaha, ity agnau hutva, manthe samsravam avanayati. pranaya svaha, vasisthayai svaha, ity agnau hutva, manthe samsravam avanayati. vace svaha, pratisthayai svaha, ity agnau hutva, manthe samsravam avanayati. caksuse svaha sampade svaha, ity agnau hutva, manthe samsravam avanayati. srotrasya svaha, ayatanaya svaha, ity agnau hutva, manthe samsravam avanayati. manase svaha, prajatyai svaha, ity agnau hutva, manthe samsravam avanayati. restase svaha, ity agnau hutva, manthe samsravam avanayati.

2. *"Svaha, to the oldest. Svaha to the greatest," saying thus, he offers an oblation in the fire and pours the reminder (of the ghee stuck to the ladle) into the mortar (Mantha).*

"Svaha to the breath. Svaha to the most excellent," saying thus, he offers an oblation in the fire and pours the reminder (of the ghee stuck to the ladle) into the mortar (Mantha).

"Svaha to the speech. Svaha to the well-established," saying thus, he offers an oblation in the fire and pours the reminder (of the ghee stuck to the ladle) into the mortar (Mantha).

"Svaha to the eye. Svaha to the prosperous saying thus, he offers an oblation in the fire and pours the reminder (of the ghee stuck to the ladle) into the mortar (Mantha).

"Svaha to the ear. Svaha to the abode," saying thus, he offers an oblation in the fire and pours the reminder (of the ghee stuck to the ladle) into the mortar (Mantha).

"Svaha to the mind. Svaha to the procreation," saying thus, he offers an oblation in the fire and pours the reminder (of the ghee stuck to the ladle) into the mortar (Mantha).

"Svaha to the semen," saying thus, he offers an oblation in the fire and pours the reminder (of the ghee stuck to the ladle) into the mortar (Mantha).

Notes: The Offerings are made to the breath, extolling him as the oldest, the greatest, the most excellent (Vasishta), etc.

3. agnaye svaha, ity agnau hutva, manthe samsravam avanayati. somaya svaha, ity agnau hutva, manthe samsravam avanayati. bhuh svaha, ity agnau hutva, manthe samsravam avanayati. bhuvah svaha, ity agnau hutva, manthe samsravam avanayati. svah svaha, ity agnau hutva, manthe samsravam avanayati. bhur bhuva svah svaha, ity agnau hutva, manthe samsravam avanayati. brahmane svaha, ity agnau hutva, manthe samsravam avanayati. ksatraya svaha, ity agnau hutva, manthe samsravam avanayati. bhutaya svaha, ity agnau hutva, manthe samsravam avanayati. bhavisyate svaha, ity agnau hutva, manthe samsravam avanayati. visvaya svaha, ity agnau hutva, manthe samsravam avanayati. sarvaya svaha, ity agnau hutva, manthe samsravam avanayati. prajapataye svaha, ity agnau hutva, manthe samsravam avanayati.

3. "To the fire, svaha," saying thus, he offers an oblation in the fire and pours the reminder (of the ghee stuck to the ladle) into the mortar (Mantha).

"To the moon, svaha," saying thus, he offers an oblation in the fire and pours the reminder (of the ghee stuck to the ladle) into the mortar (Mantha).

"To the earth, svaha," saying thus, he offers an oblation in the fire and pours the reminder (of the ghee stuck to the ladle) into the mortar (Mantha).

"To the mid-region, svaha," saying thus, he offers an oblation in the fire and pours the reminder (of the ghee stuck to the ladle) into the mortar (Mantha).

"To the sky, svaha," saying thus, he offers an oblation in the fire and pours the reminder (of the ghee stuck to the ladle) into the mortar (Mantha).

"To the earth, the mid-region and sky, svaha," saying thus, he offers an oblation in the fire and pours the reminder (of the ghee stuck to the ladle) into the mortar (Mantha).

"To the Brahmana, svaha," *saying thus, he offers an oblation in the fire and pours the reminder (of the ghee stuck to the ladle) into the mortar (Mantha).*

"To the Kshatriya, svaha," *saying thus, he offers an oblation in the fire and pours the reminder (of the ghee stuck to the ladle) into the mortar (Mantha).*

"To the Past, svaha," *saying thus, he offers an oblation in the fire and pours the reminder (of the ghee stuck to the ladle) into the mortar (Mantha).*

"To the Future, svaha," *saying thus, he offers an oblation in the fire and pours the reminder (of the ghee stuck to the ladle) into the mortar (Mantha).*

"To the universe, svaha," *saying thus, he offers an oblation in the fire and pours the reminder (of the ghee stuck to the ladle) into the mortar (Mantha).*

"To the all, svaha," *saying thus, he offers an oblation in the fire and pours the reminder (of the ghee stuck to the ladle) into the mortar (Mantha).*

"To Prajapati, svaha," *saying thus, he offers an oblation in the fire and pours the reminder (of the ghee stuck to the ladle) into the mortar (Mantha).*

Notes: The offerings are made to the deity who represents the reproductive fire.

4. athainam abhimrsati, bhramad asi, jvalad asi, purnam asi, prastabhdam asi, eka-sabham asi, hinkrtram asi, hinkriyamanam asi, udgitham asi, dugityamanam asi, sravitam asi, pratyasravitam asi, ardre samdiptam asi, vibhur asi, prabhur asi, annam asi, jyotir asi, nidhanam asi, samvargo siti.

4. *Then he touches it (the mixture of herbal paste), saying, "You are the moving, you are the burning, you are the full, you are still, you are the one assembly place, you are the sound of Hin. You are the making of the sound of Hin. You are the high chant, Udgita. You are the chanting of the Udgita. You are the Sravita chant. You are the Prasavita counter-chant. You are the dazzling light in the water-laden cloud. You are the all-pervading. You are the ruler. You are food. You are light. You are death. You are that in which all things merge.*

Notes: The moving one is the breath. The burning one is the fire. The one that is full is the mid-region. The one that is still is space. The one assembly place is the earth. The sound Hin is made by a Prastotr priest at the beginning of a sacrifice. Udgita refers to the Samans sung loudly by the Udgatir priests during a sacrifice, extolling the deities. Sravita is a recital by an Adhvaryu priest. Prasavita is sung by a Agnidhra priest in response to Sravita. The herbal past symbolizes the subtle prana.

5. athainam udyacchati: amamsi, amam hi te mahi, sa hi rajesano'dhipatih, sa mam rajesano'dhipatim karotv iti.

5. Then raising it (he says), "You know all. We are aware of your greatness. He, indeed, is the king, the lord, and the ruler. May he make me, the king, the lord, and the ruler."

Notes: Here, the worshipper raises the mortar (Mantha) containing the remains of the herbal paste and addresses breath, extolling him as the king, the lord, and the ruler of all the organs in the body.

6. athainam acamati: tat savitur varenyam: madhu vata rtayate, madhu ksaranti sindhavah, madhvir nah santv osadhih; bhuh svaha; bhargo devasya dhimahi; madhu naktam utosasah, madumat parthivam rajah, madhu dyaur astu nah pita; bhuva svaha; dhiyo yo nah pracodayat; madhuman no vanspatih, madhuman astu suryah, madhvir gavo bhavantu nah, svah svaheti. sarvam ca savitrim anvaha, sarvas ca madhumatih aham evedam sarvam bhuyasam, bhur bhuvah svah svaheti, antata acamya, pani praksalya, jaghanenagnim prak-sirah samvisati: pratar adityam upatisthate: disam eka-pundarikam asi, aham manusyanam eka-pundarikam bhuyasam iti. yathetam etya, jaghanenagnim asino vamsam japati.

6. Then he takes a sip, saying, "That adorable sun... Honey-bearing winds and honey-bearing rivers bring forth honey for the righteous. May the herbs be filled with honey for us. To the earth, Svaha. Let us meditate on that divine splendor. May the nights and days be filled with honey. May the dust of the earth be sweet as honey. May heaven, our Father, be honey to us. To the mid-region, Svaha. May he illuminate our intellect. May the trees be filled with honey. May the sun be filled with honey. May the cows be filled with honey. To the heaven, Svaha." Then he repeats the whole Gayatri and all the verses on the doctrine of honey (Madhumati) and says, "May I, indeed, be all this. To the earth, to the mid-region, and to the sky, Svaha." Then he drinks it completely to the last sip, washes his hands, and lies down behind the fire, with his head towards the east. In the morning, he worships the sun, "Among the quarters, you are the one lotus. May I become one lotus among men." Then, he returns by the same path, sits behind the fire, and recites the lineage (of his family).

7. tam haitam uddalaka arunir vajasaneyaya yajnavalkya yantevasina uktvovaca; api ya enam suske sthanau nisincet, jayeran sakhah, praroheyuh palasaniti.

7. Then Uddalaka Aruni taught this to his pupil, Vajasaneya Yajnavalkya, and said, "If one sprinkles this even on a dry stump, branches will grow, and leaves will sprout."

Notes: The paste, thus sanctified, now represents the rejuvenating power of the life force, prana. It can revive even a dying twig. Probably, the sacrifice was meant to rejuvenate the body by energizing the vital energy flowing in it.

8. etam u haiva vajasaneyo yajnavalkyo madhukaya paingyayantevasina uktvovaca, api ya enam suske sthanau nisincet jayeran sakhah paroheyuh palasaniti.

8. Then Vajasaneya Yajnavalkya taught this to his pupil, Madhuka Paingya, and said, "If one sprinkles this even on a dry stump, branches will grow, and leaves will sprout."

9. etam u haiva madhukah paingyas culaya bhagavittaye 'nteva-sina uktvovaca, api ya enam suske sthanau nisincet jayeran sakhah praroheyuh palasaniti.

9. Then Madhuka Paingya taught this to his pupil, Cula Bhagavitti, and said, "If one sprinkles this even on a dry stump, branches will grow and leaves will sprout."

10. etam u haiva cul bhagavittir janakaya ayasthuna yantevasina uktvovaca, api ya enam suske sthanau nisincet jayeran sakhah praroheyuh pasaniti.

10. Then Cula Bhagavitti taught this to his pupil, Janaki Ayasthuna, and said, "If one sprinkles this even on a dry stump, branches will grow, and leaves will sprout."

11. etam u haiva janakir ayasthunah satyakamaya jabala yantevasina uktvovaca, api ya enam suske sthanau nisincet jayeran sakhah praroheyuh pasaniti.

11. Then Janaki Ayasthuna taught this to his pupil, Satyakama Jabala, and said, "If one sprinkles this even on a dry stump, branches will grow, and leaves will sprout."

12. etam u haiva satyakamo jabalo'ntevasibhya uktvovaca, api ya enam suske sthanau nisincet jayeran sakhah praroheyuh pasaniti. tam etam naputraya vanante;vasine va bruyat.

12. Then Satyakama Jabala taught this to his pupils and said, "If one sprinkles this even on a dry stump, branches will grow, and leaves will sprout." One must not teach this to anyone who is not a son or who is not a pupil."

Notes: Shankaracharya says that of the six qualified people (a student, a knower of the Vedas, an intelligent person, one who pays, a son, and one who teaches another branch of learning in exchange), only a son and a pupil are qualified to know this secret.

13. catur audumbaro bhavati; audumbarah sruvah, audumbaras camasah, audumbara idhmah, audumbarya upamanthanyau; dasa gramyani dhanyani bhavanti; vrihi yavas tila masa anupriyamgavo godhumas ca masuras ca khalvas ca khalakhulas ca; tan pistan dadhini madhuni ghrta upasincati, ajyasya juhoti.

13. Four are made of the wood from the fig tree. The ladle is made of wood from the fig tree; the mixing bowl is made of wood from the fig tree; the fuel is made of wood from the fig tree; and the two mixing rods are made of wood from the fig tree. These are the ten grains collected from the fields in the village: rice and barely, sesame and beans, millet and panic seeds, wheat and lentils, pulse and vetches. They should be crushed and mixed with curds, honey, and clarified butter, and offered as an oblation. That, along with clarified butter, should be poured into the fire as an oblation.

Fourth Brahmana

Methods to Obtain a Good Son

1. esam vai bhutanam prthivi rasah, prthivya apah, apam osadhyah, osadhinam puspani, puspanam phalani, phalanam purusah, purusasya retah.

I. The earth, verily, is the essence of all these beings: the water of the earth, the herbs of water, the flowers of herbs, the fruits of the flowers, the person of fruits, and the seed of humans.

Notes: The essence for the seed of humans comes from the earth through the plants., The essence is prana, the vital energy that is present in all.

2. sa ha praja-patir iksam cakre: hanta, asmai pratistham kalpayaniti; sa striyam sasrje; tam srstvadha upasta; tasmat striyam adha upasita, sa etam prancam gravanam atmana eva samudaparayat, tenainam abhyasrjat.

2. Prajapati contemplated, "Let me create a place where he can establish himself. So, he created a woman. He placed her sexual organ on the lower side. Therefore, one should perform service to a woman on the

Chapter 6

lower side. He stretched out for himself that which projects, verily, with pleasure. With that, he impregnated her.

3. tasya vedir upasthah, lomani barhih, carmadhisavane, samiddho madhyatastau muskau; sa yavan ha vai vajapeyena yajamanasya loko bhavati (tavan asyaloko bhavati), ya evam vidvan adhopahasam carati, asam strinam sukrtam vrnkte. Atha ya idam avidvan adhopahasam carati, asya striyah sukrtam vrnjate.

3. Her sexual organ is the sacrificial pit; the hair around it, the grass, skin, the soma press, and the labia are the kindling fire in the middle. Truly, the world of him who practices intercourse knowing this is as good as that of he who performs Vajapeya sacrifice. He who practices intercourse, knowing that it secures for himself the merit of the woman's good deeds, while he who indulges in the intercourse without knowing it passes on the merit of his good deeds to the women.

4. etadd ha sma vai tad vidvan uddalaka arunir aha; etad ha sma vai tad vidvan nako maudgalya aha; etadd ha sma vai tad vidvan kumara-harita aha; bahavo marya brahmanayana nirindriya visukrto'smal lokat prayanti; ya idam avidvamso'dhopahasam caranthi, bahu va idam suptasya va jagrato va retah skandati.

4. Truly, this is what Uddalaka Aruni knew when he said, truly this is what Naka Maudgalya knew when he said, and truly this is what Kamuara Harita knew when he said, "Many mortal men, Brahmanas by birth, who practice sexual intercourse without knowing this, depart from this world without potency and without merit. If one discharges the seed, a little or a lot, awake or asleep...

5. tad abhimrset, anu va mantrayeta: yan me'dya retah prthivim askantsit, yad osadhir apy asarat, yad apah, idam aham tad reta odade, punar mam aitu indriyam, punas tejah, punar bhagah punar agnir dhisnyah yathasthanam kalpantam ity anamikangustabhyam adaya, antarena stanau va bhruvau va nimrjyat.

5. One should touch it and utter this mantra, "Whatever seed that has fallen on the earth, whatever has gone into the plants or into the water, I reclaim it; let my virility, my vigor, my passion, come to me again, luster and glow come to me again. Let the fire and the altar return to their usual place.) (Saying thus) he should lift the seed with his hands and rub it in between his breasts or eyebrows.

Editor's Note: Many translators avoid translating verses 3-5 due to the explicit nature of their content. They are included here for their historical value and their possible connection with the Tantra of the later Vedic period. In Hinduism, as with everything else, sexual intercourse is also considered an act of sacrifice in which there will be the sacrificer, the sacrifice, the results of sacrifice, and the means of sacrifice. These verses are not just about sexual union but about creation and procreation.

6. atha yady udaka atmanam pasyet, tad abhimantrayeta: mayi teja indriyam yaso dravinam sukrtam itisrir ha va esa strinam yanmalodvasah. tasman malodvasasam yasasvinim abhikramyopamantrayeta.

6. Now, if he happens to see his own reflection in the water, he should recite the hymn, "Mine is the luster of the semen, fame, wealth, and the result of good works." There, indeed, is loveliness in women when they discard the impure clothes (worn during menstruation). Therefore, when she has removed her impure clothes and glowing with vigor, he should approach her and make a proposal.

7. sa ced asmai na dadyat, kama enam avakriniyat; saced asmai naiva dadyat, kamam enam yastya va panina vopahatyaikramet, indriyena te yasasa yasa adade, ity ayasa eva bhavati.

7· If she is not willing to grant his desire, he should buy her (gifts). If she is still unyielding, he should strike her with a stick or with his hand and overpower her, uttering the following mantra, "I take away your body vigor." Then, she becomes weak without strength.

8. sa aced asmai dadyat: indriyena te yasasa yasa adadhami iti; yasasvinav eva bhavatah.

8. If she consents, he should say, "Through my seed, I transmit my glory into you." Then, the two glow with vigor.

9. sa yam icchet, kamayeta meti, tasyam artham nisthaya, mukkena mukham samdhaya, upastham asya abhimrsya, japet: angad angat sambhavasi, hydayad adhijayase sa tvam anga-kasayo'si: digdha-viddham iva madaya imam amum mayi.

9. If one desires to have union with a woman thinking that she may enjoy love with him, inserting his member in her, pressing his mouth against her, caressing her lower part, he should recite, "You, who is born from every limb of mine, who is created from my heart, you are my body's essence. May she become infatuated with me as if she has been hit by a poisonous arrow."

10. atha yam icchet: na garbham dadhiteti, tasyam artham nisthaya, mukkena mukham samdhaya abhipranyapanyat, indriyena te retasa reta adada iti; areta eva bhavati.

11. Now, if he desires, "She should not become pregnant," after inserting his member into her, pressing his mouth against her, and inhaling and exhaling, he should say, "With my vigor and semen, I reclaim the semen from you." Surely, then, she will be without the seed.

11. atha yam icchet; garbham dadhitcti, tasyam artham nisthaya mukhena mukham samadhaya apanyabhipranyat; indriyena te retasa reta adadhami, ity, garbhiny eva bhavati.

11. Now, if he desires," May she become pregnant," after inserting his member into her, pressing his mouth against her, and inhaling and exhaling, he should say, "With my vigor and with my seed I deposit the semen in you." Surely, then, she will become pregnant.

12. atha yasya jayayai jarah syat, tam ced dvisyat, amapatre'gnim upasamdhaya, pratilomam sarabarhis tirtva, tasminn etah sarabhrstih pratilomah sarpisakta juhuyati; mama samidde'hausih, pranapanau na adadeasav iti. mama samiddhe'hausih, putra-pasums ta adadeasav iti. mama samiddhe'hausih istasukrte ta adade, asav iti. mama samiddhe'hausih asa-parakasau ta adade asav iti. sa va esa nirindriyo visukrto'smal lokat praiti, yam evam-vid brahmanah sapati. tasmat evamvit srotriyasya darena nopahasam icchet, uta hy evam-vit paro bhavati.

12. If a man's wife has a lover and he wants to harm him out of hatred, he should put fire in an unbaked earthen vessel, spread arrows made of reed and kusa grass in an inverse order, and offer the arrows, with their tips soaked in clarified butter, in the fire in an inverse order, saying, "You have sacrificed in my fire, I take away your incoming breath, and your outgoing breath, you so and so. You have sacrificed in my fire. I take away your sons and cattle, you so and so. You have sacrificed in my fire. I take away your sacrifices and good deeds, you so and so. You have sacrificed in my fire; I take away your hopes and expectations, you so and so." He, indeed, departs from this world without potency and without merit, whom a Brahmana who knows this curses. Therefore, one should not wish even to make fun of the wife of a person who recites the Vedas. Indeed, he who knows this becomes supreme.

13. atha yasya jayam artavam vindet, try aham kamse na pibet ahata-vasah; nainam vrsalah na vrsaly upahanyat, triratranta aplutya vrhin avaghatayet.

13. Now, when anyone's wife has monthly sickness, she should not drink from a bronze vessel for three days. No impure man or woman should touch her. She should bathe after three nights. Then, she should be made to pound rice.

Notes: Vrishala means a Sudra, a low caste person, a sinner, or a wicked or irreligious person. Vrishali means a Sudra woman, an unmarried girl under twelve years of age, a barren woman, a woman in menstruation, or a woman who has given birth to a stillborn child.

14. sa ya icchet, putro me suklo jayeta, vedam anubruvita, sarvam ayur tyad iti, ksirandanam pacayitva sarpismantam asniyatam; isvarau janavita vai.

14. He who desires that a son should be born to him with a fair complexion, who would study the Vedas and attain the full span of his life, should have rice cooked in milk, which he and his wife should eat with clarified butter. Then, they would be able to give birth (to such a son).

15. atha ya icchet, putro me kapilah pingalo jayeta, dvau vedav anubruvita, sarvam ayur iyad iti, dadhyodanam pacayitva sarpismantam asnivatam; isvarau janavita vai.

15. He who desires that a son should be born to him with a brown complexion, who would study the Vedas and attain the full span of his life, should have rice cooked in curd, which he and his wife should eat with clarified butter. Then, they would be able to give birth (to such a son).

16. atha ya icchet, putro me syamo lohitakso jayeta, trin vedan aubruvita, sarvam ayur iyad iti, udodanam pacayitva, sarpismantam asniyatam; isvarau janayita vai.

16. He who desires that a son should be born to him with a dark complexion and red eyes, who would study the Vedas and attain the full span of his life, should have rice cooked in water, which he and his wife should eat with clarified butter. Then, they would be able to give birth (to such a son).

17. atha ya icchet duhita me pandita jayeta sarvam ayur iyad iti, tilodanam pacayitva sarpismantam asniyatam, isvarau janayita vai.

17. He who desires that a daughter should be born to him, who would be a scholar and attain the full span of her life, should have rice cooked with sesame, which he and his wife should eat with clarified butter. Then, they would be able to give birth (to her).

18. atha ya icchet putro me pandito vigatah, samitim-gamah, susrusitam vacam bhasita jayeta, sarvan vedan anubruvita, sarvam ayur iyad it, mamsodanam pacayitva sarpismantam asniyatam; isvarau janayita vai, auksnena varsabhena va.

18. He who desires that a son should be born to him, who would be a scholar, who would frequent the congregations, speak delightful words, and attain the full span of his life, should have rice cooked with the meat of a vigorous and young bull or an old bull, which he and his wife should eat with clarified butter. Then, they would be able to give birth (to such a son).

19. athabhirpratar eva sthali-pakavrtajyam cestitva, shalipakasyopaghatam juhoti: agnaye svaha, anumataye svaha, devaya savitre satya-prasavaya svaha, iti; hutva uddhrtya prasnati, prasyetarasyah prayacchati; praksalya pani, udapatram purayitva tenainam trir abhyuksati; uttishato visvavaso, anyam iccha prapurvyam, sam jayam patya saha, iti.

19. Now, in the early morning, having prepared clarified butter for the sake of Sthalipaka rites, and poured Sthalipaka oblations again and again, saying, "To the fire, Svaha; to Anumati, Svaha, to the divine Savitr, the creator of truth, Svaha." Having made the offering, he then eats (the remnants of the food). Having eaten, he then offers to his wife (whatever is left). Having washed his hands, he fills up the water vessel and sprinkles her thrice with the water, saying, "Arise Visvavasu and find out another young woman who is a wife and lives with her husband."

20. athainam abhipadyate: amo'ham asmi, sa tvam; sa tvam asi, amo'ham; samaham asmi, rk vam; dyaur aham, prthivi tvam; tav ehi samrabhavahai, saha reto dadhavahai pumse putraya vittaye iti.

20. Then, he embraces her, saying, "I am breath, and you are speech; you are speech, and I am breath; I am Saman, and you are Rik; I am the heaven, and you are the earth; come, let us be together so that I can give you my seed and we may have a male child.

21. athasya uru vihapayati: vijihitham dyavaprthivi, iti tasyam artham nisthaya, mukhena mukham samdhaya, trir enam anulomam anumarsti: visnur yonim kalpayatu, tvasta rupani pimsatu asincatu praja-patih, dhata garbham dadhatu te: garbham dhehi, sinivali; garbham dhehi, prthustuke, garbham te asvinau devau adhattam puskara-srajau.

22. Then he spreads her thighs apart, saying, "Spread yourselves apart like heaven and earth." After establishing his member in her and pressing his mouth against her, he strokes her three times in the direction of her hair, saying, "Let Vishnu prepare your womb, let Tvastr create the forms, let Prajapati impregnate you, let Dhatr place the seed in your womb. O Sinivali, place the fetus, place the seed O broad plaited one. Place the fetus, O Asvins, who are crowned with lotus wreaths.

22. hiranmayi arani yabhyam nirmanthatam asvinau; tam te garbham havamahe dasame masi sutaye: yathagni-garbha

prthivi, yatha dyaur indrena garbhini vayur disam yatha garbhah, evam garbham dadhami te asav iti.

22. *The flame that the Asvins brought forth with the friction of the two golden sticks, such a germ I invoke as the fetus for you for delivery in the tenth month. Just as the earth has the germ of fire in its womb, just as the sky has the germ of rains and the wind has the germ of directions, so do I place the germ in you, so and so.*

23. sosyantim adbhir adhyuksati, yatha vayuh puskarinim samingayati sarvatah eva te garbha ejatu sahavaitu jarayuna: indrasyayam vrajah krtah sargalah saparisrayah, tam, indra, nirjahi garbhena savaram saheti.

23. *When she is ready to deliver, he sprinkles her with water, saying, just as the wind stirs a pond from all sides, so may your fetus stir and come out with the outer membrane. This is the handiwork of Indra. Let him come forth, O Indra, with the baby and the afterbirth.*

24. jate'gnim upasamadhaya, anka adhaya kamse prsad-ajyam samniya, prsad-ajyasyopaghatam juhoti; asmin sahasram pusyasam edhamanah sve grhe asyopasandyam ma chaitsit prajaya ca pasubhis ca, svadha: mayi pranams tvayi manasa juhomi, svaha: yat karmanatyariricam, yad va nyunam ihakaram, agnistat svistakrd vidvan, svistam suhuktam karotu ham: svaha.

24. *When (the son is) born, he should arrange a fire, take him in his lap, mix curd and clarified butter in a bronze cup, and pour the oblations repeatedly into the fire, saying, "May I flourish through this one and nourish a thousand in my house. May fortune, offspring, and cattle never depart from his line. Svaha. I pour my breath into your mind. Svaha. If I have overstepped my limits or failed to meet the requirements, may the Fire, the all-knowing, the beneficent, make it just right and good for us. Svaha."*

25. athasya daksinam karnam abhinidhaya; vag vag it tirh. Atha dadhi madhu ghrtam samniya anantarhitena jata-upena prasayati; bhus te dadhami, bhuvas te adhami, svas te dadhami bhur bhuva svah sarvam tvayi dadhamiti.

25. *Then, bringing his mouth closer to the child's right ear, he should say thrice, "Speech, Speech." Then, mixing curd, honey and clarified butter together, he should feed the child with a golden spoon, saying, "I give you the earth. I give you the mid-region. I give you the heaven. I give you all that is there in the earth, in the mid-region, and in the heaven."*

26. athasya nama karoti vedo' siti; tad asya tad guhyam eva nama bhavati.

26. Then he gives him a name, "You are Veda" That, indeed, becomes his secret name.

27. athainam matre pradaya stanam prayacchati; yas te stanah sasayo yo mayobhuh, yo tatnadha vasuvid yah, sudatrah, yena visva pusyasi varyani, sarasvati, tam iha dhatave kah.

27. Then he presents him to his mother and gives him her breast, saying, "Your breast, which is inexhaustible, refreshing, abundant, generous, and through which you nourish all who are worthy, O Sarasvati, please bring it here for suckling.

28. athasya mataram abhimantrayate: ilasi maitravaruni; vire viram ajijanat, sa tvam viravati bhava, yasmin viravato'karat. iti, tam va etam ahuh; atipita atabhuh, atipitamaho batabhuh. paramam bata kastham prapat, sriya yasasa brahma-varcasena, ya evam vido brahmanasya putro jayata iti.

28. Then he chants this for the mother, "You are Ila, who descended from Mitra and Varuna. You have given birth to a great child and thereby become the mother of a great child. You have given me a great child as my son. May you become the mother of many children." They speak of such a son, "You have surpassed your father, and you have surpassed your grandfather." Truly, he attains the highest level of prosperity, fame and the vigor of Brahman, who is born as the son of a Brahmanu who is a knower of this.

Fifth Brahmana

The Line of Teachers and Students

Editor's Note: This section contains the line of teachers of the whole Upanishad. Again, here also the original Sanskrit verses are omitted to avoid redundancy.

1. Now, as to the line of teachers: The son of Pautimasi (received it) from the son of Katyayani. The son of Katyayani from the son of Gautarni. The son of Gautami from the son of Bharadvaji. The son of Bharadvaji from the son of Parasari. The son of Parasari from the son of Aupasvasti. The son of Aupasvasti from the son of Parasari. The son of Parasari from the son of Katyayani. The son of Katyayani from the son of Kausiki. The son of Kausiki from the son of Alambi and the son of Vaiyaghrapadi. The son of Vaiyaghrapadi from the son of Kanvi and the son of Kapi. The son of Kapi-

2. From the son of Atreyi. The son of Atreyi from the son of Gautami. The son of Gautami from the son of Bharadvaji. The son of Bharadvaji from the son of Parasari·. The son of Parasari from the son of Vatsi. The son of Vatsi from the son of another Parasari. The son of Parasari from the son of Varkaruni. The son of Varkaruni from the son of Varkaruni. The son of Varkaruni from the son of Artabhagi. The son of Artabhagi from the son of Samigi. The son of Saungi from the son of Samkrti. The son of Samkrti from the son of Alambayani. The son of Alambayani again from the son of Alambi. The son of Alambi from the son of Jayanti. The son of Jayanti from the son of Mandukayani. The son of Mandukayani from the son of Manduki. The son of Manduki from the son of Sandili. The son of Sandili from the son of Rathitari. The son of Rathitari from the son of Bhaluki. The son of Bhaluki from the two sons of Krauncki. The two sons of Krauncki from the son of Vaidabhrti. The son of Vaidabhrti from the son of Karsakeyi. The son of Karsakeyi from the son of Pracinayogi. The son of Pracinayogi from the son of Sanjivi. The son of Sanjivi from Asurivasin, the son of Prasni. The son of Prasni from Asurayana. Asurayana from Asuri. Asuri-

3. From Yajnavalkya. Yajnavalkya from Uddalaka. Uddalaka from Aruna. Aruna from Upavesi. Upavesi from Kusri. Kusri from Vajasravas. Vajasravas from Jihvavat Badhyoga. Jihvavat Badhyoga from Asita Varsagana. Asita Varsagana from Harita Kasyapa. Harita Kasyapa from Silpa Kasyapa. Silpa Kasyapa from Kasyapa Nidhruva. Kasyapa Nidhruva from Vac. Vac from Ambhini. Ambhini from Aditya. These white Yajuses received from the sun are explained by Yajnavalkya of Vajasaneya tradition.

4. It is the same up to the son of Sanjivi. The son of Sanjivi from Manukayani. Mandukayani from Mandavya. Mandvya from Kautsa. Kautsa from Mahitthi. Mahitthi from Vamakakasyana. Vamakakasyana from Sandilya. Sandilya from Vatsya. Vatsya from Kusri. Kusri from Yajnavacas Rajastambayana. Yajnavacas Rajastambayana from Tura Kavali. Tura Kavali from Prajapati. Prajapati from Brahma. Brahma is self-born. Salutation to Brahma.

Notes: This is a long line of teacher tradition stretching back to Brahma and the beginning of creation. According to Shankara, the teachers in this section were named after their mothers instead of their fathers because, in the ceremony mentioned in the previous section, credit was given to mothers for giving birth to the great children who are mentioned here.

Bibliography

Brihadaranyaka Upanishad

Brahmananda, Swami. The philosophy of Sage Yajnavalkya: a free rendering of the Yajnavalkya-Kanda of the Brihadaranyaka Upanishad as expounded in the Atma Purana. Shivanandanagar, Distt. Tehri-Garhwal, U.P., India: Divine Life Society, 1981.

Coomaraswamy, Ananda. A new approach to the Vedas. London: Luzac & co., 1933.

Francis, X. D'Sa, and S.J. Word-index to Bṛhad-Āranyaka Upaniṣad. Pune, India: Institute for the Study of Religion, 1996.

Johnson, Charles. The song of life. Flushing, N.Y.: The Author, 1901.

Krishnananda, Swami. The Brhadāranyaka upanishad: an interpretative exposition. Shivanandanagar, Distt. Tehri-Garhwal, U.P., India: Divine Life Society, 1984.

Krishnanda, Swami. The essence of the Brihadaranyaka Upanishad. Shivanandanagar, India: Divine Life Society, 1977.

Lal, P. The Brhadaranyaka Upanisad transcreated from the Sanskrit. Kolkata, India: Writers Workshop; [Thompson, Conn.: agents in the U.S., Inter Culture Associates, 1974].

Mādhavānanda, Swami, and Sastri, Kuppuswami, Introd. The Bṛhadāranyaka Upaniṣad, with the commentary of Śaṅkarācārya. Kolkata, India: Advaita Ashrama, 1965.

R.T, Vyas. Bṛhadāranyaka upaniṣad: a critical study. Vadodara, India: Oriental Institute, 1987.

Roer, E., Dvivedi, Manilal N., pref. Bṛhadāranyaka-Upaniṣad: text in Sanskrit and translation with notes in English from the commentaries of Śaṅkarācārya and the gloss of Ānandagiri. Delhi, India: Bharatiya Kala Prakashan, 2000.

Sharma, B.N.K. The Bṛhadāranyaka upaniṣad expounded from Śrī Madhvācārya's perspective. Bangalore, India: Dvaita Vedanta Studies and Research Foundation, 1988.

Sharma, R.C., Poddar, Bimla, and Ghosa, Pranati [ed.]: Bṛhadāranyakopaniṣad: Seminar proceedings. Varanasi, India: Jñāna Pravāha, Centre for Cultural Studies, c2004.

Sivananda, Swami. The Brihadaranyaka Upanishad: Sanskrit text, English translation, and commentary. Shivanandanagar, Distt. Tehri-Garhwal, U.P., India: Divine Life Society, 1985.

General Reference

Aiyar, Narayanasvami K. Thirty minor Upaniṣads: revised edition includes Sanskrit texts, English translation. Delhi, India: Parimal Publications, 1997.

Ananthacharya, Chakravarti. Philosophy of Upanishads. Bangalore, India: Ultra Publications, 1999.

Archak, K.B. Upaniṣad and Śaivism. New Delhi, india: Sundeep Prakashan, 2002.

Aurobindo, Sri. The Upanishads, with Sanskrit text, English translation and commentary. Twin Lakes, WI: Lotus Light Publications, 1996.

Barnett, L. D. Brahma-knowledge, an outline of the philosophy of the Vedānta as set forth by the Upanishads and by Shankara.London, J. Murray, 1911.

Basham, A.L. The Origins and Development of Classical Hinduism. New York: Oxford University Press, 1991.

Bhattacharya, A.N. One hundred and twelve Upaniṣads and their philosophy: a critical exposition of Upaniṣadic philosophy with original text in Devanāgarī. Delhi, India: Parimal Publications, 1987.

Brown, George William. The human body in the Upanishads. Jubbulpore, India, The Christian Mission Press, 1921.

Chakravarti, Sures Chandra. The philosophy of the Upanishads. Delhi, India: Nag Publishers, 1979.

Deodikar, Sanjay Govind. Upanisads and early Buddhism. Delhi, India: Eastern Book Linkers, 1992.

Desai, S.G. A critical study of the later Upanishads. Mumbai, India: Bharatiya Vidya Bhavan, 1996.

Deussen, Paul, and Rev. Geden, A. S. The philosophy of the Upanishads. Edinburgh, Clark, 1908.

Deussen, Paul, and Bedekar, V.M., and Palsule, G.B. Sixty Upaniṣads of the Veda. Delhi, India: Motilal Banarsidass, 1980.

Devi, Chitrita. Upanishads for all. New Delhi, India: S. Chand [1973, i.e., 1972].

Diwakar, R.R., and Radhakrishnan, S., Intro. The Upanisads in story and dialogue. Mumbai, India: Hindi Kitabs, 1950.

Easwaran, Eknath. Essence of the Upanishads: A Key to Indian Spirituality. Canada: Nilgiri Press & Blue Mountain Center of Meditation, 2009.

Bibliography

_____. The Upanishads: The Classics of Indian Spirituality. Canada: The Blue Mountain Center of Meditation, 1987, 2007.

_____., Nagler, Michael N., fwd. The Upanishads. Tomales, CA: Nilgiri Press, 2007.

Egnes, Thomas, and Reddy, Kumuda. Eternal Stories from the Upanishads. New Delhi, India: Smriti Books, 2002.

Elenjimittam, Anthony. The Upanishads: Isa, Katha, Mundaka, Mandukya, with an introduction and commentary. Mumbai, India: Aquinas Publications, 1977.

Frawley, David. The creative vision of the early Upanisads. Denver, Colo.: D. Frawley, 1982.

Gambhirananda, Swami. Eight Upanishads: With the Commentary of Shankaracaya, Vol 1 and 2. Kolkata, India: Advaita Ashrama, 2003 and 2004.

Ghose, Aurobindo Sri. The Upanishads. Pondicherry, India: Aurobindo Ashram Trust, 1996.

Giri, Swami Satyeswarananda. The Upanishads. San Diego: Sanskrit Classics, 2006.

Gren-Eklund, Gunilla. A study of nominal sentences in the oldest Upanisads.Uppsala : Univ.; Stockholm : Almqvist & Wiksell international (distr.), 1978.

Grover, Usha. Symbolism in the Āranyakas and their impact on the Upaniṣads: a remarkable cultural upheaval which ever inspires the future thought. New Delhi: Guruvar Publications, 1987.

Hock, Henrich Hans. An early Upaniṣadic reader: with notes, glossary, and an appendix of related Vedic texts. Delhi, India: Motilal Banarsidass Publishers, 2007.

Hume, Robert Ernest. The thirteen principal Upanishads [microform]: translated from the Sanskrit with an outline of the philosophy of the Upanishads and an annotated bibliography. London; New York: Oxford University Press, 1931.

Johnston, Charles. The great Upanishads. New York: Quarterly Book Department [c1927].

Kadankavil, Kurian T. The quest of the real: a study of the philosophical methodology of Mundakopanishad. Bangalore, India: Dharmaram Publications, 1975.

Keith, Arthur Berriedale. The religion and philosophy of the Veda and Upanishads. Cambridge, Mass.: Harvard University Press, 1925.

Bibliography

Keith, Arthur Berriedale. The religion and philosophy of the Veda and Upanishads. Cambridge, Mass., Harvard university press; London, H. Milford, Oxford university press, 1925.

Krishnamurti, V.G. From J. Krishnamurti to the Upanishads: world order for the 21st century: an Indian vision. Kolkata, India: Writers Workshop, 1990.

Kriyananda, Swami Saraswati. Nine principal Upanishads, with text, translitteration [sic], translation, and notes. Monghyr, India: Bihar School of Yoga, 1975.

Kulkarni, T.R. Upanishads and yoga; an empirical approach to the understanding. Mumbai, India: Bharatiya Vidya Bhavan, 1972.

Madhavananda, Swami. Minor Upanishads. With original text, introd., English rendering and comments. Kolkata, India: Advaita Ashrama, 1968.

Majumdār, Sridhar. The Vedanta philosophy: in English with original sutras and explanatory quotations from Upanishads, Bhagavad Gītā etc. and their English translations. Varanasi, India: Chowkhamba Sanskrit Series Office, 2000.

Manohar, Mrinalini Vivek. The earlier and later Upaniṣads: a comparative study. Delhi, India: Bharatiya Kala Prakashan, 2011.

Mascaro, Juan. The Upanishads. New York: Penguin Putnam Inc., 1965.

Mead, G.R.S., and Chaṭṭopādhyāya, Jagadīsha Chandra (Roy Choudhuri). The Upanishads / translated into English, with a preamble and arguments. Adyar, Madras, India: Theosophical Publishing House, 1930.

Milburn, R. Gordon. The religious mysticism of the Upanishads. London, Theosophical Publishing House, 1924.

Mukherji Anil Kumar, Das, Saroj Kumar, fwd. Upanishad in the eyes of Rabindra Nath Tagore: an anthology of the poet Tagore's writings, interpretative of and related to Upanishadic verse. Kolkata, India: Dasgupta, 1975.

Mukhopadhyaya, Govindagopal. Studies in the Upaniṣads. Kathmandu, Nepal: Distributed by Pilgrims Book House, 1999.

Muller, Max F. Sacred Books of the East, Vol. 1. Oxford: Clarenden Press, 1900.

_____. The Upanishads. New York: Christian Literature Co., 1897.

Muni, Angirasa. The Upanisads / introduction and translation. Fort Wayne, IN: Sacred Books, 1999.

Bibliography

Narla, V.R. An essay on the Upanishads: a critical study. Hyderabad, India: Narla Institute of New Thought, c1989.

Nikam, N. A. Ten principal Upanishads: some fundamental ideas: a dialectical and analytical study. Mumbai, India: Somaiya Publications, 1974.

Nikhilananda, Swami. Upanishads, Vol.1-4. New York: Ramakrishna Vivekanada Center, 1986, 1990, 1990, 1994.

Olivelle, Patrick. The early Upaniṣads: annotated text and translation. New Delhi, India: Munshiram Manoharlal Publishers, 1998.

Olivelle, Patrick. The early Upanisads: annotated text and translation. New York: Oxford University Press, 1998.

Olivelle, Patrick. Upanishads: A new Translation. Oxford, New York: Oxford University Press, 1996.

Pandit, M.P. Upanishads: Gateways of Knowledge. Wilmot, WI: Lotus Light Publications, 1988.

Paramananda, Swami. The Upanishads: Translated and commentated. Volume 1. Boston, MA: The Vedanta Center, 1919.

Parrinder, Geoffrey. The wisdom of the forest: selections from the Hindu Upanishads. New York: New Directions Pub. Corp., 1976.

_____. The wisdom of the forest: sages of the Indian Upanishads / translated [from the Sanskrit]. London: Sheldon Press, 1975.

_____. Upanishads, Gita and Bible: a comparative study of Hindu and Christian scriptures. London: Sheldon Press, 1975.

Pathak, Meena P. (Meena Pinakin). study of Taittirīya Upanisad. Delhi: Bharatiya Kala Prakashan, 1999.

Prabhavananda, Swami. The Upanishads: Breath of the Eternal. New York: Penguin Putnam Inc., 2002.

Raja, C. Kunhan, ed., and Pandits of Adayar Library. Daśopanishads, with the commentary of Sri Upanishad-brahma-yogin. Chennai, India: Adyar Library (Theosophical Society) 1935-36.

Puligandla, R. "That thou art": the wisdom of the Upanishads. Fremont, Calif.: Asian Humanities Press, c2002.

Puligandla. R. Reality and mysticism: perspectives in the Upanisads. the University of Michigan, MI: D K Printworld (P) Limited, 1997.

Pundalik, Pandit Madhav. Mystic approach to the Veda and the Upanishads. Chennai, India: Sri Aurobindo Library [1952].

Purohit, Swami. The ten principal Upanishads Put into English. New York: Macmillan, 1975, c1937.

Bibliography

Radhakrishnan, S. Indian philosophy. London, Allen & Unwin; New York, Humanities Press [1966].

_____. The philosophy of the Upanisads, with a foreword by Rabindranath Tagore and an Introduction by Edmond Holmes. London, G. Allen & Unwin ltd.; New York, The Macmillan Company [1935].

_____. The Principal Upanishads: Edited With Introduction, Text, Translation and Notes. New Delhi, India: HarperCollins Publishers, India, 1994

Raghavachar, S.S. Sri Ramanuja on the Upanishads. Chennai, India: Prof. M. Rangacharya Memorial Trust; [can be had of M. C. Krishnan, 1972].

Rajagopalachari, C. Upanishads for the lay reader. New Delhi, India: Hindustan Times [1956].

Rajagopalachari, Chakravarti. Upanishads. Mumbai, India: Bharatiya Vidya Bhavan, 1991.

Rama, Swami. Wisdom of the ancient sages: Mundaka Upanishad. Honesdale, Pa.: Himalayan International Institute of Yoga Science and Philosophy of the U.S.A., c1990.

Ranade, R.D. A constructive survey of Upanishadic philosophy, being an introduction to the thought of the Upanishads. Mumbai, India: Bharatiya Vidya Bhavan, 1968.

Reddy, Madhusudan. Yoga of the rishis: the Upanishadic approach to death and immortality. Hyderabad, India: Institute of Human Study; Delhi: Distributed by Indian Books Centre, 1985.

Rehman, Saif-Ur. Indian philosophy: some common concepts in the Vedas, Upanishads & early Buddhism. [Lahore]: [publisher not identified], [2012?].

Rodrigues, Antonio F.X. In search of meaning: a phenomenological reading of the Upanishads. Bangalore, India: Redemptorist Publications India, [198-?].

Roebuck, Valerie. The Upanishads. London, New York: Penguin Books, 2003.

Roer, E., ed. The Twelve Principal Upaniṣads: text in Devanāgari and translation with notes in English from the commentaries of Śaṅkarācārya, and the gloss of Ānandagiri. Delhi, India: Nag Publishers, 1978-1979.

Sarasvati, Svami Satya Prakash. Parables and dialogues from the Upaniṣads. Delhi, India: S. Chand, 1975.

Saraswati, Swami Sivananda. The essence of the principal Upanishads. Rishikesh, India: Yoga-Vedanta Forest Academy, Divine Life Society, 1961.

Scharfstein, Ben-Ami A comparative history of world philosophy: from the Upanishads to Kant. Albany: State University of New York Press, c1998.

Sen, Pritam. God's love in Upanishad philosophies. Mumbai, India: Bharatiya Vidya Bhavan, 1995.

Seru, S. L. The thirteen Principal Upanisads: an introduction on Vedanta-sara text with English translation and notes. Delhi, India: Nag Publishers, 1997.

Sharma, Shubhra. Life in the Upanishads. New Delhi, India: Ahinav Publications, 1985.

Shearer, Alistair & Russell, Peter; photos. by Lannoy, Richard. The Upanishads. New York: Harper & Row, c1978.

Shearer, Alistair and Russell, Peter. The Upanishads. Bell Tower, New York: Sacred Teachings, 2003.

Singh, Maan. The Upaniṣadic etymologies. Delhi: Nirmal Publication, 1994.

Singh, Satya Prakash. Upanisadic symbolism. New Delhi, India: Meharchand Lachhmandas, 1981.

Sircar, Mahendranath. Hindu mysticism according to the Upaniṣads. New Delhi: Oriental Books Reprint Corp.: distributed by Munshiram Manoharlal Publishers, 1974.

Sreeram, Lala. The metaphysics of the Upanishads, or Vichar Sagar/ translated with copious notes. New Delhi: Asian Publication Services, 1979.

Sri Upanishad-brahma-yogin. The Yoga Upanishads, with the commentary of. [Madras] Pub. for the Adyar library (Theosophical Society) 1920.

Srinivasachari, P.N. The wisdom of the Upanisads. Madras: Sri Krishna Library, 1947.

Subrahmanian, V.K. The Upanishads and the Bible. New Delhi: Abhinav Publications, 2002.

Swāmi, Shree Purohit, and Yeats, W. B. The ten principal Upanishads; put into English. London: Faber, 1970.

Tathagatananda, Swami. Journey of the Upanishads to the West. New York, NY: Vedanta Society, 2002.

Thachil, Jose. The Upaniṣads, a socio-religious appraisal. New Delhi, India: Intercultural Publications, 1993.

Brihadaranyaka Upanishad

Bibliography

Vasus, Srisa Chandra. The Upaniṣads with the commentary of Madh-vachãrya: part I, Īśa, Katha, Praśna, Muṇḍaka and Māṅḍuka. Allahabad, India: Panini Office, 1909.

V, Jayaram. Brahman. New Albany, OH: Pure Life Vision LLC, 2010.

V, Jayaram. Chandogya Upanishad. New Albany, OH: Pure Life Vision LLC, 2013.

V, Jayaram. Bhagavadgita: Unveiling the Gita's Secrets, New Albany, OH: Pure Life Vision LLC, 2024

Vidyaranva, Srisa Chandra. Studies in the first six Upanisads and the Isa and Kena Upanisads, with the commentary of Shankara. Allahabad, India: Panini Office, 1919 [i.e. 1918].

Witz, Klaus G. The supreme wisdom of the Upaniṣads: an introduction. Delhi, India: Motilal Banarsidass Publishers, 1998.

Cover Page Symbolism

The cover page illustration by Jayaram V depicts the earth, the heaven, and the moon, with the constellation of stars in the background. The heaven and the earth are connected by a tree in inverse form, with its roots in heaven and branches on earth. It represents the Asvattha tree, which is described in the Katha Upanishad as the tree of creation. The image of a horse in heaven represents Brahman, described in the first chapter of this Upanishad as Brahman with four feet. The five roots and the five branches refer to the fivefold division of creation (pancikarana), five elements, five senses, and five breaths.